MARKING THE HOURS

Oratio de noie iesu.

Miserere mei deus & salua me.

O Jesu spes penitentium. Spes mea in die afflictionis. Non confundar in eternum quia in te domine speraui. Nullus enim sperauit in te & cōfusus est.

Miserere mei deus & salua me.

O Jesu rex gloriose inter sanctos tuos qui semper es laudabilis et tamen ineffabilis: tu in nobis es domine & nomen sanctum tuum inuocatū est super nos/ne derelinquas nos domine deus noster. Ut in die iudicij nos collocare digneris inter sanctos & electos tuos rex benedicte. Uersus. Jesu rex clementissime: tu corda nostra posside. R. Ut tibi laudes debitas reddamus omni tempore. Oratio.

Sancti nominis tui domine timorem pariter & amorē fac nos habere perpetuum: quia nunq̄ tua gubernatione destituis/quos in soliditate tue dilectiōis instituis.

Omnipotens sempiterne de⁹/dirige actus nostros in beneplacito tuo: ut in nomine dilecti filij tui mereamur bonis operibus abundare. Per eundem dominum nostrum Jesum christum filium tuum. Qui tecum viuit & regnat in unitate spiritussancti deus. Per omnia secula seculorum. Amen.

O iesu.
Intra pectus meum
Et munda cor meum
Sis defensorium/
Uirtus/auxilium/
Salus fidelium.
Amen.

4 the yere endes say our lordes prayer after all yere. prayer for all christen soles on wednesday within the said yere fast bread and water.

[illegible] friday [illegible] fast.

Oratio deuotissima ad sanctam trinitatem.

[illegible] psalmes once. iij pat. nost. & one crede [illegible] say [illegible] one yere. With [illegible] and iij collecte [illegible]

Oro ad sanctā trinitatē. Fo.

A... s
idiuidu
tas/de⁹
lis. E
as ago
me ad
nē et b
dinē t
re dig
ut sim
milis
riā in
tiā &
Hec t
nio p
colo/
2cup
mem
remi
inte

te intueor. Per voluntatem te diligo teq̄
Per memoriā que est parens intelligētie
similis deus pater eterne lucis et summe
dñi nostri iesu christi. Per intellectū qui
memorie/sum tibi similis dñe iesu christe
pientia a patre genita. Per volūtatem q
dentia & directio amantis in amatū/& am
pulat cum amato: sum tibi similis spūs sa
clite/qui es patris & filii amor/ concordia
tus. Da igitur mihi beatissima trinitas
ciendi id ad quod factus sum: ut meminer
gam te/& intelligā te. Da michi fidem rec
firmam/charitatē perfectam: ut per spem
memoria/per fidem illuminetur intellig
charitatē inflāmetur volūtas. O beata t
serere michi: & oibus ppinquis meis/bñf
Sap.

MARKING THE HOURS

English People and their Prayers 1240–1570

Eamon Duffy

YALE UNIVERSITY PRESS
NEW HAVEN AND LONDON

Published with assistance from the foundation established in memory of Oliver Baty Cunningham of the Class of 1917, Yale College.

Typeset in SNP Best-set Typesetter Ltd., Hong Kong
Designed by Sally Salvesen
Printed in Singapore by CS Graphics

Library of Congress Cataloging-in-Publication Data
Duffy, Eamon.
Marking the hours : English people and their prayers, 1240–1570 : the Riddell lectures 2002 / Eamon Duffy.
p. cm.
Includes bibliographical references (p. ••) and index.
ISBN 0-300-11714-0 (alk. paper)
1. Books of hours–England. 2. Marginalia–England.
3. Prayer–England–History. 4. England–Religious life and customs.
I. Title.
BX2080.D84 2006
242.0942′0902–dc22

2006006209

FRONTISPIECE MARGINAL PIETY?

This 1531 printed Book of Hours was one of the best-selling lines of the publisher François Regnault. Owned in the 1530s by the Whiston family of Dinton, it remained in use by Catholics long after the reformation, as its battered and thumbed condition suggests. One of these later owners added a devotion for the souls of the dead (left, lower page), involving fasting on bread and water on Wednesdays and Fridays, and reciting daily the Pater Noster, Creed, Litany and De Profundis Psalm.

Stonyhurst College T7/26, S3/9 RSTC 15970, Regnault, Paris, 1531 fol clxiv (verso) and clxv. Page size 10 × 6 cm

FOR MY SISTER

MARY

WITH LOVE

CONTENTS

PREFACE

Almost 800 manuscript Books of Hours survive from the English Middle Ages. These Latin books, often gloriously illuminated, were the indispensable devotional accessory of well-to-do lay people in the later Middle Ages. They have always been favourite collectors' items, and examples are to be found in most of the world's great libraries. With the invention of print, the Book of Hours, once the exclusive prerogative of the rich, became affordable by anyone aspiring to respectability. Thousands of these printed Books of Hours have also survived, and both the manuscript and printed versions provide valuable clues to the beliefs and devotional habits of medieval people – not least to the innermost thoughts of women, who formed a large proportion of the medieval market for such books.

I began looking at Books of Hours more than fifteen years ago, while preparing a study of late medieval religion, published as The Stripping of the Altars. I was struck then by how many of these books contained often crude manuscript material added by successive owners. Some of this was no more than pen-trials and doodles – 'Joe soap his book', scribbled long after the religion which the books represented had been forgotten or repudiated, and the books themselves seemed no longer sacred. One example in the Bodleian Library in Oxford was even signed in biro! But most of the additions dated from the middle ages, and were far more revealing. Family notes were common: people used their Books of Hours to record deaths, births, and marriages. I still recall the surge of emotion with which, turning the pages of one such book, I saw written in a neat fifteenth-century hand against a date in the calendar for November, 'My mother departed to God'. My own mother had died not long before, and for a moment the centuries between me and the fifteenth-century book-owner were gone, swallowed up in the universal human experience of loss.

But the additions were very varied: portraits of the owners, or customised prayers into which their names had been inserted: extra prayers in Latin, French or English, added to the fly-leaves or margins: detailed information about times of births for use in the casting of horoscopes: charms and cures and recipes: notes on financial transactions (people often swore solemn oaths on their prayer-books, so they were a good place to record agreements): holy pictures and pilgrim souvenirs, glued or stitched in: requests for prayers and affectionate remembrance: the range seemed endless. Here was an extraordinary archive, a series of unexpected windows into the hearts and souls of the men and women who long ago had used these books to pray. I decided to look systematically at as many of these books as possible, to see what sense could be made of all these additions.

The history of prayer, with which this book is much concerned, is as difficult to write as the history of sex, and for some of the same reasons. Both activities are intensely personal and in the nature of things not readily accessible to objective analysis. As a consequence, the history of prayer, like that of sex, is prone to elicit from historians a good deal of slack thought and overheated comment. I have tried to avoid both dangers by focussing on a very concrete body of evidence. The Book of Hours was beyond all question the most intimate and important book of the late Middle Ages, and that intimacy has left its physical trace in the margins, fly-leaves and blank spaces of those which survive. It is that material, those marginalia, which form the core of my concern here. The people I shall be concerned with vandalised their books, as we should say, in ways which make the art historian draw breath sharply in disapproval. But it is primarily to that vandalism that I want to attend, for in it we have the trace of use, and a set of clues to what it was brought the first owners of these books to use them at all.

So, most of the books to which I will be discussing are a librarian's nightmare, and my book itself is a tribute to scribbles, an attempt to trace a history written, quite literally, in the margins. This will emphatically not be an exercise in art history, as writings about Books of Hours normally are. In the course of preparing this work I encountered time and again the tolerant bafflement of librarians and curators, amazed that anyone should concern themselves with the very marks, scratches and blots which spoiled otherwise beautiful books. I necessarily commissioned a good deal of photography from the manuscript and rare books departments of many great libraries, and I treasure a puzzled email from a kind member of staff at the greatest of them, who told me that she felt sure some mistake had been made. The order I had placed for photographs, she wrote, listed pages on which the pictures had unfortunately been scraped or blotted or cut out completely, and some had no pictures at all, only ugly scribblings. So she wondered if I had inadvertently written down the wrong folio numbers, and suggested that I might prefer pictures of some of the more handsome adjacent pages. In the same way, another kindly librarian, querying the folio numbers I had listed for photography, asked, 'but why did someone scribble on them anyway?' When I explained that these were catholic books being censored by Tudor protestants, she paused for thought, then commented tersely: 'well, I only hope they were their own, and not borrowed from a library'!

We will in fact be considering some beautiful books in what follows, but beauty is not my concern, and I have little to say about the pictures which are sometimes the chief glory and almost always a key dimension of these books. Instead, I want to take my reader on a journey through the odd but revealing things that people write in, on, or outside their books, hoping, in the process, to catch a glimpse of the inner lives of people who lived in an even more turbulent age than our own.

Marking the Hours is an expanded version of the 2002 Riddell lectures in the University of Newcastle, incorporating material first aired in the 1999 Shannon-Clerk lecture at Washington and Lee University, Lexington, Virginia. I am grateful to both Universities for the invitation to give these prestigious lectures, and for the warmth of the hospitality I received in both institutions. Parts of the argument have also been aired in a number of other locations, including the University of the South at Sewanee, the international Medieval Congress at Kalamazoo, and the Summer Conference of the Ecclesiastical History Society. I have benefited greatly from the comments of members of all these auditories.

The Riddell Lectures in particular have a long and stellar pedigree, and my predecessors as Riddell Lecturer include such luminaries as the late Nora Chadwick, the late Christopher Hill, and the happily still quick Archbishop of Canterbury. In offering my small candle in the wake of their blazing torches, I take comfort from the fact that at least my lectures have lovely pictures to commend them. Though I have fleshed out the argument and added illustrative material, I have not tried to disguise the origins of the book as a series of lectures, and what is offered here is an overview of an enormous and complicated body of material, rather than an attempt at an exhaustive treatment.

As always, I am deeply indebted to my friend and editor at Yale, Sally Salvesen, who designed the book and suggested the title. My many debts to the kindly librarians at all the many institutions whose Books of Hours I have consulted are incalculable, but I owe particular debts of gratitude to the Librarians and staff of the British Library, the Bodleian Library, the Bienecke Library at Yale, the Cambridge University Library, Downside Abbey, the Fitzwilliam Museum, the Pierpont Morgan Library, Stonyhurst College, Ushaw College Durham, and York Minster. Richard Marks, Nicholas Rogers, and Nigel Morgan read drafts of Marking the Hours, and generously shared their great learning with me. They are, however, individually and collectively guiltless of the blemishes which remain.

Eamon Duffy
Easter 2006

LIST OF ILLUSTRATIONS

Part I

TOWARDS A HISTORY OF INTIMACY

I

A BOOK FOR LAY PEOPLE

The Book of Hours is one of the most glamorous and most familiar artefacts of the Middle Ages. With its illuminated initials, jewel-like colours and rich and sometimes literally bejewelled covers, it is an art work in its own right, and also features as a 'prop' in a myriad late medieval and renaissance paintings. In those pictures the Book of Hours functions not as a merely accidental piece of decoration, but as an instantly recognisable symbol of recollectedness, interiority and prayer [Pl. 1].

Walk round the medieval and renaissance rooms of any great picture-gallery, and you will see images of Books of Hours laid on prayer-desks before devoutly kneeling donors, held in the hands of attendant saints, or being prayed from by the Virgin Mary herself as the Angel surprises her at her devotions in a hundred Annunciation scenes.[1] Books of Hours, often known by their Latin name, 'Horae', or the familiar English name 'Primer' (to rhyme with 'dimmer'), survive in their myriads, and are found in every major collection of ancient books – almost 800 manuscript books of hours made for use in England are scattered in libraries all over the world, and surviving printed versions produced for the English market in the two generations before the reformation are even more abundant.[2] Nineteenth-century book- and art-collectors loved them. Compact yet highly coloured, ranging from the modest to the breathtakingly lavish, they

1.
The display of piety was a feature of the sober court of Henry VII. Both the Queen (Elizabeth of York) and the King's mother (Lady Margaret Beaufort) were trend-setters of contemporary devotional fashion, and both of them gave and received Books of Hours as gifts. In this posthumous portrait, Lady Margaret is portrayed in the costume of a vowess (widow sworn to chastity) and her religious dedication is symbolised by the richly decorated Book of Hours she holds in her hand.

Lady Margaret Beaufort with a Book of Hours, Christ's College Cambridge

might contain a mere handful of pictures, or a more or less complete compendium of medieval Christian iconography. Into relatively modern times Books of Hours still came regularly on to the art market, at prices which might be afforded even by only modestly rich collectors.

By and large, however, it was their pictures and border-decorations that attracted, rather than their text. Written in Latin, the texts the books existed to transmit were seldom of primary interest to the majority of those who sought them out, except perhaps in their faint whiff of the exotic, or the book's generic function as a relic of a romanticised Middle Ages, or, alternatively, the dark ages of popery. Anyone who has had occasion to handle any quantity of such books will be familiar with misleading eighteenth- and nineteenth-century binding labels, and even with elderly catalogue entries, describing such books, quite mistakenly, as 'Missals'.

But the attraction of the Book of Hours is not merely posthumous. The Book of Hours was the most popular book of the late Middle Ages, and the contents of such books provide a key, till recently largely neglected, to understanding the prayer-life, and therefore some of the innermost thoughts and most sacred privacies of late medieval people, women as well as men.[3] Books of Hours have been described by one historian of the medieval book as 'Books for everybody'.[4] This is perhaps to exaggerate a little the breadth of their appeal: to begin with at least any Book of Hours cost a fortune, and they were owned only by the rich. But that situation did not last: by the fifteenth century, cheaper versions for a wider market were being produced, and by the early Tudor period an unbound printed Book of Hours could probably be bought for 3d or 4d. In 1500, a London pauper woman, Avis Godfrey, was accused of stealing a 'premar' from Elizabeth Sekett, a domestic servant. She denied the charge, claiming she had picked the book up in Pudding Lane, but this fraught exchange suggests that the Book of Hours might be owned by a serving girl and desired by a pauper, though in the latter case possibly simply as a piece of disposable property.[5] So, even if not quite 'books for everybody', they penetrated a long way down the social scale and they were undoubtedly, as we shall see, books for anyone who mattered, or anyone who aspired to matter.

This popularity is in itself very surprising, for the Book of Hours was a Latin book, consciously modelled on the Latin books used by the clergy in the Church's formal services. We do not nowadays associate the inner lives of ordinary people with Latin literacy and the imitation of the clergy. So the Book of Hours can be regarded in two directly contrasting ways. On one reading, it can be understood as the physical embodiment of a remarkable medieval laicisation of clerical forms of prayer, the adaptation of the Church's complex liturgy for use by men and women from many walks of life, and of many levels of education. Conversely, one might view the evolution of such a book as a major monument to a baffling imaginative and religious failure, the imprisonment of medieval lay devotion within the constrictions of an inappropriate clerical straitjacket. People power, or aping of the clergy? It will, I hope, become clear that I myself tend to the former view, but readers will be able to form their own judgement in the light of what follows.

The principal contents of the Book of Hours were in fact originally private devotions which had, by the twelfth century, become a routine and often obligatory extension of the Monastic round of worship or *Opus Dei*. Monks and canons (clerics living in community under a rule) were obliged to the weekly recitation of more or less the entire Psalter in a complex arrangement divided into the seven major daily offices of Matins (or 'Vigils', originally recited in the night), Lauds (the dawn office), Prime, Terce, Sext and Nones (the shorter 'day' offices), Vespers (the evening office), plus the short bed-time service of Compline. Most of these formal offices varied considerably with the liturgical seasons, involving an elaborate system of variable psalms, prayer-texts, hymns and antiphons with their accompanying music, all of which was contained in a formidable battery of books. Even the priest's Breviary or *Portiforium*, intended, as these names suggest, as a convenient and portable compendium of these elaborate services, was a dauntingly copious, complex and bewildering book, written in double columns and normally divided into summer and winter volumes. Involving an expert knowledge of the rules for variation encapsulated in the Latin rubrics, and requiring much turning to and fro to find the right page on the right day, the breviary was less than ideal as a vehicle for lay prayer.

By the twelfth century, however, monks and canons were also often obliged to recite shorter groups of psalms such as the Penitential psalms or the so-called 'Gradual' psalms, and some short devotional offices, above all the 'Little Hours of the Virgin', as well as to recite the office for the dead daily in memory of deceased brethren, all this on top of the Office proper. These additional services, like the formal Office, were similarly arranged round the liturgical 'Hours', and were sometimes recited immediately after them. They were, however, far simpler in structure, the texts shorter, the psalms fewer, varying hardly or not at all with the seasons. They might therefore even be recited from memory, but were more commonly written out in small books suitable for use in private rather than in choir.[6] These utilitarian collections were the ultimate ancestors of the gorgeous later elaborations of the Book of Hours. Shorter, simpler and almost unvarying, yet containing many of the most accessible, eloquent and affecting of the psalms, between them the 'Little Hours' of the Virgin, the Gradual Psalms, Penitential Psalms, Litany of the Saints, and the Office of the Dead would become the basis for the most popular book of the Middle Ages, a short and simple 'breviary' for lay folk.

By the early thirteenth century Western Europe as a whole, and England with the rest, was in the full flood of the great expansion of religious provision for lay people which we associate with the Fourth Lateran Council (1215), and the popular Christianity of the friars.[7] Significant numbers of devout lay people, especially among the leisured and well-heeled, and perhaps especially among wealthy women, were responding to the heightened mood of religious seriousness, and looking to the new religious orders to give that mood point and direction. Growing numbers of lay people were interested in the pursuit of a serious interior religious life, and sufficient numbers of these lay people were literate to provide a market for religious books specially designed to cater for their needs.[8]

Our first major medieval source for the religious life of English people other than monks or nuns is a treatise of guidance written in English, and for women, sometime during the second quarter of the thirteenth century. This devotional manual was the work of an anonymous male religious, friendly to the new mendicant orders though probably not himself a friar. It was originally designed for the guidance of three pious women, sisters from the same family. We can deduce from what he wrote that these ladies were daughters of a gentry household, who had renounced the world and were living together in modest comfort as recluses, attended by their maid-servants under the financial protection of a local lord, perhaps a relative. Nothing else is known for certain of the author or his first readers, though there are some reasons to think he may have been an Augustinian canon, and to judge by the dialect in which the treatise was written, he lived in the west of England, somewhere near the Welsh border. *Ancrene Wisse* 'A Guide for Anchoresses' was so far as we can tell the first sustained treatise on the devout life to be written in English, though its original audience of genteel secluded ladies were clearly accustomed to saying their prayers in Latin, and, as their spiritual director's instructions make clear, had access to at least a simple form of the Latin Book of Hours, which was already becoming and would be increasingly the favoured devotional tool of the well-to-do.

Much of the later development of the Book of Hours was foreshadowed in the devotional regime prescribed for this group of early thirteenth-century 'ancresses'.[9] The author assumes that these pious women will attend devoutly while the clergy of the church to which their hermitage was attached recite the daily offices from the breviary.[10] But he stipulates that they should listen to, but not audibly join in, these clerical devotions. Their own personal pattern of prayer was to be structured instead round the daily recitation of the simpler and shorter Little Hours of the Virgin in Latin, and he assumes that they would all have their own books or rolls for this purpose. 'Let each one say her Hours as she has written them out.' They were also to recite regularly the two parts of the Office of the Dead, known from their opening words, *Placebo* and *Dirige*, since this commemoration was a feature of the prayer routine in religious houses, which lay people could usefully imitate, 'and you can do so too'. Alongside these offices he recommends also the regular recital of the seven penitential psalms, of the fifteen 'Gradual' psalms,[11] and of a series of prayers in honour of the holy cross, the five wounds of Christ, and the joys of the Virgin. Here, in one of the earliest of all discussions of the pattern of daily prayer for women, the development of later medieval piety is already mapped out. Prayers drawing on precisely these sources and themes were to dominate the core contents of the Book of Hours for the rest of the Middle Ages.

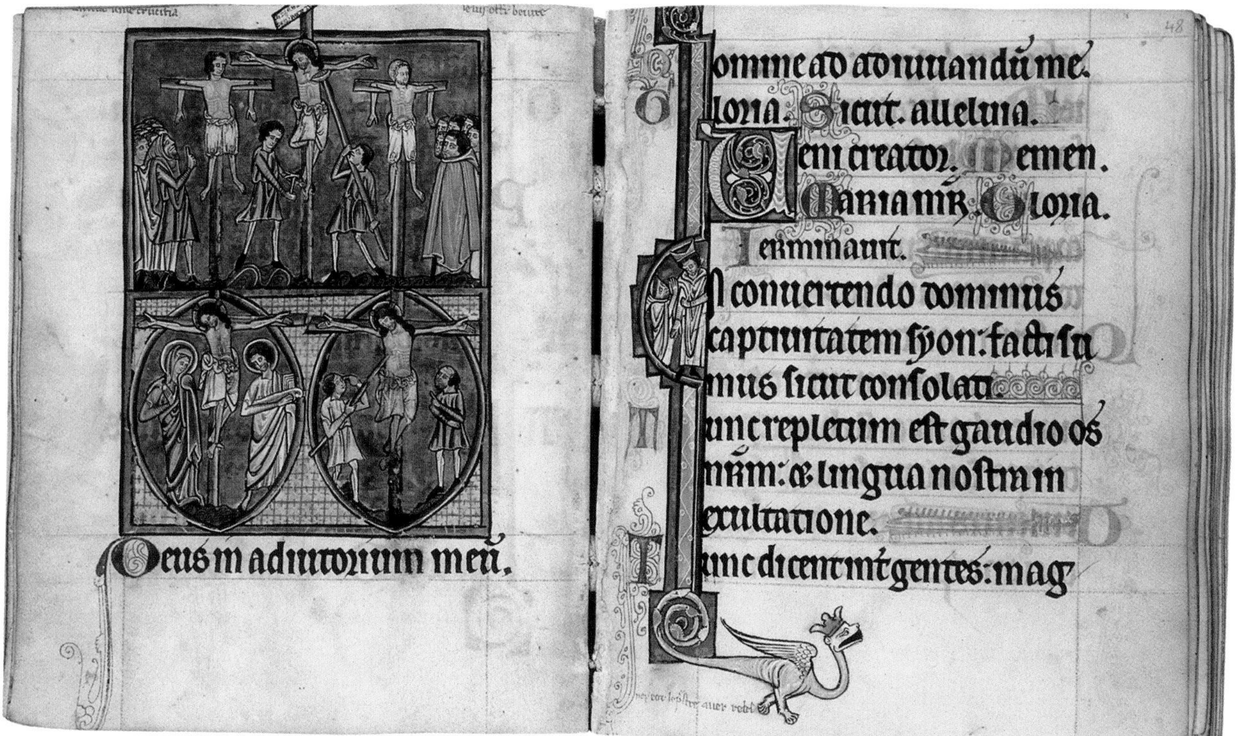

2. THE EMERGENCE OF THE FORMAT
Written and illuminated in Oxford *c.* 1240 by the commercial scribe William de Brailes, the De Brailes Hours may be the earliest surviving free-standing Book of Hours (without Psalter) made for an English user. Here the opening of Nones (the liturgical hour at which, by tradition, Christ died on the Cross) is marked by a series of miniatures of the Passion. In the margin of the opposite page is one of a sequence of drawings illustrating a miracle story of St Thomas Becket.

British Library Add 49999, De Brailes Hours fos. 47v–48. Page size 15 × 12 cm

But to begin with, the precise selection of material for inclusion in Books of Hours varied from book to book, reflecting the devotional choices of those who had often commissioned them. And remarkably, a high proportion of the surviving examples of these earliest Books of Hours in England were made for women. The likely social provenance of what may well be the very first of these surviving English Books of Hours is suggestive in this regard [Pl. 2]. It was produced in Oxford around the year 1240 by William de Brailes, a commercial illuminator and scribe working in the warren of stationers' shops round the church of St Mary the Virgin.[12] To judge by the decorative scheme, the book was commissioned by or for a woman whose name may have been Susanna (though the evidence that this was her name is decidedly circumstantial and tenuous), and whose family were possibly parishioners and benefactors of the parish church of St Laurence, North Hinksey.[13] A sequence of illustrations in the illuminated capitals of the Gradual Psalms associated with intercession for

3. A LITERATE WOMEN AT PRAYER
The patron for whom the De Brailes Hours was made was a woman, who is represented in the book four times. Here she is in supplication in the opening initial of the Penitential Psalm 101 (102), beginning appropriately 'Lord hear my prayer'. Representations of women owners are surprisingly common in early Books of Hours.

British Library Add Ms 49999, De Brailes Hours fo. f 75. Page size 15 × 12 cm

the dead tells the otherwise unknown story of a wealthy burgess and benefactor of the parish of St Laurence, whose soul is delivered by alms and the intercession of an anchoress attached to the church of St Laurence. The parish church of North Hinksey is the only one in the Oxford area dedicated to St Laurence, so if (as is by no means certain) the story is intended to have a local resonance, Hinksey must be the intended location. The illustrations begin with the opening words of Psalm 129 (130), the '*De Profundis*' which is the principle Catholic prayer for the dead: it seems likely that the burgess concerned was a deceased member of 'Susanna's' own family, perhaps her father. Fact or fiction, given the centrality of the anchoress's role in this little drama, we have clearly not moved far from the devotional world of *Ancrene Wisse*.[14] However that may be, 'Susanna', who is repeatedly depicted in a posture of prayer in the illuminated initials of the book [Pl. 3],[15] was almost certainly a client of the Dominicans, for she had spiritual advisers in the Oxford house: vernacular (French) Prayers to the Virgin were added on blank pages at the back of the book at the same time as the main commission. They begin with a reminder to say an Our Father, and a Hail Mary for three Dominicans, Richard of Newark, Richard of Westey and Bartholomew of Grimston, for all friars, Preachers and Minors alike, and for her confessors [Pl. 4].[16]

This first surviving English Book of Hours, with its handy small format, simple layout and large clear script may well have had an abiding influence on the layout and format of subsequent books of hours, but its contents were meagre by later standards. Though it included the Little Hours of the Virgin, the Penitential and Gradual

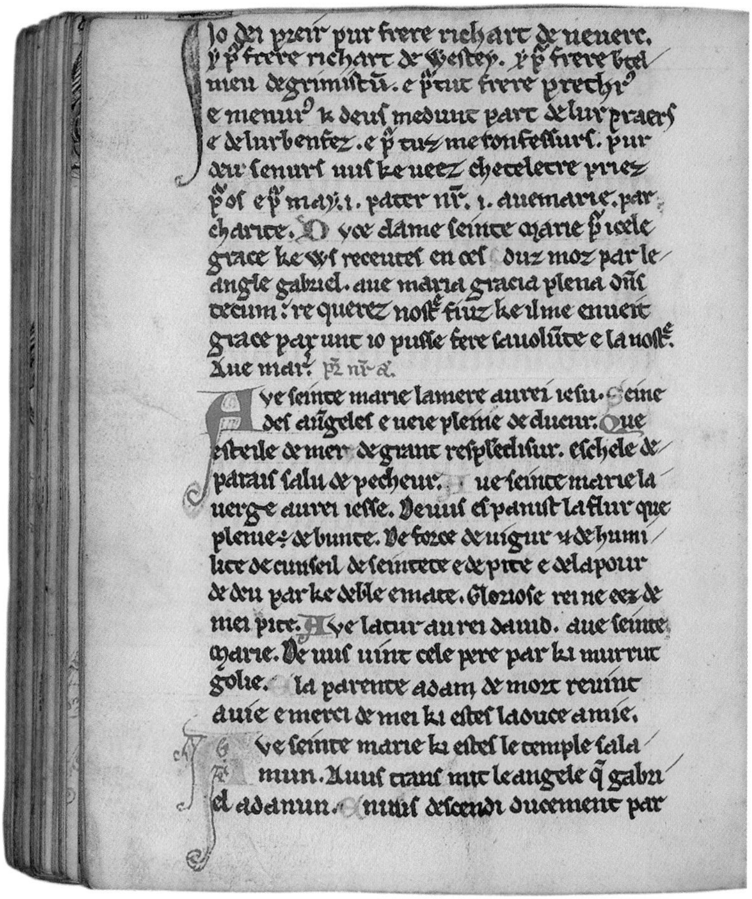

Psalms, and the Litany of the Saints, all destined to be staples of the fully developed Book of Hours, it lacked both a Calendar, indispensable for any well-ordered devotional life, and also the Office of the Dead. The owner perhaps had access to either or both of these missing elements in another form, such as an illuminated Psalter.

Very few Books of Hours survive for England for the century after 1240, and one recent count found fewer than three dozen in all before the end of the thirteenth century.[17] In the century after William de Brailes' first book, the form and content of the Book of Hours was still evolving, and there is therefore a striking variation in the content of the earliest books, for every commission was a fresh beginning, and the wishes and needs of patrons were relatively unconstrained by convention. All the earliest books contain the Little Office of the Virgin, but there consistency ends. The Marston Hours, produced in East Anglia about 1250, has the Hours of the Virgin and the short hours of the Holy Spirit: a subsequent owner a generation or so on added the Penitential Psalms and the Litany.[18] The De Vere Hours, by contrast, probably produced in the Fenlands sixty years after the De Brailes Hours, is a bruiser of a book, ten and a quarter inches by seven, and even in its present modest leather binding weighing in at a massive 2.8 kilos. It could never have been comfortable to hold for long in the hands, and must have been used on a cushioned desk or prie-dieu. It is almost as elaborate as a breviary, containing many seasonal variations to the Hours of the Virgin, and including not only the Litany, Gradual and Penitential Psalms, and the Office of the Dead, but also a series of minor offices – of the Trinity, the Holy Spirit, the Nativity, the Purification and the Assumption of the Virgin, and of the Passion of Christ.[19] And if few of these early books rivalled the De Vere Hours in the choice of special services it provided, many include idiosyncratic and even exotic items, including devotions to local or unofficial saints, and many vernacular prayers and rhymes.[20] As the core contents of the books stabilised, these idiosyncratic materials would be excluded, but patrons continued to value this sort of devotional personalisation, and as we shall see, materials of this kind were to recur throughout the Middle Ages, added to Books of Hours on end gatherings, blank pages, and flyleaves.

Many of the Books of Hours which date from thirteenth century England can be associated with women, and no fewer than six of those made before 1300 contain what appear to be portraits of their female owners. Several suggest a connection between their owners and the religious orders, especially the friars.[21] At this stage, all Books of Hours, whether or not they had a portrait of the owner, were of course expensive, because they were copied and coloured by hand on folded sheets of vellum made from the laboriously prepared skins of a small flock of sheep or herd of calves. They therefore took time to establish themselves widely in lay regard, though the accidents of survival make attempts at statistical precision here illusory. However, it is clear that after the Black Death lay interest in such books, or perhaps just lay purchasing power, was growing, and from the early fifteenth century onwards, Books of Hours were being produced in large numbers for the English market, as for the rest of western Europe. They become an increasingly common devotional accessory, largely superseding the Psalters which till then had been the most popular prayer-book for wealthy and literate lay people.[22]

From the beginning, in a devotional culture in which images played a dominant role, Books of Hours were often lavishly decorated with elaborate borders, initials and miniatures. These will not be our main concern in this book, but we need to register their centrality for the first users of these books. If *Horae* were at an obvious level expressions of the religion of the word, and of a newly awakened lay appetite for a more active and personalised devotional regime, they were also very much part of the religion of the image, and the pictures were often at least as important to their users as the texts they accompanied.

4. CUSTOMISED PRAYERS AND SPIRITUAL GUIDES
The De Brailes Hours was modified while still in preparation, to bring the evening office of vespers into line with the Dominican rite, perhaps in order to allow the female owner to pray with her Dominican advisers. A series of prayers to the Virgin in French (the vernacular language of this upper-class English owner) added at the end of the book begins by naming three Oxford Dominicans, and prays for all Dominicans and Franciscans, a mark of the role of the Friars in the spiritual awakening of the thirteenth century which encouraged lay use of Books of Hours.

British Library Add Ms 49999, De Brailes Hours fo. 102v. Page size 15 × 12 cm

5. SCRIPTURE SCENES FOR THE HOURS

The Hours of the Virgin were traditionally marked by eight scenes from the Infancy of Christ, beginning with his Conception at the Annunciation at the start of Matins, culminating with the Virgin's Coronation in Heaven at Compline. In this mid-fourteenth-century English book, with a long history of female ownership, the morning office of Lauds opens with the standard miniature of the Visitation of Mary to her cousin Elizabeth.

Fitzwilliam Museum Ms 48, Carew-Poyntz Hours fo. 97v. Page size 18 × 11 cm

The illustrative schemes in such books were often carefully planned and expensively executed to enhance comprehension.[23] Early Books of Hours often had sequences which might counterpoint or gloss the prayer texts around the pictures, or which might have a devotional value independent of the text – the story of Susannah or the life of the Virgin in the De Brailes Hours, the miracles of the Virgin Mary in the Neville of Hornby Hours, or the scenes from the Nativity or Passion stories which became a staple item in many *Horae*.[24]

One very obvious use for illustrations and illuminated initials was as a guide to the user of the book, providing a marker for the opening of each of the Hours. Early in the history of the Book of Hours these illustrations at the opening of the Hours of the Virgin became standardised – a Nativity sequence which included the Annunciation

6. SCRIPTURE SCENES FOR THE HOURS

From the later fourteenth century, the Hours of the Virgin in Books of Hours for the English market are normally preceded by scenes from the Passion rather than from Christ's Infancy. In this handsome example made in a London workshop *c.* 1405–10, Vespers begins with the standard depiction of the Deposition of Christ from the Cross, probably painted by the best German artist working in London in the reigns of Henry IV and Henry V, Herman Scheere.

Cambridge University Library Ee 1 14, fo. 44. Page size 21 × 14cm

at the start of Matins, the Visitation (visit of Mary to her cousin Elizabeth) at Lauds, the birth of Jesus at Prime, the annunciation by the angels to the shepherds at Terce, the adoration of the Magi at Sext, the presentation of the infant Jesus in the temple at Nones, the flight of the Holy Family into Egypt at Vespers, and the coronation of the Virgin in heaven at Compline [Pl. 5].

A second sequence, intended as subjects for meditation on the sufferings and death of Christ, and derived from a devotional work by a saintly thirteenth-century Archbishop of Canterbury, Edmund of Abingdon, allocated the major events of the Passion to the eight liturgical Hours, starting with the Agony in the Garden at Matins and finishing with the laying of Christ's body in the tomb at Compline [Pl. 6]. These scenes were considered specially appropriate for the

7. THE DEVOTIONAL GAZE

The pictures in Books of Hours both enhanced the texts they accompanied and worked independently of them. Many images were designed specifically to arouse intense devotional feeling in those who gazed at them. In this late-fifteenth-century book made for use in the Norwich diocese, the solemn and arresting face of Christ on the 'Vernicle' or 'Veronica's Veil' accompanies a verse meditation on the Divine glory revealed in the Incarnation.

Fitzwilliam Museum Ms 55 fo. 122v, Holy Face and Hymn 'Salve Sancta Facies'. Page size 20 × 14cm

8. A BOOK FOR URBAN WOMEN

Three of the four donor pictures in the Bolton Hours, produced in York *c.* 1405–15, feature the patroness without her husband, suggesting that the book was primarily intended for female use. Here the patroness kneels before St Zita of Lucca (labelled St Sytha). Zita was a servant-girl, whose cult was associated with women, the household and the recovery of lost keys.

York Minster Library Add 2 Ms 40v. Page size 15 × 11 cm

Hours of the Cross, which were often included as an additional item in Books of Hours or in a short form were interpolated in the Hours of the Virgin. But in England they were more often than not substituted as the frontispieces to each of the Hours of the Virgin in place of the Nativity scenes: very lavish books might have both.[25]

In addition to these sequences of scriptural scenes, Books of Hours from their very beginning also included single images which might function either in association with services and devotions, or as focuses of devout contemplation in their own right. Images of the saints with their identifying emblems might mark the appropriate suffrages or commemorations within the daily offices, the commendations and Litany might be preceded by a depiction of the Last Judgement, and the office of the dead by an image of the funeral liturgy. In addition, in the course of the later Middle Ages a repertoire of powerful single devotional images emerged as routine elements in the Books of Hours: the *Arma Christi* or Instruments of the Passion; the Image of Pity or Mass of St Gregory; the 'Vernicle', Veronica or Holy Face of Jesus; the wounds of Jesus in hands, feet and (especially) side [Pl. 7].[26] Many of these were routinely used to preface or accompany particular prayers: the Image of Pity or Mass of St Gregory to accompany the Psalms of the Passion or the so-called prayers of St Gregory,[27] addressed to the Wounds of Christ; the Vernicle to accompany the hymn *Salve Sancta Facies*; Christ in Judgement to preface the Penitential Psalms, and so on. The most copiously illustrated surviving English Book of Hours of the fifteenth century is the Bolton Hours. This was produced in York before 1420 for a mercantile family, probably in the Michaelgate area, and had over seventy pictures, admittedly rather naively drawn: more than forty of them were full page miniatures, making the book as much a picture book as a collection of texts [Pl. 8].

In addition to miniatures of the Holy Face and the Sacred Heart and Wounds of Jesus, they included the usual sequences from both the Infancy and the Passion of Christ before the Hours, portraits of the patron's family in prayer before the Holy Trinity and favourite saints such as the 'martyred' Archbishop Richard Scrope of York or the women's saint, Zita of Lucca, sequences of the Apostles and of helper saints like Christopher (protector of travellers) and Apollonia (for relief from toothache). The book seems to have been the special

9. HOURS OF MARY OF BURGUNDY
The miniature before the Hours of the Cross from a sumptuous Primer made in the later 1470s for Mary of Burgundy, wife of the emperor Maximilian I and step-daughter of the Englishwoman Margaret of York. Here the scene of the nailing of Christ to the cross is framed by statuettes of Old Testament typological scenes. These, with an assortment of bric-a-brac which includes a rosary and a Book of Hours, symbolise a typical mixed late-medieval lay devotional regime of rote-prayer, meditation and the recitation of the Hours.

Vienna, Österreichische Nationalbibliothek, Codex Vindobonensis 1857 (Hours of Mary of Burgundy) fol 43v. Page size 23 × 16 cms

possession of the women of the family, which may account for the presence in it of several other images of women saints, and of saints favoured specially by women. These included the newly canonised Swedish visionary, St Brigid, whose controversial Revelations were establishing themselves, in York as elsewhere, as a crucial devotional resource. Even as the Bolton Hours was being compiled, Brigid's sanctity was being debated at the Council of Constance, and she herself was providing a role-model for the extraordinary East Anglian mystical pilgrim, Margery Kempe.[28]

Such pictures were of course more than bookmarks or holy wallpaper. They were intended as aids to mental prayer, supplementary to or independent of the text to which they were prefixed. They were designed to stir religious emotion and arouse gratitude to God or sorrow for sins, every detail to be gazed at, prayed over and ruminated on. Consequently, image and text might operate independently as well as in concert, and the 'devotional gaze' on a sacred 'close-up' was a crucial element in the piety even of the sophisticated and the literate in the late Middle Ages.[29] In a Latin book whose precise meaning might be only partially or imperfectly understood by its lay user, the role of the pictures must often have been at least as important as the words of the services themselves.

Once again, the very format of these books encourages us to resist simplistic polarities. It is tempting to see the rise of the Book of Hours as in some sense a triumph of literacy over rote devotion, the rise of the religion of the book at the expense, at least among the well-to-do, of the less literate religion of the image or the bead. This however, is a temptation which should be resisted, for image, bead and book continued to coexist, and to be used by the same people.

The very first surviving English book of Hours had contained an injunction to its owner to recite Hail Maries for her Dominican spiritual guides, and this injunction to the book-owner to repeat Our Fathers and Hail Maries is an example of the overlap between the religion of the bead and of the book. It would be often replicated throughout the subsequent history of the Book of Hours. Two centuries on, two of the best-known illustrations in Mary of Burgundy's lavish Book of Hours carefully locate the use of the book within a devotional regime which included, with no apparent sense of hierarchy, the recitation of the rosary, the use of devotional images, the recitation of the liturgical office and the cultivation of extended devotional meditation on the Passion [Pls 9, 18].[30]

The author of *Ancrene Wisse* took it for granted that his pious ladies would routinely recite decades of Paters and Aves alongside or instead of their daily recitation of Our Lady's Matins, and that they would have images and relics on the altars before which they prayed.[31] Preaching at the funeral of Joan, Lady Cobham in 1344, John Sheppey, Bishop of Rochester, reported the mixed nature of her prayer-regime, liturgical, devotional, and rote-repetitious, with her Book of Hours at its centre: 'on no day would she willingly come down from her chamber or speak with any stranger, until she had said matins and the Hours of Our Lady, the Seven Psalms and the Litany, almost every day': then at Mass, 'when the priest was silent', she said some private prayers in French – no doubt from texts in her book – 'and some Paternosters and Hail Maries'.[32]

10. & 11. DEVOTIONAL DISPLAY
Books of Hours were often as much tokens of worldly wealth as of spiritual devotion. In this sumptuous book, produced in England for an aristocratic couple at the beginning of the fourteenth century, the size of the pages, the lavish use of gold, the heraldic display of armorial shields, and portraits of the couple on either side of the throne of God and of the wife kneeling in the initial of the Hours of the Trinity, combine to announce the high status of the book's owners.

Cambridge Fitzwilliam Museum Ms 242, (Pabenham-Clifford / Grey Fitzpayne Hours) fos. 28v, 29r. Page size 25 × 17 cm

The presence and importance of pictures, textual illumination and marginal decoration made Books of Hours especially costly, and to begin with they certainly were the preserve of royalty and aristocracy, or the wealthiest members of the urban elite, like the Boltons. Indeed, the cost was often not so much a drawback of such books, as part of their *point*, and their decorative schemes were often designed to draw

attention to wealth and dynastic alliances as much as religious preferences – a glance at the heraldic elaboration and the lavish use of gold in sumptuous early examples like the Pabenham-Clifford (formerly Grey Fitzpayne) Hours [Pls. 10, 11] makes this point eloquently. Here indeed was a manifestation of social as well as of devotional elitism.[33] Possession of more than one Book of Hours was common, and

12. A BOOK FOR THE BOURGEOIS
The Bolton Hours contains obits of the family of the mercer, John Bolton, successively chamberlain, M.P. and Mayor of York, and was made for his family, or that of another York city grandee. Here, as in the Pabenham-Clifford Hours, the donor and his family kneel in prayer before the Trinity, but although still a luxury item for the well-to-do, this York book is intended for townspeople, not for aristocrats.

York Minster Library Add Ms 2 fo. 33. Page size 15 × 11 cm

perhaps reflected routine use of relatively humble books, and the confinement of the use of large and highly ornamented books to occasions of state. Bequests of such books sometimes make special provision for the bequest of 'my best primer' or 'my big best primer' to a favoured recipient.[34]

Large and lavish manuscript Books of Hours like these would go on being produced well into the late fifteenth century.[35] Nevertheless, the Book of Hours also moved inexorably and decisively down-market. This, it should be noticed, is a development that long predates print, for already by the early fifteenth century Books of Hours were being effectively mass-produced in stationers' shops across Europe, but especially in France and the Netherlands.[36] So, before and after print, the Book of Hours was everywhere in the late Middle Ages. In the late fourteenth century the French poet Eustache Deschamps satirised this appetite, which he thought was specially strong in women, for the last word in devotional display:

13. WOMEN AT PRAYER
In Memling's picture Sir John Donne of Kidwelly and his wife Elizabeth, wearing prestigious livery collars of Edward IV, kneel before the Virgin and Child. Sir John owned a Book of Hours which survives in the library of the University of Louvain. Here, Lady Donne holds her Hours open before her, an instantly recognisable symbol of devout contemplation. Double columns identify the Virgin Mary's larger book as a Breviary or Bible rather than a Book of Hours.

Hans Memling, Donne Triptych. National Gallery, London, 6275

Get me an Hours of the Virgin,
Matched to my high degree,
The finest the craftsmen can manage
As graceful and gorgeous as me:
Paint it with gold and with azure
With gold clasps to fasten it down,
So the people will gasp when I use it,
'That's the prettiest prayer-book in town.'[37]

But by the early fifteenth century Books of Hours had become much more widely accessible, and examples were routinely owned and used by wealthy townsmen and-women. We know of many late fourteenth- or fifteenth-century books of hours commissioned for or bought by members of the urban elites, and some of these survive, such as the Bolton Hours, or the Browne Hours, a ready-made book customised in the 1460s for the Stamford merchant, John Browne, bound with silver-gilt and crystal clasps, and embossed with his merchant's mark [Pl. 16, 17].[38]

Unsurprisingly, the cost of Books of Hours might vary widely. Medieval book prices are notoriously elusive, but probate valuations from late medieval York give us some sense of the range of prices at any rate for secondhand Books of Hours. So the Primer 'with devotions' of Thomas Overdo, a York baker who died in 1444, was valued at 9s, as against the 6s 8d estimated for the primer covered with red velvet belonging to Thomas Morton, canon of York Minster. Cheaper still was the sixpence estimated as the value of the primer left by John Collan, a York goldsmith who died in 1490, and whose Book of Hours was in all probability one of the printed versions only recently available.[39] Given this steady growth in accessibility, by the late Middle Ages, wealthy bourgeois women felt naked unless they too possessed an example of this most chic of devotional fashion accessories. Its social cachet sprang from its iconic function. Wherever we turn in representations of later medieval and renaissance lay prayer, the Book of Hours is present, for example, in Memling's well-known Donne Triptych of 1478, showing Sir John Donne and his wife, Elizabeth Donne née Hastings, in prayer before the Virgin and Child [Pl. 13]. Lady Donne's rapt state of prayer is symbolised here by her Book of Hours, now sadly lost, though her husband's Book of Hours, made for him shortly after this altarpiece was painted, survives, as does the even more magnificent example made for Lady Donne's ill-fated brother, Sir William Hastings (executed in 1483), and now in the British Library.[40]

2

DEVOTIONAL INTIMACY: A BOOK OF REMEMBRANCE

Books of Hours were, from the start, intensely personal objects, carried about, when small enough, in a sleeve or at the belt, passed from hand to hand, a personal dimension indicated in the bequest by a fifteenth-century London merchant of 'my primer with gilt clasps *whereon I am wont to say my service*' or the York merchant's wife Agnes Hull, who left 'my primer which I use daily' to her daughter, or the London wax-chandler Roger Elmsley who in 1434 left to a favourite godchild 'a prymmer to serve God with'. In 1395 the Hampshire widow, Lady Alice West, who had taken a vow of chastity after her husband's death, bequeathed to her son Thomas 'a peyre Matyns bookis and a peire bedes, and a rynge with which I was yspousyd to God, which were my lordes his fadres'.[1] The 'matins book' here is Our Lady's Matins, the Primer or Book of Hours, and that cluster of religious and domestic sanctities (combining, it should be noted once again, the religion of bead and book) is entirely characteristic of the devotional world of which the Book of Hours was the principal token. This process of transmission within families and kinship groups might go on for generations and even centuries.

But books were also passed on outside families. Since many devout people had more than one book of hours, in addition to passing them on to children, they might be given or bequeathed to god-children, friends, chaplains, or servants. A printed Book of Hours published in 1528 and now in the Pierpont Morgan Library in New York nicely epitomises this sort of transmission history. Given by Catherine of Aragon to a lady in waiting, it had then moved on through that recipient's family: an inscription on the flyleaf records that 'Thys boke was good queen Katrins boke and she gave yt to Mrs Coke hir woman and she gave yt to Katryne Ogle hyr dawghter and she gave yt to Roger Ogle her husband and the sayd Roger wyll that at my deth she shall have the sayd boke ageyn and non other to have yt.'[2]

Roger Ogle, evidently an opponent of the Henrician reformation, was clearly concerned to keep this devotional relic of 'Good Queen Catherine' in the family, but books often did gravitate outside the families for which they were made, and in the process more often than not moved down-market, not least because the very dynastic additions – portraits, coats of arms and obit entries – which at first made them emblems and expression of elite religion, combined now to lower their value, and constituted a problem for new users. There is in the Bodleian a once handsome but long since battered and disbound late fourteenth-century Book of Hours produced in an Oxford stationers for the Wyllylie family, minor Shropshire gentry from the Much Wenlock area. The book passed by marriage from the Wyllylies into the Parlour family, hereditary foresters of Morfe: obits for members of both tribes were entered into the calendar. By the later fifteenth-century, however, the Parlours had evidently fallen on hard times, either financially or genetically, for the book moved altogether out of the family, and was acquired, probably by purchase, by another Shropshire household, the Wegges. They or whoever sold the book to them carefully dealt with the removable traces of the earlier history of the book by pumicing out of the vellum all the Wyllylie and Parlour obits, which can now only be read under ultra-violet light. The new owners were still gentry, but not nearly so grand as the Wyllylies, as is evidenced by their willingness to buy a century-old prayer-book secondhand rather than commissioning a new book of their own. They started afresh, however, entering their own series of obits at the turn of the fifteenth and sixteenth centuries. An Egge daughter married into the Corberts early in the sixteenth century, and another married a Ward. The book, still in use and by now into its second set of covers, moved on in the female line, and therefore in the course of the later sixteenth century accumulated Egge, Corbert and Ward obits and birthday entries, till at length the family evidently conformed to the new religion, and new entries ceased altogether.[3]

In the same way, a handsome manuscript Book of Hours produced *c.* 1450 for Ann, daughter of Richard Duke of York, and Duchess of Exeter, and now in the library of Sidney Sussex College, Cambridge, had by the mid-Tudor period fetched up in a middle-class household in Ipswich, where its flyleaves and blanks were being used as a copybook to instruct young Edmond Church in handwriting and good manners.[4] We catch a glimpse of the economic realities behind this sort of social descent in the note added to a tiny Book of Hours made originally for Richard Plantagenet, Duke of York (d. 1460), and now at Ushaw College, Durham, which records that an early sixteenth-century owner, Edward Ashton of Chadderton, had picked it up secondhand for three shillings, well within the buying-power of even a modest yeoman or city merchant or shop-keeper.[5]

But there was no need for merchants, shopkeepers or country gentry to resort to the sellers of secondhand books to acquire a Book of Hours. From the end of the fourteenth century the stationers' shops of the Low Countries and Northern France were catering for a mass market, producing manuscript books on vellum with a largely plain or lightly decorated text, and where such full-page illustrations as were provided were bulk-bought in sets by the stationers, and tipped into the volumes to dress them up. Nearly two hundred of such assembly-line books for England survive [Pls. 14, 15], and a large proportion of their known owners were, as Nicholas Rogers, the leading authority on these books has observed, 'middling merchants and local gentry, people with social pretensions who would be attracted by something which looked more expensive than it really was.'[6]

All this ensured that in the course of the fifteenth century the Book of Hours and the religion it represented ceased to be the monopoly of aristocracy and the upper gentry, and became an integral part of the religious experience of the urban and rural 'middling sort': the King's Lynn housewife and small-time brewer Margery Kempe owned a Book of Hours, and, as we have seen, they are a common bequest in the wills of merchants and better off shopkeepers. But the decisive democratising of the Book of Hours came at the end

14. ASSEMBLY LINE PIETY

A late fourteenth or early fifteenth-century example of the modestly produced Flemish Books of Hours for the English market, with a comparatively plain text and tipped-in full-page illuminations. Here, in a standard pairing, a picture of the Trinity accompanies a popular prayer for protection against enemies. One of the book's many owners has corrected the text by adding in the margin the opening words of Psalm 129 (130), *De Profundis*, omitted by the original scribe.

Cambridge University Library Ii 6 2 fo. 10v–11. Page size 19 × 13 cm

15. ASSEMBLY LINE PIETY

A book using pictures from the same workshop as Plate 14 (note the canopy over both images). The *Imago Pietatis* or 'Image of Pity', the wounded Christ surrounded by the 'Instruments of the Passions', is prefixed to a series of devotions to the Cross and Passion of Christ. The Image of Pity often carried an accompanying indulgence, promising spiritual reward to all who 'piteously behold' the image [see Pls. 17, 20, 28].

British Library Sloane 2683 fo. 65v–66. Page size 20 × 12 cm of the fifteenth century, with the arrival of print. Books of Hours became, in terms of numbers of editions, quite simply and without any rival the chief product of the new technology.[7]

All these people, then, high and low, aristocratic and plebeian, were using the same book. That book contained a standardised selection of psalms, antiphons, hymns and prayers, arranged for recitation in honour of Mary at each of the eight monastic divisions or hours of the day. To these 'hours' of the Virgin were added the office for the dead or *Placebo et Dirige* (Vespers Matins, and Lauds of the dead), the short Hours of the Cross, which in books for the English market were usually inserted between the Hours of the Virgin, the long Psalm 118 (119) called the Commendations of the soul, the seven Penitential Psalms and the Litany of the Saints, the fifteen Gradual Psalms, and a series of individual 'suffrages' or short prayers to saints, especially to the Virgin Mary. These made up the core contents of the Book of Hours, which by the later fifteenth century had expanded to become a compendium of popular devotions. By then most included also a series of devotions (with accompanying illustrations) to the Trinity, the Wounds, the Passion and the Veronica or Holy Face of Jesus, prayers to the Virgin such as the popular prayers beginning *Obsecro Te*, and *O Intemerata*, hymns to and about Mary, such as the well-known poem on the passion, the *Stabat Mater*, or the Marian hymn against the plague *Stella Coeli extirpavit*. Many also included eucharistic devotions like the *Anima Christi*, ('Soul of Christ, sanctify me, Body of Christ, save me . . .') designed to be recited at Mass, and almost all contained the shortened version of the Psalter known as St Jerome's Psalter, which included almost 200 verses from the psalms, including the whole of Psalm 50 (51), the *Miserere*, and which normally carried a prefatory legend which guaranteed the user protection against the devil and untimely death.

As we have seen, Books of Hours were, to begin with, precious objects, whose expensive gold illumination, heraldic emblems and fine binding placed them among the most valuable objects an individual might own [Pls. 16, 17]. They were often covered with a protective chemise,[8] and in a famous illustration from the Hours of Mary of Burgundy from the 1470s, you see just such a book with its chemise in use [Pl. 18].[9]

But of course, such wonderful books were always great rarities. In

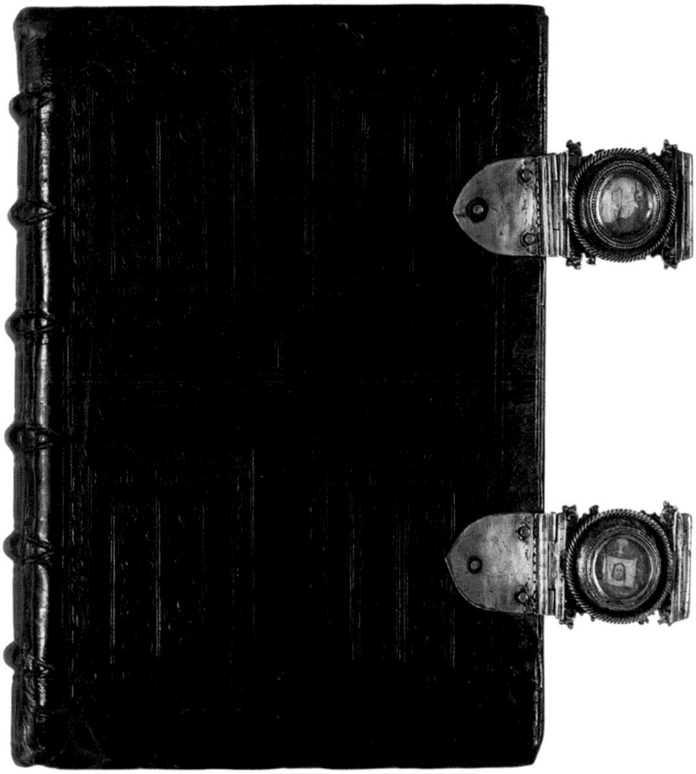

16.
Most Books of Hours have lost their original bindings, but the Browne Hours, imported from Bruges in the 1460s for the Stamford merchant John Browne, retains the customised binding added to this 'off the shelf' book to personalise it for its first purchaser. The binding, by the Bruges craftsman Anthonis van Gavere (died 1505) is in blind-stamped calf, and has silver-gilt clasps with miniatures of the Virgin and Child and of St Veronica under crystal. On the reverse Browne's name and merchant's mark are engraved.

Philadelphia Free Library, Widener Ms 3, Browne Hours, cover

17. A PIOUS BUSINESSMAN
The Browne Hours is a gaudy example of the books mass-produced for the English market in Bruges in the later fifteenth century. It was customised for John Browne *c.* 1460 with a rich binding, and by the inclusion of this prefatory miniature of the legendary Mass of St Gregory, in which Browne and his wife Agnes feature as witnesses of the miracle. Browne's merchant's mark is in the left-hand margin. A later owner scraped out the Pope's tiara and defaced the indulgence rubric on the page opposite, in obedience to Henry VIII's repudiation of papal obedience.

Philadelphia Free Library, Widener Ms 3, Browne Hours, fo. 7v. Page size 23 × 17 cm

18. MARY OF BURGUNDY AT PRAYER her precious Primer protected by its chemise: lap-dog and jewels suggest the domestic use of the Book of Hours, while, through the window, the visionary scene of Mary and her entourage at prayer to the Virgin (here a figure of the Church) in a sacred building symbolises a wider ecclesiastical context for such prayer. The miniature prefaces a prayer to the Virgin attributed to the English saint Thomas Becket.

Vienna, Österreichische Nationalbibliothek, Codex Vindobonensis 1857 (Hours of Mary of Burgundy) fo. 14v, Page size 23 × 16 cms

the fifteenth and sixteenth centuries most Books of Hours were humbler objects, mass-produced with no illustrations, few illustrations or just bad illustrations.[10] Books of this kind[11] of course, though superficially flashy and designed to impress, might be aesthetically poor enough things, embellished with stiffly drawn and crudely coloured pictures, as in the Bolton Hours. The advent of print, however, and of books with full or half-page illustrations and ornamental borders produced from detailed metal plates, meant that the effect of richness and sumptuousness could be achieved at a much lesser cost. Indeed, print made possible inexpensive Books of Hours which were incomparably more sophisticated than all but the most lavish manuscript books, capable of rivalling some of the great aristocratic commissions of the high Middle Ages. By the early years of the sixteenth century, French publishers producing multiple editions of Books of Hours for a variety of European markets, including England, were employing artists of the calibre of the so-called '*Master of the Très Petites Heures*' of Anne of Brittany, and producing books of unsurpassed sumptuousness.[12] Such books could be enhanced by hand-colouring the printed illustrations, to imitate the effect of manuscript illumination [Pls. 19, 20]. So by the sixteenth century every prosperous shopkeeper who aspired to devotional gentility might have their own splendid Book of Hours at, relatively speaking, bargain prices, and with a degree of iconographic complexity which, till the advent of print, had been available only to the most aristocratic (or at any rate monied) book-owners.

Before printing, as we have seen, the personal character of these books was often signalled by the inclusion of prayers specially composed or adapted for their owners. A book commissioned for a woman might have the Latin grammatical forms in the feminine gender, or the owner's Christian name might even be incorporated directly into

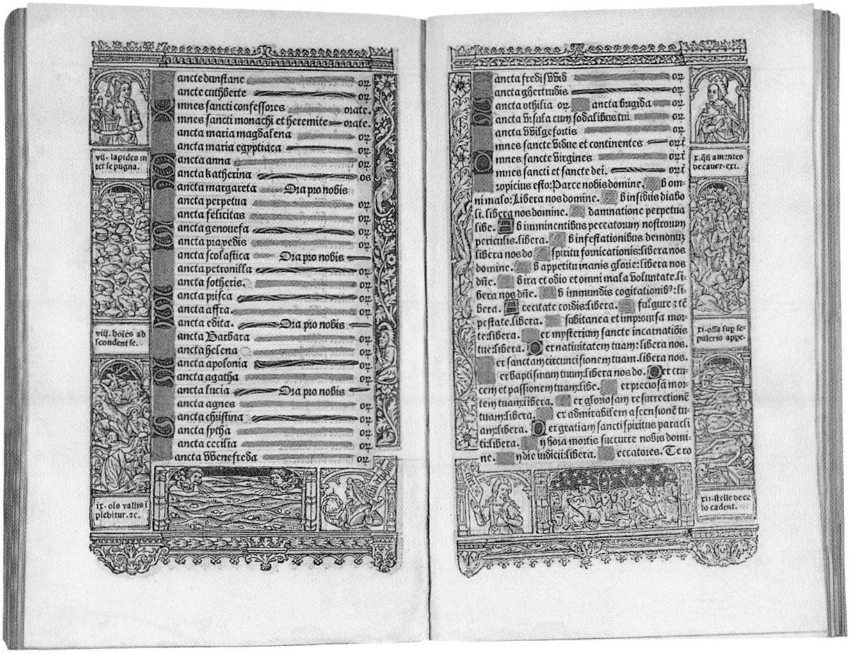

19. PRINT RIVALLING MANUSCRIPT

Several surviving copies of this splendid edition of the Sarum *Horae* of 1520 are printed on vellum rather than paper. The book was printed by Nicholas Higman for Simon Vostre, a Paris-based international publisher who specialised in luxury Books of Hours. The borders to the Litany of the Saints here depict the Fifteen Signs of the End of the World, a popular theme in late medieval art and a regular item in the decoration of French-printed Books of Hours.

British Library C 41 e 9 sigs K6v–k7 (RSTC 15926). Page size 20 × 11 cm

20. PRINT IMITATING MANUSCRIPT

The borders, initials and half-page illuminations of this book printed in 1494 in Paris for the English market have been hand-coloured, to resemble an illuminated manuscript book. The Mass of St Gregory here prefaces a set of prayers to the Crucified Christ attributed to St Bede, a common pairing. The book's first owner was John George, a gentleman with property in Cirencester and Bawdington, who wrote his name on the flyleaf in 1495.

British Library 1A40311 (RSTC 15879)' unpaginated. Page size 14 × 8 cm

21. FROM HAND TO HAND
Made in London *c.* 1405–10, this book was acquired *c.* 1440 by a man named Nicholas, living in Bury St Edmund's (the feast of the dedication of the parish church of St Mary, Bury St Edmund's, was added to the calendar for 4 October). A Bury scribe added a new supplement of prayers to the book, including this popular invocation of the Trinity against spiritual and material enemies. Nicholas's name, included as part of the text, has later been scratched out, and replaced with the letter R, the initial of a subsequent owner.

Cambridge University Library Ee 1 14 fo. 120r. Page size 21 × 15 cm

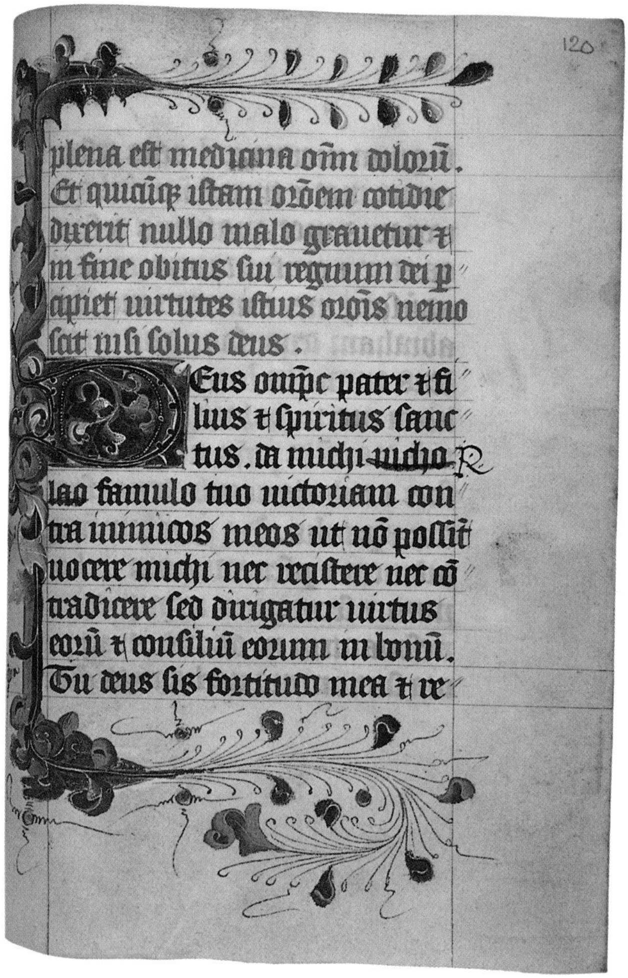

the prayers. Many late medieval prayers for help against enemies or protection against spiritual and material evils actually required the petitioner to name themselves in this way – to say their name. This might be achieved by leaving a blank space which the user filled in by speaking the name, and the blank might have a capital initial N for *nomen*. But where patrons requested it, the name was often written out in full, as an integral part of the text by the scribe. The ostentatious De Bois Hours, written and illuminated in the 1330s for Hawisia De Bois, and crusted with her family's armorial bearings, also contains a series of prayers for protection personalised by the inclusion of Hawisia's name – 'libera me Hawisiam famulam tuam ab omne opere malo',[13] and a similar example is the long prayer against enemies added to the secondhand Book of Hours which Richard III may have had with him at Bosworth Field, and which is written throughout using his name, with the formula 'me, your servant Richard'.[14] In the event, the prayer didn't work, of course, and after the battle the book was given by the victorious enemy Henry VII to his mother the Lady Margaret Beaufort. The new Queen Mother evidently acquired Richard's book as a trophy rather than a devotional aid, and I doubt if she prayed with it much; at any rate she did not bother to scratch out Richard's name very thoroughly, though she did write her own on the back flyleaf – 'In the honor of God and sainte Edmonde/Pray for Margaret Richmonde', a mark of proprietorship which was itself scratched out in due course by a subsequent owner – also in all probability a woman.[15] But where a book was in continuing use, the writing in of names might well create problems when the book duly passed to another user, as in fact most Books of Hours eventually did. One early fifteenth-century London-produced book in the Cambridge University Library, for example, was expanded in the 1440s for an East-Anglian owner. The new material included a well-known prayer to the Trinity for protection, which had the commissioning owner's Christian name, Nicholas, written as part of the text throughout: a still later owner has scratched through the name wherever it occurs, substituting what is presumably their own initial, 'R' [Pl. 21].[16]

Even before a book changed hands this customising might create problems. The Tudor matron Anne Withypole owned several books of hours, manuscript and printed, two of which survive. A manuscript book now in Ipswich Public Library contains a particularly embarrassing change of name and circumstance, though in this case not that of the owner. Mistress Withypole was a much married woman, and Paul Withypole, protégé of Cardinal Wolsey and one of the most important figures in the city of London under Henry VIII, was her third husband.[17] Her printed Book of Hours contains calendar entries recording her marriages to William Rede and to Paul Withypole (the entry on her marriage to Rede, it has to be said, being a good deal warmer than that recording her subsequent marriage to Withypole) [Pls. 22, 23].

In the body of the manuscript book, there is an edifying Latin prayer for marital harmony, which she evidently used for all her

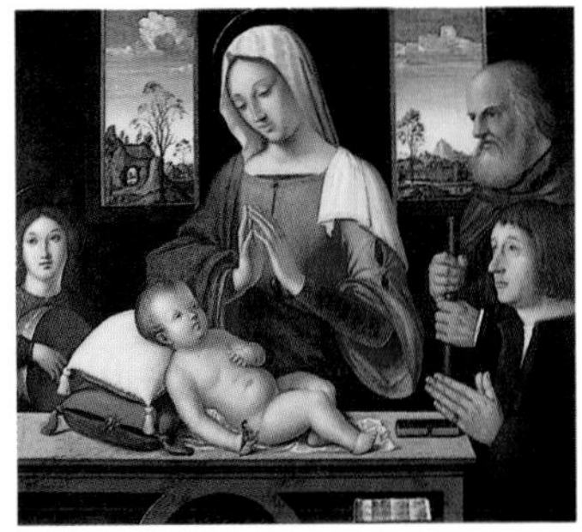

22. A PIOUS ACCESSORY
Paul Withypole was a prominent Merchant Taylor and M.P. for the City of London during the Reformation Parliament. He regularly loaned money to Henry VIII and was an associate of Thomas Cromwell. In this domestic altarpiece, commissioned from a Venetian painter, his piety as well as his prestige is on show. Withypole's clasped and closed Book of Hours lies before him on the table on which the Holy Child rests. Two Books of Hours owned by Withypole's much-married wife Anne, one printed [Pl. 23] and one manuscript, survive.

Antonio de Solario, Withypole Altarpiece, 1514. Bristol Museums and Art Gallery. Panel size 77 × 89 cm

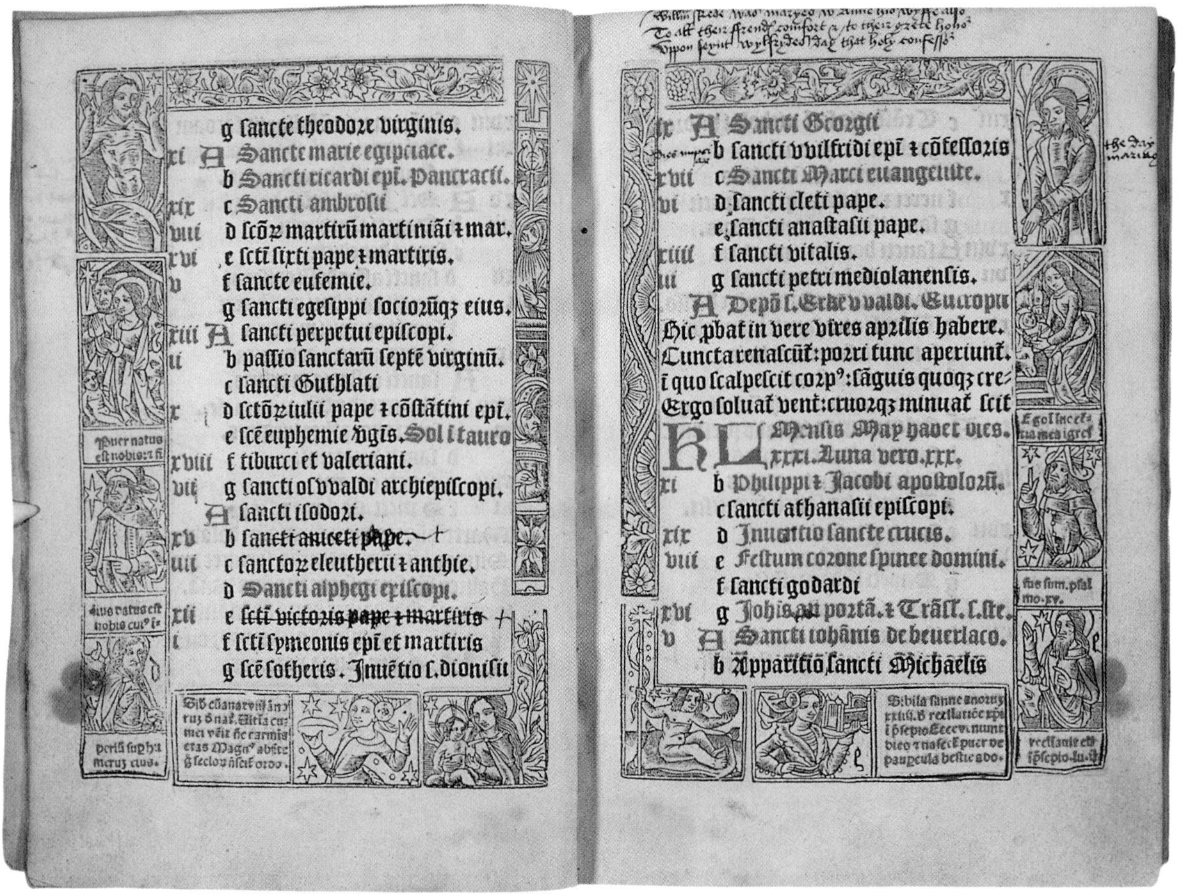

g sancte theodore virginis.
xi A Sancte marie egipciace.
b Sancti ricardi epi. Pancracii.
xix c Sancti ambrosii
viii d scor martiru martiniani & mar.
xvi e scti sixti pape & martiris.
v f sancte eufemie.
g sancti egesippi sociorumqz eius.
xiii A sancti perpetui episcopi.
ii b passio sanctaru septe virginu.
c sancti Guthlaci
x d sctorz iulii pape & costatini epi.
e sce euphemie vgis. Sol i tauro
xviii f tiburci et valeriani.
vii g sancti osvvaldi archiepiscopi.
A sancti isodori.
xv b sancti aniceti pape.
iiii c sanctorz eleutherii & anthie.
d Sancti alphegi episcopi.
xii e scti victoris pape & martiris
i f scti symeonis epi et martiris
g sce sotheris. Inuetio s. dionisii

xx A Sancti Georgii
b sancti vvilfridi epi & cofessoris
xvii c Sancti Marci euangeliste.
vi d sancti cleti pape.
e sancti anastasii pape.
xiiii f sancti vitalis.
iii g sancti petri mediolanensis.
A Depo s. Erkevvaldi. Eutropii
Hic pbat in vere vires aprilis habere.
Cuncta renascuntur: pori tunc aperiuntur.
In quo scalpescit corp9: sanguis quoqz cre-
Ergo soluatur vena: cruorqz minuatur scit
KL Mensis May habet dies. xxxi. Luna vero. xxx.
xi b Philippi & Jacobi apostolorum.
c sancti athanasii episcopi.
xix d Inuentio sancte crucis.
viii e Festum corone spinee domini.
f sancti godardi
xvi g Johis ant porta. & Trasl. s. ste.
v A Sancti iohannis de beuerlaco.
b Apparitio sancti Michaelis

husbands. The phrase in the prayer which asks for 'true concord and love between me and my husband' (*veram concordiam et verum amorem inter me et maritus meum*), has a blotted and scratched erasure, over which she has inserted the name of her third husband, 'Paulum'.[18]

In more expensive manuscripts, the personal character of the Book of Hours was sometimes expressed by commissioning a portrait, or at any rate a stylised representation, of the owner at prayer. As we have seen, this was already so in the earliest surviving English Book of Hours, the De Brailes Hours, where the first owner appears four times in the book.[19] In the Pabenham-Clifford (Grey Fitzpayne) Hours, the original owner, Joan Clifford of Frampton, appears with her husband John Pabenham – they were married round about 1314.[20]

In the mid-fifteenth-century Talbot Hours John Talbot, 1st Earl of Shrewsbury, and his wife Margaret Beauchamp, kneel in adoration

23. DOMESTIC PIETIES
Anne Withypole, Paul's wife, was the daughter of a minor Suffolk gentry family (Curson of Brightwell) and widow of a Cambridgeshire gentleman (William Freville) and a Boston merchant, William Rede. She inscribed the calendar of this printed book of Hours with memoranda of Tudor dynastic events and with family notes. Here (top right) she records her (second) marriage to William Rede 'to all their frendes comfort and to their grete honor, upon Seynt Wylfrydes day, that holy confessor'. Note also the deletion of the title 'Papa' wherever it occurs, in compliance with royal command after 1534.

RSTC 15880, Bodleian Douce 24 Sigs Aiv(v)–Av. Page size 16 × 11 cm

24. DYNASTIC PIETY
A distinctive long format, perhaps derived from prayer-rolls, characterises several fifteenth-century Books of Hours made for members of the Talbot family. This example, written in Rouen *c.* 1444 for John Talbot, Earl of Shrewsbury, was one of a pair made for him and his wife Margaret Beauchamp. Both books contain similar heraldic frontispieces, in which the donors are presented to the Virgin and Child by their patron saints, over a panel containing their arms, garter emblems and entwined monograms. Margaret Talbot is accompanied by her name-saint, and John Talbot by St George, patron of the Order of the Garter, of which Talbot was a Knight.

Cambridge Fitzwilliam Museum, Talbot Hours fo. 7v. Page size 27 × 11 cm

of the Virgin and Child under the tutelage of their patron saints – her name-saint Margaret behind Lady Talbot, with St George as patron of England, and of the Order of the Garter in particular, behind John Talbot. Below them left and right are the arms of Talbot and Beauchamp, and at the bottom, the crowned monogram of John and Margaret. This is about as elaborate a system of reference to status, alliance and identity as you can get [Pl. 24].

By the end of the Middle Ages this custom of visual allusion to the owner or donor had become much more post-modernistically self-referential. The owner frequently not only appears at prayer in their own prayer book, but is portrayed in the very act of using the book which contains the picture. This is so in the well-known picture of Mary of Burgundy using her own Book of Hours. In the same way, Henry VIII's sister, Margaret Tudor, Queen of Scotland, features in

25. THE VIRGIN'S HOURS
The Angel's greeting to Mary at the Annunciation, *Ave Maria Gratia Plena*, 'Hail Mary full of grace', formed the opening words of one of the most frequently recited of all prayers, and was a constant refrain in the Hours of the Virgin. Depictions of the Virgin reading as the angel greeted her often included books modelled on the Book of Hours, and enabled the user of such books to identify their own prayer with that of the Virgin herself.

Master of Urgel Cathedral c. 1490, Museu Nacional d'Art de Catalunya

a Book of Hours made for her and her husband King James IV around 1500, saying the Hail Mary, for on the altarpiece before which she kneels is portrayed the Annunciation, in which the Angel Gabriel spoke the Hail Mary.[21]

The inclusion of portraits of the owner in a Book of Hours was of course the exclusive preserve of the rich, and like the use of specific names in prayer texts, only occurs in custom-made books. But most later manuscript Books of Hours were mass-produced, and of course such customising could not happen at all in a printed book. It is also worth remembering that by the end of the Middle Ages most Books of Hours were in fact printed. By 1530 there had been at least 760 separate printed editions of the Book of Hours, 114 of them produced for England alone.[22] In any case, a Book of Hours which contained any illustrations at all did contain an idealised surrogate portrait, applicable to every user. Any Book of Hours was liable to have a picture of the Annunciation in it, when the Angel Gabriel appeared to Mary to tell her that she had been chosen to be the Mother of Christ. By the end of the Middle Ages, Mary in the Annunciation is very frequently portrayed as surprised in the very act of praying from a book. The text she is reading was by tradition taken from the prophecy of a virginal birth in Isaiah chapter 11, and in many Annunciation scenes Mary is reading the prophecy from a Bible or Breviary, recognisable by their large size and double columns. But by the later Middle Ages the book in her hand or on a desk before her has shrunk to a single column on each page, and has been illuminated or bound as a Book of Hours. In representations of the Annunciation with donors, the book used by the Virgin often corresponds exactly to the Books of Hours depicted before the donors [Pl. 25].[23]

There was a double self-referentiality here, to the pray-er, and to the prayer they **were** reciting. The main component of the Book of Hours was of course the Little Office of the Blessed Virgin, and the

refrain that runs through that office was the most popular of all prayers, the Hail Mary, *Ave Maria, Gratia Plena*, the opening of which was made up from the words of the Angel Gabriel at the Annunciation. That reference is picked up and played with in a French Book of Hours now in the Walters Collection in Baltimore, where the owner had her portrait included physically within the Annunciation scene [Pl. 26].

On one half of a double page spread the owner of the book kneels, reading from the book, attended by the Angel Gabriel. On the facing page, the Virgin kneels at a small domestic altar on which she has laid her book of hours. Gabriel begins his message *Ave Gratia Plena, Dominus Tecum*, written on a scroll issuing from his mouth, but he pauses to present the owner of the book. She kneels at a carpeted desk with her book open before her: and below her are once again the words of the Hail Mary, at the opening of Matins. The female user of the book therefore no longer simply recites the Hail Mary, she has

26.
In this Annunciation scene at the opening of Matins of the Virgin, the owner of the book is depicted as a devout spectator of the biblical episode. Reciting the Hail Mary, she is introduced to the Virgin by the Angel Gabriel, also uttering the same words as he announces the incarnation of Christ in the Virgin's womb. The image encapsulates the involvement with the sacred drama which many late devotional regimes aspired to.

Walters Art Gallery, Baltimore, Ms 267 fo. 13v–14

27. DEVOTIONAL ACCRETION
In the 1490s a London scribe added a new supplement of prayers to update a century-old Book of Hours for a new owner, Sir Thomas Lewkenor of Trotton in Sussex. This depiction of the Side-Wound of Jesus was also added to the original part of the book. The Side-Wound occupied a place in late medieval piety similar to that of the Sacred Heart of Jesus in modern Catholic devotion. The image has been attached to the vellum page with five stitches, perhaps an allusion to the five wounds of Jesus. The English inscription reads 'The mesure of the wonde of our Lorde ihesu crist/[that] he suffurde on the crose for oure redempcion'.

Lambeth Palace Ms 545 fos. 78v–79. Page size 15 × 10 cm

climbed inside it, and has become part of the scene which her prayer evokes and commemorates.[24]

But even if the owner of a Book of Hours could not impress their personality on their book by the inclusion in its design of specially personalised prayers or commissioned portraits, they might leave a personal mark all the same. Almost half the 300 Books of Hours in the Bibliothèque Nationale de France in Paris have manuscript annotations and additions of some sort, and it was very common indeed for English owners too to annotate their books. Such additions might amount to no more than the insertion of some regional or personal patron saint in the standardised calendar, but they often include devotional material added by the owner. The Lewkenor Hours, originally the product of a London workshop in the 1390s, was expanded for a new owner with a series of prayers and devotional images in the 1490s. The owner for whom these alterations was carried out was Sir Thomas Lewkenor, of Trotton in Sussex, a servant of the Lady Margaret Beaufort who shared many of his mistress's religious tastes. Sir Thomas's additions included an image of the side-wound of Christ, drawn on parchment and neatly stitched on to a blank page in the book [Pls. 27, 28, 29].[25]

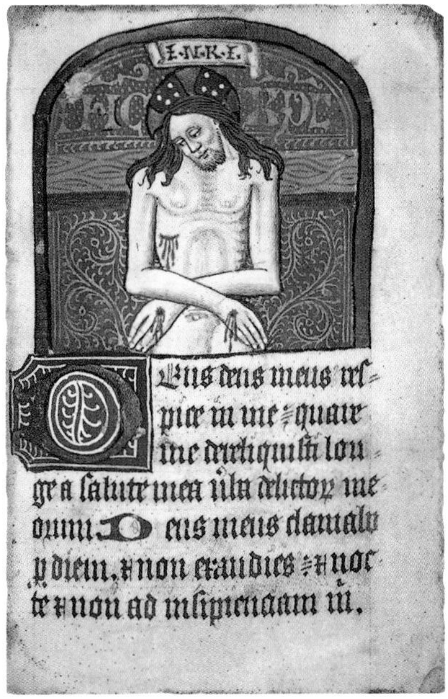

28. DEVOTIONAL ACCRETION
The additions to Sir Thomas's book include pictures as well as words. Here the Psalms of the Passion are preceded by the Image of Pity. This version of the *Imago Pietatis* is closely modelled on a small Byzantine mosaic icon displayed as a miraculous image in the basilica of Santa Croce in Rome.

Lambeth Palace Ms 545 fo. 144. Page size 15 × 10 cm

A more complex addition was a devotion to the Cross which incorporated both the text of the hymn used at the shrine of the Holy Cross at Bromholm, and a pilgrim souvenir card from the shrine, superimposing a drawing of the shrine reliquary on top of the text of the hymn.[26] Carefully pasted into the book, the Lewkenor Hours pilgrim card is an extraordinary testimony both to personal devotional adaptation of the standard content of the Book of Hours, and to the convergence of popular and elite religion at the end of the Middle Ages. Later still, in what appears to be a regretful allusion to the destruction of the shrine, a subsequent female owner wrote across the bottom of the card 'Thys ys the holie cros that ys or sped'; in an unconscious association of sacred and secular intimacies, the same woman, Mary Everard, noted later in the book that 'In my cofer [are] xij payers and a shet.'[27]

There is an obvious deliberation about this process of customising a book by adding devotional memorabilia in the Lewkenor Hours – Sir Thomas clearly commissioned the devotions to the Cross to provide a context for his treasured souvenir card. Occasionally such pilgrimage memorabilia might even be built into the specifications for Books of Hours in the first place. The wealthy East Anglian owner

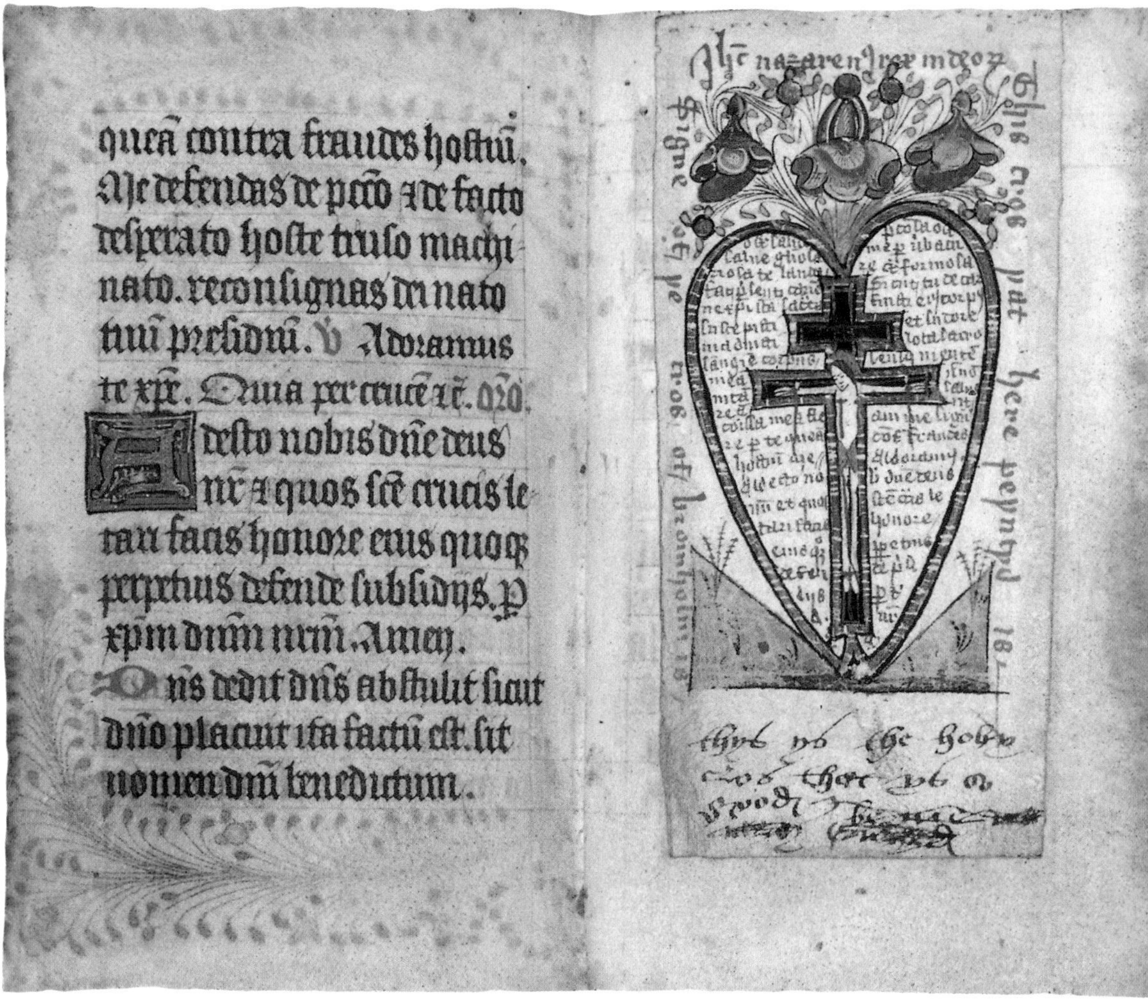

29. DEVOTIONAL ACCRETION

The most remarkable addition to the Lewkenor Hours is a pilgrim devotional card from the East Anglian shrine of the Holy Cross at the Cluniac Priory of Bromholm, pasted on to a page apparently left blank for the purpose at the end of a Latin devotion invoking the Cross as a protection against the snares of the devil. The card depicts the conventional patriarchal (two-barred) cross-reliquary in which fragments of the cross were normally displayed, superimposed on a hymn used at the shrine, and the English inscription 'This cros that here peyntyd is/Signe of the cros of Bromholme is'.

Lambeth Palace Ms 545 fos. 184v–185. Page size 15 × 10 cm

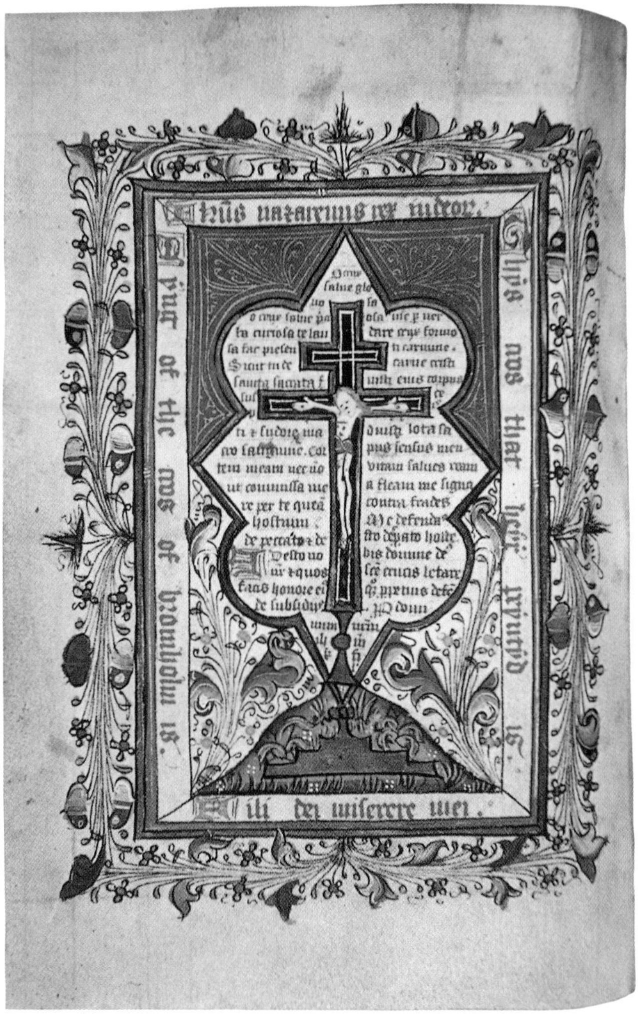

30. POPULAR AND ELITE
This handsome Book of Hours was produced *c.* 1480 in England for a patron in the diocese of Norwich, whose calendar it contains. Though sparingly illustrated, it contains this full-page replica of a Bromholm pilgrim card, very similar to the real card pasted into the Lewkenor Hours [Pl. 29]. The integration of such a commissioned image into the design of an expensive book of this kind, with its allusion to a popular East Anglian pilgrimage site, vividly highlights the convergence of popular and elite piety in fifteenth-century England.

Fitzwilliam Museum, Cambridge Ms 55, fo. 57v. Page size 20 × 14 cm

who commissioned an illustrated Book of Hours now in the Fitzwilliam Museum evidently also had a devotion to Bromholm, one of the most famous of all East Anglian shrines. They commissioned the artist who painted the illuminations for the book to copy an almost identical pilgrim card to that pasted into the Lewkener Hours and incorporate it into the scheme of illustrations, not as a pasted enclosure, but as an integral part of the book' the frame around this 'fake' pilgrim card paste-in explaining that 'Thys cros that heyr peynted is/Syng [sign] of the cros of bromholm is' [Pl. 30].[28]

This sort of inclusion, providing in some sense a 'virtual' pilgrimage for the sedentary user of the book, might occur in even the

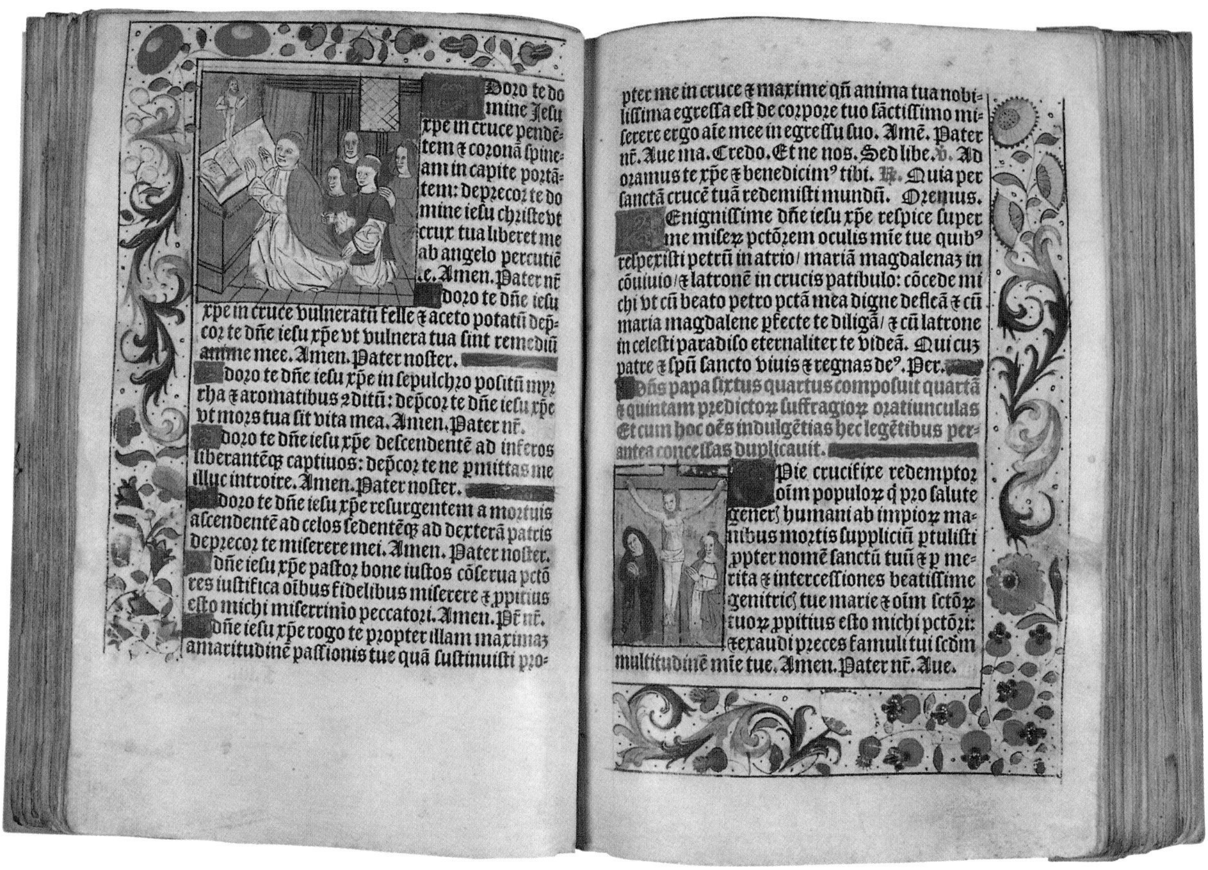

31.
By 1503, when Wynkyn de Worde printed this Sarum Hours, French publishers were beginning to invade the English market, and their products often outclassed English books like this one in quality of design and illustration [cf. Pl. 20]. De Worde's book, printed on vellum and with its illustrations and floral borders hand-coloured, has not yet parted company with the elite devotional world of the illuminated manuscript.

British Library C 41 e 8 (RSTC 15899) fos. 4v–5. Page size 16 × 10 cm

most lavish books – Mary of Burgundy had a picture and prayer to the miraculous host of Dijon added to her book.[29] But such devotional gestures can also be found in the most modest books. In a printed *Horae* from the press of Wynkyn de Worde now in the British Library, the owner has added a crudely hand-coloured indulgenced image of Christ as Man of Sorrows, the so-called *Imago Pietatis*, on the end flyleaf. On the opposite page, jottings invoke some of the owner's favourite devotions: 'haly kyng herry', 'sanct George', Master John Schorne, Saint Margaret, the Image of the 'Rode of Chestre', '*Sancta Maria Vergine*', and Christ as *Salvator Mundi* [Pls. 31, 32].[30] And in fact most additions to such books were simple hand-written text like those invocations, rather than extra illuminations [Pl. 33].

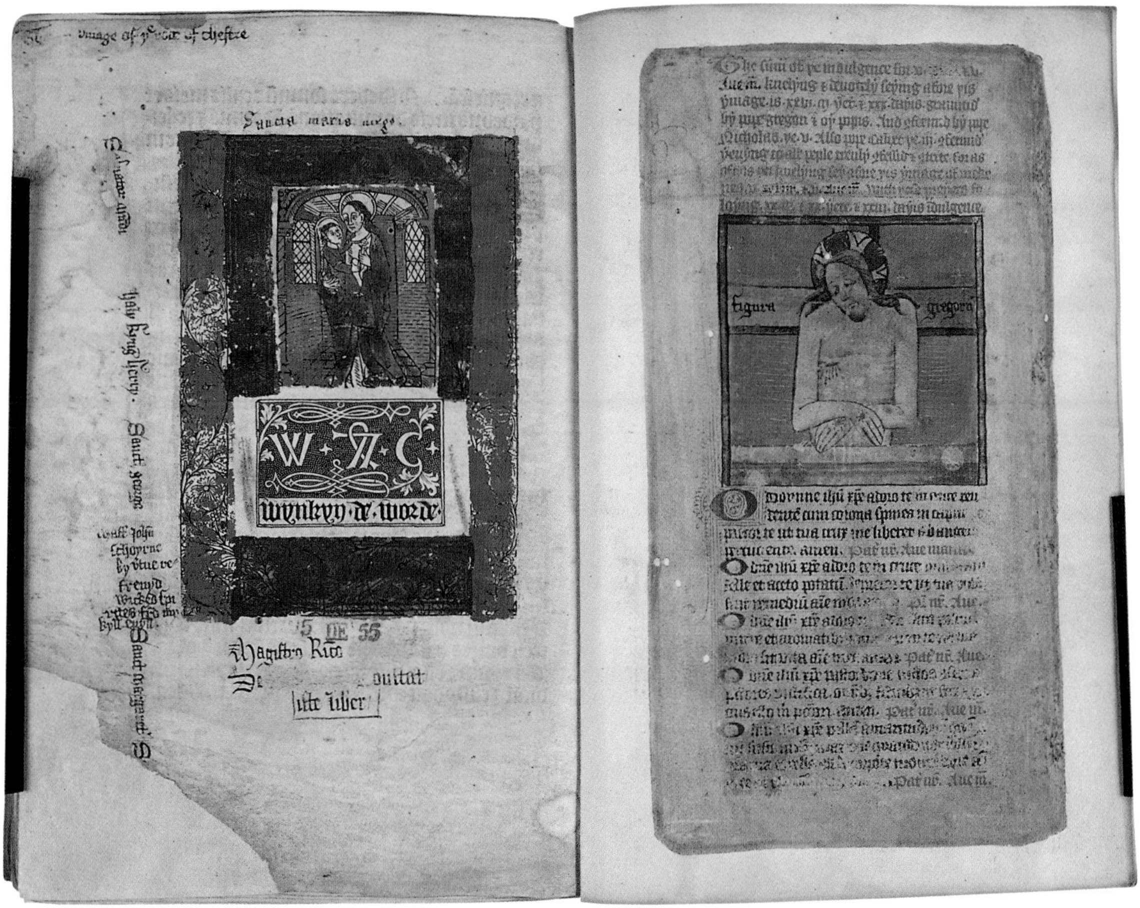

Some of this material we should be inclined to call secular, like the jottings on the triumphs of Henry VII which Anne Withypole added to the calendar of her printed Book of Hours now in the Bodleian Library,[31] or the dates of notable battles in the Wars of the Roses, and the notables killed there, written into the calendar of Fitzwilliam 54,[32] or, more mundanely, Mary Everard's notes on bed-linen and blankets which we have already encountered in the Lewkenor Hours, or the notes on rents due and payments made on the back flyleaves of a late fifteenth-century Book of Hours in the Fitzwilliam Museum [Pl. 34].[33]

Notes on agreements, debts and contractual obligations of this kind are a regular item in such jottings, even in books manifestly still in devotional use, rather than merely used as a convenient (because redundant) source of paper. They possibly reflect the fact that Books

32.
The owner of this comparatively luxurious printed Book of Hours has jotted the names of a series of saints and of shrines ('image of the Rode of Chestre, Master John Schorne') on the colophon page, and opposite has pasted-in a down-market printed broadsheet of the Image of Pity with the indulgence and the so-called Prayer of St Bede which often accompanies it.

British Library C 41 e 8 (RSTC 15899), back fly

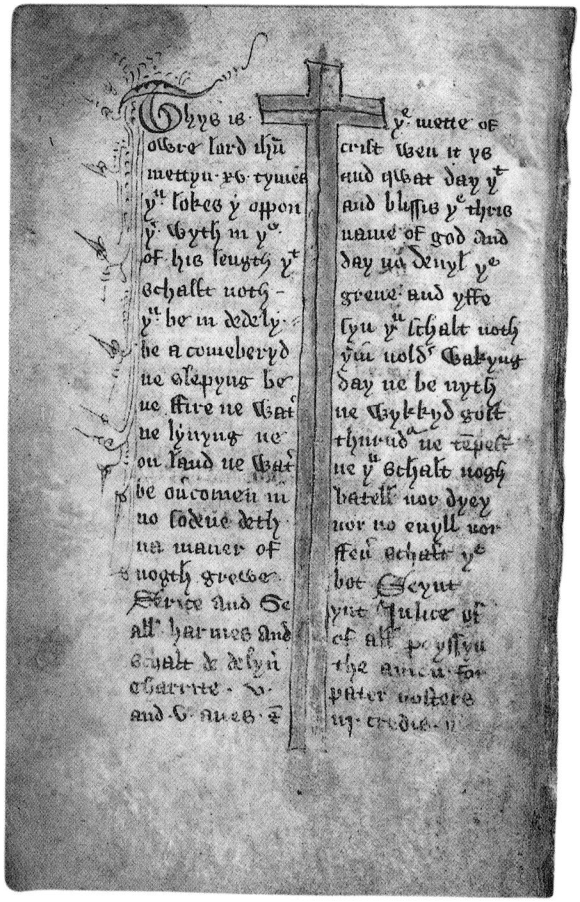

33. DEVOTIONAL ACCRETION
Written originally for a female member of the family of Sir John Carew, who fought at Cressy, this late fourteenth-century book passed in the female line by marriage into the Poyntz family. A late fifteenth-century inscription to Katherine Carew (née Huddersfield) from her half-sister Elizabeth Poyntz, asks for prayers (f. 86). The book acquired many added devotions as it passed from hand to hand. On this fly-leaf a drawing of the Cross said to be exactly one fifteenth of the height of Christ is copied as a talisman, with promises of miraculous protection and blessing. 'Measured' images of this kind were a common feature of popular piety in late medieval England [cf. Pl. 27].

Cambridge Fitzwilliam Museum Ms 48 (Carew-Poyntz Hours) fo. 2v. Page size 18 × 11 cm

34. RESPECTABILITY AND POWER
The alliance between piety and power is reflected in the calendar pages of Anne Withypole's Book of Hours, recording not only family events like marriages and births, but also key Tudor dynastic events, beginning with the landing of Henry VII at Milford Haven in 1484, the defeat of rebels at Stoke before Newark (here lower left) and the death of the Earl of Lincoln. Very similar jottings are found in other contemporary elite Books of Hours, including the Beaufort Hours, which belonged to Lady Margaret Beaufort.

Bodleian Library, Oxford, Douce 24 Sigs Avi (v)–Avii (r)

of Hours were sometimes used instead of Gospel books for swearing solemn oaths and obligations. But Fitzwilliam 54 also has a series of dates of births of the Skipwith family of South Ormsby added to the calendar, and stretching from 1510 to 1623. Most of the 'secular' material in the Books of Hours is family material of this sort, the records of births, deaths and, less often, marriages. But it is probably a mistake anyway to think of such entries as secular. They found their way into calendars in the first place primarily in the form of obits, often no more than a bare note of the name and date of decease, but which might be more personal, like the note made against 27 November in the calendar of one such book, which simply says, 'my moder departed to God' [Pl. 35].[34]

Such entries of course were not a matter of simple mnemonics. They were a call to prayer, a reminder of the obligation to intercede

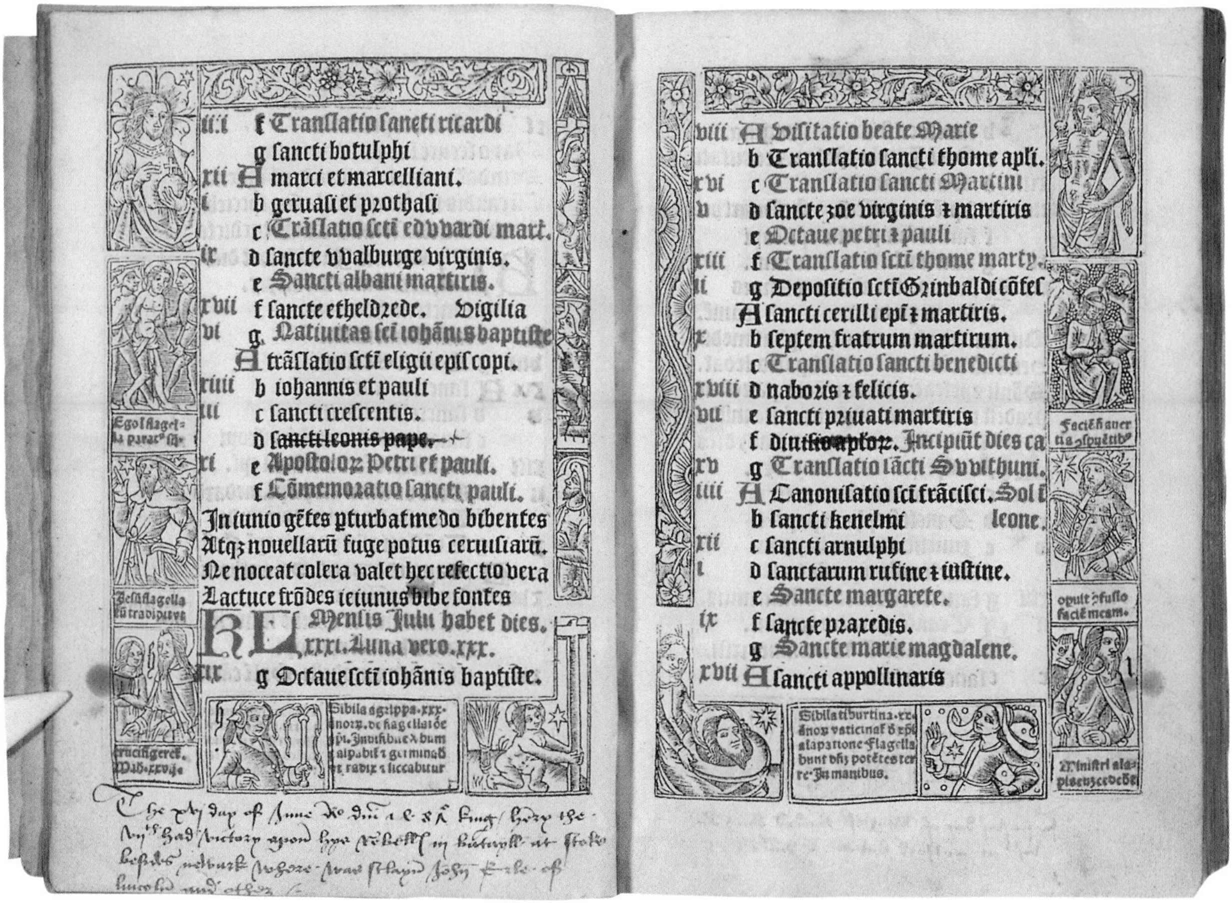

for the repose of the soul of the person commemorated. Birth entries, though they became almost as common, had on the face of it no such function, and certainly did have the straightforwardly practical purpose of determining seniority among inheritors and, in some cases, of providing precise information for the casting of horoscopes – hence in many such entries the careful note of the precise time as well as the day and date of birth. But they might and usually did also qualify as religious, and help determine a child's name, by noting the saint's day on which they had been born, or by blending the facts with a prayer. Flyleaf jottings in a Book of Hours which belonged to the Derham family of Crimplesham in Norfolk record the births of sons and daughters with astrological precision, and with devotion: 'Thomas my son was born the xiii day of Januarii the yere of our lorde 1488 on a Tewesday at nyght, between viii and ix: god make hym a good man:

that day callid sent hillary ys day', or on St Alban's day 1492 the birth of 'Frawnses my son, god make him his servaunt'.[35]

Behind such sentiments lay a devotional ethos in which the recitation of the little hours had an important role, as a symbol of religious devotion and decency. It is made explicit in the bequest by the Rutland landowner Roger Flower, not of a simple Book of Hours but of the fuller 'portoos' or breviary, to his son Thomas in 1425, 'charging him, on my blessing, that he keep hit, terme of his lif, so that God woll her after sende him devocion to say his service theron, as I have done, that thenne he may have such a good honest boke of his owne.' And should this son predecease him, 'I woll thanne my eldest son have it to the same entent. And I pray to the blessed trinite for his endles mercye and goodnesse he sende my children grace to be goode men and wemmen, and to yelde him gode soules, thorough the helpe and praier of oure lady seint Marye, and of all the seyntes of hevene.'[36] The gift of a prayer-book here was part of a complex of feelings – concern for the spiritual well-being of the child, the desire to hand on a personal and treasured object as a sign of affection and request for remembrance, and the provision of a concrete emblem of dynastic continuity. All these are in evidence in the devotional bequests of Henry IV's sister-in-law Eleanor Duchess of Gloucester, who left her daughter Joan a bed and a Book of Hours 'with two clasps of gold enamelled with my arms, which book I have often used, with my blessing', and to her son Humphrey 'a psalter well and richly illumined . . . and the arms of my lord and father enamelled on the clasps . . . which psalter was left to me to remain to my heirs, and from heir to heir'.[37] Anne Withypole's printed Book of Hours records, lovingly, her marriage to William Rede, to 'all their ffrends comfort and their grete honor upon seynt Wylfredes day, that holy confessor'. Widowed, she subsequently remarried Paul Withypole, but she evidently handed the book on to her son by William Rede, for Thomas Rede inscribed the book 'Though I come last, Pray for me fast: Thomas Rede'.[38]

In the same way, in 1495 Sir Brian Roucliffe, one of the Barons of the Exchequer, bequeathed to his son John a large Book of Hours made about 1408/9, his 'Great Primer' ('*magnum Primarium*') into which he had copied a number of additional English devotions including a unique poem to St Henry VI. The book, which is now in

35. REMEMBRANCE AND INTIMACY 'Obits' (reminders to pray for a person on the anniversary of their death) are very common additions to Books of Hours, normally a simple record of the deceased's name and titles added to the calendar. Touchingly, the owner of this early fifteenth-century book has written against 27 November, 'my moder departyd to god'. Two other common types of marginalia are also in evidence here: the addition of the feast of the Translation of St Etheldreda on 17 October (perhaps because the book's owner lived in or near the Ely Diocese) and the deletion of the title 'Papa' (Pope) after the name of St Callistus (14 October), following Henry VIII's break with Rome.

Cambridge University Library Ee 1 14, October/November calendar. Page size 21 × 15 cm

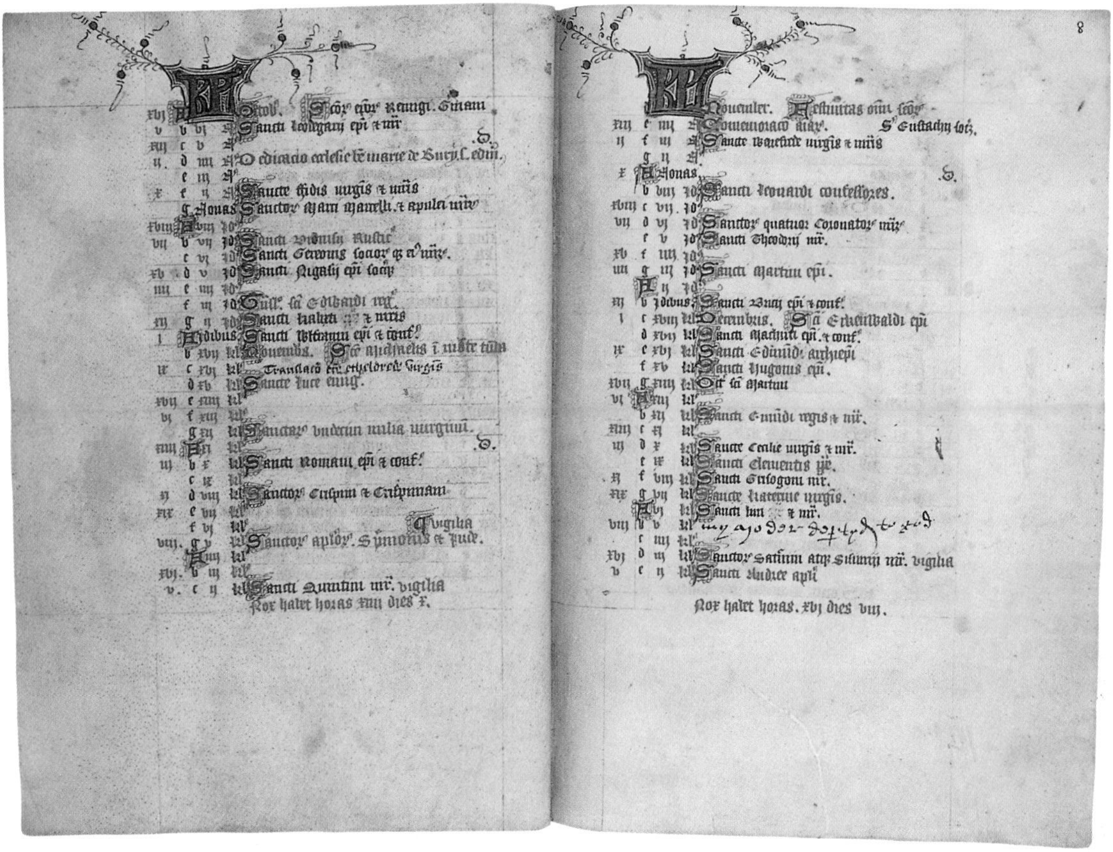

the Library of Ushaw College Durham, had come to him through his wife's family, for he notes that it had belonged to his mother-in-law, Margaret Burgh, and that she had got it from Mistress Elizabeth Elyngham, one of the executors of his father-in-law's will, so perhaps an aunt or godmother, and in all probability the first purchaser of the manuscript.[39] Passing on this manifestly treasured prayer-book, Sir Brian was transmitting to his son an heirloom with resonances and encoded affections on both the maternal and paternal sides of the family.

Piety and family pride, spiritual and worldly concerns, are here hard to separate, and indeed, in these sorts of contexts medieval people did not neatly divide the world into sacred and secular dimensions. Even a simple practical request for the return of the book in the event of loss might be cast in devotional mode, like the rhyme entered alongside a series of added prayers on the flyleaf of a book now in the Cambridge University Library:

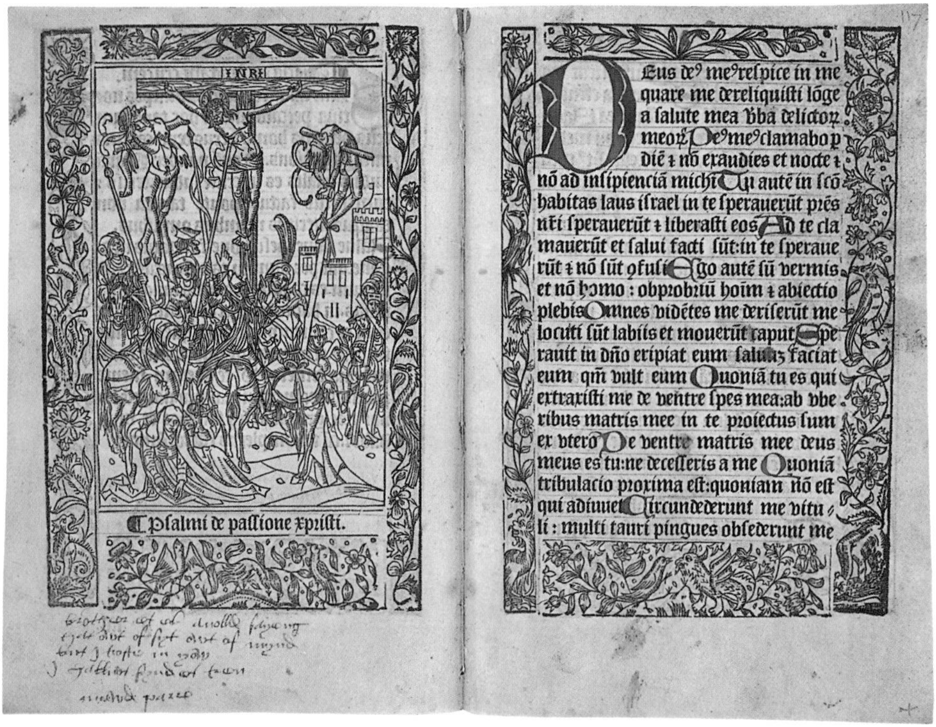
Psalmi de passione xpristi.

Deus de⁹ me⁹ respice in me quare me dereliquisti lõge a salute mea vba delictoꝝ meoꝝ. De⁹ me⁹ clamabo p diē ꝛ nō exaudies et nocte ꝛ nō ad insipienciā michi Tu autē in scō habitas laus israel In te sperauerūt pres nri sperauerūt ꝛ liberasti eos Ad te clamauerūt et salui facti sūt: in te sperauerūt ꝛ nō sūt cōfusi Ego autē sū vermis et nō homo : obprobriū hoim ꝛ abiectio plebis Omnes videtes me deriserūt me locuti sūt labiis et mouerūt caput Sperauit in dño eripiat eum saluū faciat eum qm vult eum Quoniā tu es qui extraxisti me de ventre spes mea: ab vberibus matris mee in te proiectus sum ex vtero De ventre matris mee deus meus es tu: ne decesseris a me Quoniā tribulacio proxima est: quoniam nō est qui adiuuet Circundederunt me vituli : multi tauri pingues obsederunt me

inimicos diligere qui eius commemoracionē celebram⁹ qui nouit eciam pro persecutoribus suis exorare dominum nostrum ihesum xpristū filiū tuum. an [illegible] sanguinē [illegible] p te impendit fac nos [illegible] thomas ascendit. V Gloria ꝛ honore vt supra. Deus p [illegible] gladiis martir ꝛ pontifex thomas gladiis ipiorum occubuit. presta qs vt omnes qui eius implorāt auxiliū pie peticiōis sue salutarē cōsequant effectū Per. an Beatus nicholaus adhuc puerulus multo ieiunio macerabat corp⁹. V Ora p nobis beate nicholae Vt digni efficiamur pmissionibus xpi Oremus

Deus q̄ beatū nicholaū piū pontificē tuū i numeris decorasti miraculis tribue nobis qs vt ei⁹ meritis ꝛ pcib⁹ a gehenne incendiis liberemur P. an Maria ergo vnxit pedes ihesu et extersit capillis capitis sui et domus impleta est ex odore vnguenti V. Dimissa sunt ei peccata multa Quoniā dilexit multū Oro Largire nobis clementissime pat quo sicut beata maria magdalena vnigenitū tuū sup oia diligendo suoꝝ obtinuit veniā peccaminū ita nobis apud miaꝫ tuā sempiternam impetret beatitudinē P. an. Virgo scā katherina grecie gemma vrbe alexandria costi regis erat filia. V. Ora p nobis beata katherina Vt dig.

c iiii

Who so ever thys book fynd,
I pray hum have thys in hys mynde,
For huys love that dyed on tre,
Save thys booke and bryng yt to me
William Barbor of New Bokenham.[40]

The living as well as the dead might call for prayer. Because Books of Hours were such personal items, in daily use and often a gift or bequest from loved ones, they were an especially appropriate place for gestures of affection. Fitzwilliam Ms 56 is a handsome Book of Hours which was once the property of the Henrician courtier, Robert Ratcliffe, Viscount Fitzwalter, the first Earl of Sussex, who died in 1542. His book carries inscriptions from two of his three wives, the fullest at the foot of folio 159, where his third wife Mary Arundell wrote

Good my lord I shall you heartely pray,
to remember me when ye thys oryson say
as sche that ys your unfayned lovynge wyfe
and so schall remayne durynge my lyfe, Mary Sussex.[41]

Cambridge University Library houses a handsome Book of Hours *printed* on vellum in 1494 by Wynken de Worde, given by Mabel Lady Dacre to her nephew Thomas Parr, and passed on after his death by his widow Maud to his brother Sir William Parr, later Baron Parr of Horton, uncle to Queen Catherine Parr. Sir William certainly used the book, and as he did so will have been reminded of his family obligations, for his sister-in-law and her children had inscribed the book for him. Maud wrote, rather sternly,

Brother et es another sayenge
That owt of syt owt of mynd
But I troste in you
I shall not fynd it true
Maud Perre.

His niece Catherine, the future queen, placed a more affectionate memento appropriately at the foot of a suffrage and picture of her name-saint, St Katherine of Alexandria [Pls. 36, 37],

Oncle wen you do on thys loke
Pray you remember wo wrote thys in your boke
Your lovynge nys Katheryn parr.[42]

The *conventional* character of such gestures is obvious enough –

36.
Devout remembrance might be a very practical and urgent affair. Donating her late husband's printed Hours to his brother, Sir William Parr, Maud Parr urges him not to forget her or her children: 'owt of syt owt of mynd/But I troste in you/I shall not fynd it true'. Her gift inscription is strategically placed at the foot of the best illustration in the book, the fine crucifixion scene prefacing the Psalms of the Passion.

Cambridge University Library RSTC 15875, Inc 4.J.1.2 [3750], unpaginated. Page size 16 × 10 cm

37.
Henry VIII's future (and final) queen, Catherine Parr, here places an affectionate request for remembrance in her uncle William's Hours, appropriately immediately under a devotion addressed to St Katherine of Alexandria. Handsomely printed on vellum, this was Wynkyn de Worde's first Book of Hours, and contained the popular supplement of prayers which Caxton had produced under the sponsorship of Henry VII's queen, Elizabeth of York, and of his mother, Lady Margaret Beaufort.

Cambridge University Library RSTC 15875, Inc 4.J.1.2 [3750] unpaginated

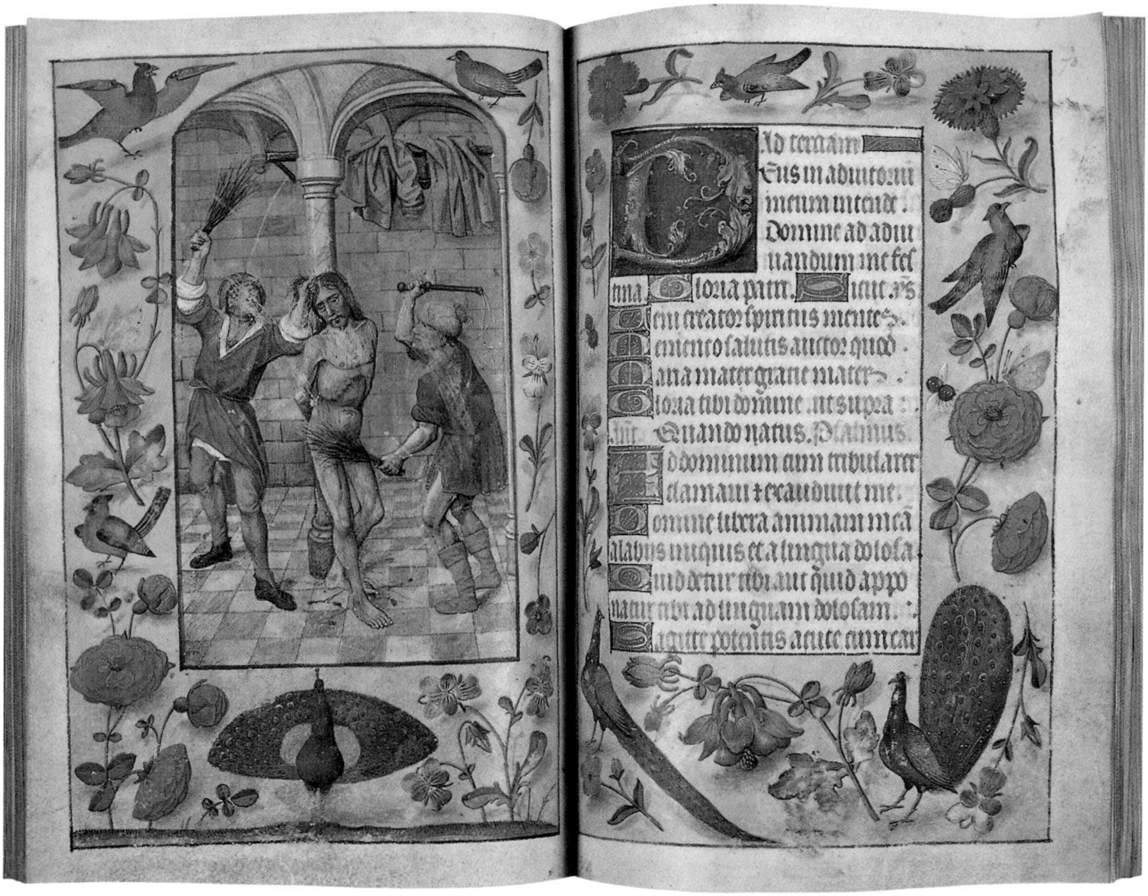

38. CONSPICUOUS PIETY
This magnificent Book of Hours was made in Antwerp in the late 1490s. With its full-page illuminations and sumptuous borders decorated with birds and flowers, it represents the most luxurious end of the trade in Flemish Books for England. It belonged to a lady in waiting at the courts of Henry VII and Henry VIII, and contains many pious autographs. The book is open at the beginning of Terce, illustrated, as was usual in manuscript books for the English market, with a miniature of the Flagellation of Christ.

British Library Add 17012, fos. 72v–73. Page size 20 × 14cm

Catherine's brother William put a similar message on the foot of the next page, and we need not suppose these family inscriptions represents an especially intense piety. Nevertheless, the transmission of the book was clearly a matter of consequence for all concerned, and the custom shows that the conventions of affectionate remembrance at prayer were specifically linked to the use of very personal books such as these. In a Paris Primer of 1495 now in the British Library someone has written 'I whas and ys and ever schell be youwre awne true bedewomen tyll I dee'.[43] In another printed Book of Hours of 1495, now in the Bodleian, an inscription runs 'My nowne good nese I requer you to remember me yor lovynge aunte margret

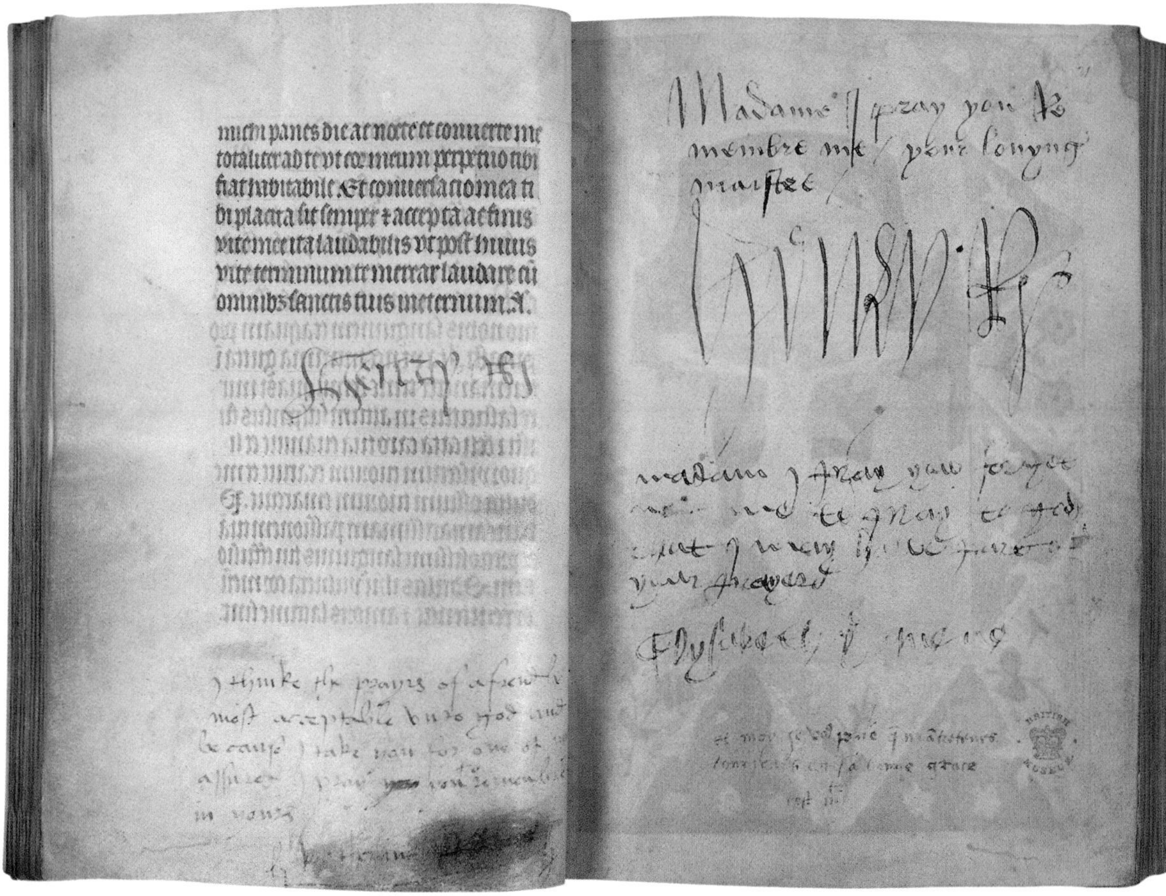

39. FIDELITY AT COURT
A page of pious remembrances from Henry VII, Henry VIII, Elizabeth of York and, most poignantly (bottom left) Katherine of Aragon, requesting the prayers of her 'most assured' friend, who subsequently blotted Katherine's name and title out, after Henry VIII had divorced her.

British Library Add 17012, fos. 20v–21. Page size 20 × 14cm

grey'.[44] And in a printed Book of Hours of 1498 in the Folger, Henry VII's queen Elizabeth of York wrote 'Madam I pray yow remember me in youwr god prayers yowr mastres Elysabeth R'.[45] Henry himself gave his daughter Margaret a Book of Hours inscribed 'Remembre yor kynde and lovynge fader in yor prayers. Henry Ky', and 'Pray for your loving fader that gave you thys boke and I geve you att all tymes godds blessing and myne. Henry Ky.'[46]

An entry of this sort clearly moves us in the direction of the autograph album, and such inscriptions were clearly recognised expressions of royal condescension to favoured servants. Books of Hours were used publicly. They were meant to be looked at by others, and they were often used in public places. George Cavendish, servant and biographer of Cardinal Wolsey, tells of a vivid encounter with

Thomas Cromwell, in a window-alcove in the great chamber of the palace at Esher, where Cromwell sat weeping and saying his hours, in the aftermath of the fall of his patron Wolsey, a public display of traditionalist piety which, as Cavendish sardonically noted in the light of Cromwell's subsequent career 'would since have been a very strange sight'.[47] Unsuprisingly therefore, the Book of Hours could become the location for public assurances of affection, trophy signatures, not least in the court. Henry VII's wife, Elizabeth, seems to have made the gift or exchange of such books a regular mark of favour, and a sumptuous manuscript Book of Hours owned by a Tudor court lady is a monument to these sorts of public gestures of affection. On one page King Henry VII has written 'Madam, I pray you remember me your lovyng master, Henry Rex': underneath Elizabeth of York has added 'Madam I pray you for you forget not me, to pray to God that I may have grace of your prayers, Elizabeth the Queene'.[48] Other members of the Court added their own pious autographs. On folio 180 Thomas Manners, Lord Roos, wrote

> Madam wan you ar dysposyd to pray
> remember your assured sarvant always, T Roos.

Lower down the same page Francis Poyntz added

> Madame when ye most devoutyst be
> have yn remembrance f and p.[49]

But the most touching additions to the book bring us into the heart of the reformation crisis, which will be the subject of a later chapter. At the foot of folio 20v Queen Katherine of Aragon has written

> I thinke the prayers of a frend the most acceptable unto God and because I take you for one of myn assured I pray you remember me in yours. Katherine the queen.

At the end of the book, the princess Mary wrote

> I have red that no body lyvethe as he shulde doo but he that folowethe vertu and y reckenyng you to be one of them I pray you to remembre me in your devocyons.

It is part of the heartlessness of Tudor history that the signatures and titles of both Katherine and Mary, the court lady's *assured friends*, have been carefully and ruthlessly blotted out [Pls. 38, 39].[50]

3

DEVOTIONAL ISOLATION?

With such inscriptions, and the sometimes fragile fidelities they promised or invoked, we are in a world of devotional intimacy and friendship, real or pretended. What was the spatial setting for such intimacies – where is all this devotion going on? Mary of Burgundy, pictured at prayer in her own Book of Hours, appears to be in her own 'closet' or private room, jewellery and clothing scattered before her, her lap-dog on her lap [Pl. 18]. We know what sort of prayer she is saying, because her portrait serves as frontispiece to a devotion on the joys of the Virgin Mary which regularly appears in Books of Hours, and was supposedly revealed to Thomas Becket in a vision of the Virgin. Using this prayer seems to transport Mary of Burgundy herself into a visionary setting, which we see through the window – into a public church where she and her attendants kneel before the Virgin and Child, larger than life. As in Petrus Christus's well-known image of a young man praying from a book of hours [Pl. 40],[1] Mary of Burgundy's picture shows us the user of the Book of Hours in the first place as a solitary, in line with the Dominical instruction on prayer in the Gospel of St Matthew: *Tu autem cum orabis intra in cubiculum tuum et cluso ostio tuo ora Patrem tuum in abscondito* (But thou, when thou shalt pray, enter into thy chamber and, having shut the door, pray to thy Father in secret).[2] In her vision, however, she is in a public church, surrounded by her

40. DEVOUT INTERIORITY
This portrait of a wealthy young man alone in his room praying from a Book of Hours (with its tasselled protective chemise) and behind him on the wall a coloured broadsheet of the Vernicle and its accompanying hymn *Salve Sancta Facies*, catches an important dimension of late medieval lay piety in general and the Book of Hours in particular: the quest for some approximation in secular life to the life of prayer and asceticism lived (ideally) by monks and nuns.

Petrus Christus, Portrait of a Young Man. National Gallery, London

ladies in waiting and a priest, kneeling in veneration of a type of image of the Virgin normally taken to symbolise the Church as a whole.[3] The boundaries between private and public, individual and corporate, are here permeable.

And this raises the question of whether or not the Book of Hours is not only a forum for the exchange of intimacy, an aspect of the history of privacy, but a cause, or at any rate a signal, of the growth of individualism. Some serious historians of religion have tended to think so. Professor Colin Richmond has associated the popularity of the Book of Hours with other manifestations of privatisation in religion, such as the private pew and the domestic chapel. By private pews he has in mind elaborate structures like the Harling Chapel at East Harling in Norfolk, the Spring Chapel, at Lavenham in Suffolk, or the Chudleigh Chapel at Ashton in Devon [Pl. 41].

Built inside the parish church, yet not altogether part of it, such pews constituted, Richmond considers, a private enclave in which the gentry could get on with the practice of an elite religion increasingly remote from the public religion of the rest of the parish, who

41. PRIVACY OR PROPRIETORSHIP? This chapel in the south aisle of East Harling Church was the chantry chapel and private pew of the Harling family, Lords of the Manor, and in the Middle Ages was equipped with its own altar and clergy. Chantry clergy often contributed to parochial worship as well as serving their private patrons, and historians disagree as to whether such structures were a sign of retreat from parish religion into elite privacy, or an assertion of presence (and power) in the parish community.

Harling Chapel, East Harling Norfolk

were essentially outsiders to this private and propertied religion. In there, he argues, 'they were, so to speak, getting their heads down, turning their eyes from the distractions posed by their fellow worshippers, [and] at the same time talking them off the priest and his movements and gestures. Such folk, in becoming isolated from their neighbours, were also insulating themselves against communal religion, possibly even religion *per se*, for how can you be religious on your own?'[4]

It is perfectly clear that the use of books of Hours by lay people in the late Middle Ages is indeed an aspect of the promotion of lay interiority, the personalising of religion which had been one of the aims of pastoral strategy and spiritual direction since at least the time of the reform papacy, and which is such a feature of the late medieval devotional landscape – the world of Margery Kempe.[5] The Book of Hours, as we saw at the outset of this chapter, offered lay people a share in what was essentially a monastic form of piety. The interiority of that piety was classically articulated in the opening lines of Anselm's Proslogion:

42. DEVOTIONAL DISPLAY
Books of Hours, like rosary beads, were dress accessories as well as equipment for prayer, and were frequently used in public places. Mary Wotton, wife of Sir Henry Guildford, Master of the Household to Henry VIII, was portrayed holding both by Holbein in 1527.

Hans Holbein, Mary Wotton, Lady Guildford, 1527. St Louis Art Museum, Missouri

43. A FAMILY AT PRAYER
Holbein's wonderful drawing of Thomas More's family has often been taken as a portrait of a Renaissance humanist household with its books. In fact, the entire family are almost certainly holding uniform copies of a printed Book of Hours (similar to the cheap edition by Regnault which More was to take with him into the Tower) as they prepare to recite the Hours of the Virgin together. More's daughter-in-law leans over More's father to help him find the place.

Hans Holbein, The More Family, 1527. Öffentliche Kunstsammlung, Basel

> *Eia nunc, homuncio, fuge paululum occupationes tuas . . .* Come now, little man, turn aside for a while from your daily employment, escape for a moment from the weight of your thoughts. Put aside your weighty cares, let your burdensome distractions wait, free yourself awhile for God and rest awhile in him. Enter the inner chamber of your soul, shut out everything except God and that which can help you in seeking him, and when you have shut the door, seek him. Now, my whole heart, say to God, 'I seek your face.'[6]

This is the medieval church's idealised situation for prayer and meditation, and the suggestion that its attainment represented a threat, in the form of an exclusive alternative, to the *official* religion of the community, in particular to the community of the parish, is surely wide of the mark. The late medieval church measured its success not

on how far it could *prevent* people interiorising their religion, but how far it actually succeeded in helping them to do just that: medieval bishops and pastoral theologians would have been baffled by the suggestion that increased lay devotional intensity might threaten the religion of the parish church. For interiority is by no means to be equated with individualism. People prayed their Book of Hours often, perhaps usually, alone, and indeed fifteenth-century and early Tudor devotional and conduct books often recommended the recitation of Matins or Vespers in one's closet, which, you will recall was Lady Cobham's practice. But it was almost as common for people to recite their hours in public rooms, as a dozen Tudor portraits make clear [Pl. 42] and as we glimpse in George Cavendish's anecdote about Thomas Cromwell reciting the Matins of our Lady from his Book of Hours in the window seat of the Great Chamber at Esher.[7] And the arrival of printed Books of Hours opened up new possibilities for communal recital. Most gentry and many bourgeois households would have held more than one copy of the Book of Hours, but communal recitation would have been hindered by the fact that no two manuscript books were identical, and finding one's way around them was not always a quick business. Printed books, by contrast, were uniform, had tables of contents and indices, and regularly advertised themselves as easy to navigate around – 'set out along without any searching'.[8] Moreover, since they were cheap, a single household could own multiple copies. The Holbein drawing of the household of St Thomas More in the late 1520s is one of the most famous images of a Renaissance family [Pl. 43].[9] The picture, in which almost everyone is holding a book, has been variously interpreted, not least as a Humanist household in which the written and printed word held pride of place. It has not been much noticed, however, that everyone is holding the *same* book. They have set aside books of different thicknesses and size, which lie on floor and window-ledge. The identical book in every hand is a prayer-book, in fact the Book of Hours, as is plain from the fact that Dame Alice, More's wife, is kneeling at her prayer-desk. Through Holbein's eyes, we are privileged flies on the wall at a London bourgeois household's family prayers, and the More family are about to start a *communal* recitation of Our Lady's Matins.

But it was equally common to recite one's Matins in church. Margery Kempe tells us how a falling wedge of stone from the roof of her parish church dashed her Book of Hours from her hands and concussed her as she was reciting her Matins one morning,[10] and an Italian tourist in England in the 1490s noted that literate townspeople liked to go with a companion to church and recite their Hours 'verse by verse, in a low voice, after the manner of churchmen'.[11] *After the manner of churchmen* – that, of course, was one of the essential features of the Book of Hours, and we encounter it at the very outset. The earliest surviving English Book of Hours, the De Brailes Hours, was clumsily altered as soon as it was made, spoiling the appearance by cutting away a page containing an illuminated initial and inserting pages written in a totally different hand in order to alter the psalms of Vespers of the Virgin from those customary in England to those used in the Dominican rite. This clumsy and very noticeable change, made before the whole book was bound for the first time, was most likely made so that the owner could recite Vespers along with the Dominican friars who were her spiritual advisers.[12] And since the very *raison d'être* of the Book of Hours was to offer lay people a suitably slimmed down and simplified share in the Church's official cycle of daily prayer, it was not so much a rival to the religion of the official church as an aspect of it, cementing the lay devotee more closely to the institution by encouraging him or her to participate in its formal worship.

This perhaps helps explain the otherwise apparently baffling fact that all over Europe the overwhelming majority of Books of Hours remained in Latin, and their lay users went on apparently contentedly reciting the prayers contained in these books even though they were written in a language which few of them can have understood perfectly. Translations of the Book of Hours did of course exist in French, Dutch, and even English: to judge by survivals such vernacular versions were much more common in the Low Countries than elsewhere. In England the production of such English versions was almost certainly inhibited by the prohibition which Archbishop Arundel issued in 1409 of translations of scripture, a reaction to the spread of Wycliffite or 'Lollard' heresy.[13] Although no such prohibition was in force elsewhere in Europe, still the overwhelming majority of European Books of Hours were in Latin. Indeed, the use of Latin psalms and prayers was part of their point. Lay people used these books specifically in order to share in the official liturgy of the Church. That liturgy, based on the Latin Bible, was of course itself in Latin. A special sacral aura therefore attached to Latin as the language of revelation and of worship, and that aura made lay people willing and even eager to pray privately in Latin, thereby associating themselves with the universal public worship of the Church. Lay people were of course interested in prayer in English, and often added vernacular prayers to their Latin books. But such devotions were valued as additions or supplements to the liturgical contents, which provided the backbone of the book, and a large part of its *raison d'être*.[14]

The lay person who recited these prayers was thereby being equipped to appropriate – and understand – the Latin words which they routinely heard recited by clergy and ministers in the public liturgy. This has obvious implications for the theory that such books were a symptom or a cause of rising individualism and isolation. What sense does it make to talk of idiosyncrasy and individualism,

44.
The Office of the Dead in most Books of Hours was illustrated with a scene depicting the public liturgy of death. In this early fifteenth-century example clergy and paid mourners celebrate the *Dirige* round a catafalque covered with a black pall. A female owner has written at the foot of the page 'In all tyme of nesessitye: with your prayers remember me/EDETH BREDYMAN'.

Fitzwilliam Museum, Cambridge Ms 57 fo. 127r. Page size 10 × 7 cm

when we are confronted by the spectacle of hundreds and indeed thousands of lay people reciting more or less identical prayers, chiefly liturgical, day in and day out, often in their parish churches, surrounded by the neighbours they are supposedly distancing by this very act, some at least of whom are similarly engaged in reciting the same words at the same time?

We need to remind ourselves here that precisely because they were part of the liturgy, the prayers of these books were not merely used privately. Large sections of them were regularly recited collectively as part of the public worship of the whole community, or of some of its constituent sub-groupings, such as the gilds. The key item in the Books of Hours here was the Office for the Dead, that is Vespers, Matins and Lauds of the Dead, or *Dirige* as it was known from the opening word of the opening antiphon of Matins. This service was an invariable and popular feature of Books of Hours, and unlike the Little Hours of the Virgin, which formed the first part of all such books, it was neither simplified nor abbreviated, but included the full text of the Church's official prayers for the dead. The inclusion of obit notices in the calendar of such books was a reminder to the user to recite this office on the appropriate anniversary. But the office was also one of the most familiar parts of the Church's formal liturgy, publicly recited as part of every funeral, and often subsequently on weekly, monthly and yearly commemorations. Devotional gilds often required their members to attend these recitations for deceased brethren, and literate lay people were encouraged or expected to join in. In most illustrated Books of Hours, the *Dirige* is preceded by a picture of this part of the funeral liturgy, being celebrated by clergy, often accompanied by lay people [Pl. 44].[15]

And certainly the proud owners and users of Books of Hours did not conceive themselves to be separating from their neighbours, or the public worship of the parish. In the 1520s, the wealthy Devon clothier John Greneway and his wife Joan had themselves portrayed kneeling in the porch of the parish church of St Peter at Tiverton with their Books of Hours before them [Pl. 45]. They placed those self-images with books not in the isolation of their private chantry chapel, but prominently above the south door, a key spot where marriages and the first part of baptism was celebrated, inside the splendid porch they built for their neighbours' comfort and convenience

In all tyme of nesessitye: with yor prayer remember me,
EDETH. BREDYMAN

45. A PUBLIC PRAYER BOOK
John Greneway (died 1526) was Master of the Drapers Company in London, one of the wealthiest Devon clothiers in the reign of Henry VIII and a lavish benefactor of the town and parish church of Tiverton. Here in the porch which he built (the space where weddings were celebrated) he and his wife Joan kneel before the Virgin Mary assumed into heaven; before them on their prayer-desks are their open Books of Hours.

Greneway tympanum, Church of St Peter and Paul, Tiverton

46. A LITURGICAL DEVOTION
Many late medieval and early Tudor gentry constructed tombs for themselves, which doubled as the parish's 'Easter Sepulchre', the site for the annual liturgical service of the 'burial' and resurrection of the Body of Christ in Holy Week. A number of surviving Easter Sepulchres, like this one donated by the Gounter family of Racton in Sussex, portray the donors praying from Books of Hours.

Gounter Monument c. 1520, Racton Church, Sussex

against the wind and damps of Exe valley winters. It would simply not be possible to find a more communal context in which to depict the use of a Book of Hours. In the same way, a number of early sixteenth-century Easter Sepulchres portray the donors reading from Books of Hours before the risen Christ or the Trinity [Pl. 46]. There is more than casual decoration at stake here. The Easter sepulchre was the focus of the parish community's most intense corporate adoration of the sacrament in Holy Week. To have oneself portrayed praying from the Book of Hours in such a context is a significant and deliberate choice, and hardly indicates that the book was associated with devotional isolation.[16]

A late fifteenth-century prayer added to the flyleaf of a book of hours now in Lambeth Palace Library suggests that its owner while praying at Mass understood perfectly well the communal nature of the mystery being enacted before his eyes:

> Most mercyfull Lord I beseche thee heartely off thy mercy and grace and forgyfnes of my synnes and thow wyll make me partner of the effects and graces of thy moste blessyd bodye and blode the whyche be mynysterd her in thys blessed masse also I beseche thee to mak me partener of all masys that ys seyd thys daye in thys churche and in all holly churchys. I beseche thee heartely to make me a pertener of all suffragys of holly church and of all good dedys they whychge be done off all crysten men. Jesu, Jhesu, Jhesu mercy . . .[17]

The history of the evolution of the Book of Hours itself should in any case give us pause before we associate its use with the growth of individualism and a retreat from public religion, a sort of material equivalent, say, to the spread of the *Devotio Moderna*. The devotional temperature of the fourteenth and fifteenth century was admittedly rising steadily, as late medieval Christianity went through the religious equivalent of global warming, inspired in part by the preaching and devotional regime of the Franciscans, and partly by a growing hunger for religious variety and intensity on the part of lay men and women with time, leisure, literacy, and not least, money on their hands. But if we are to judge from the evidence of Books of Hours, the result was not a move towards mysticism and interiority, but rather a twofold trend, one in the direction of greater intimacy, and another in the direction of a decidedly instrumental understanding of prayer. On the one hand, many of the prayers most commonly included in Books of Hours display a marked relish for devotional sweetness, exemplified in prayers like the *O Bone Jesu*, which approached the divinity like a lover or a family intimate, and in which penitential humility is enfolded in the language of affection and familiarity:

> O good Jesu, o sweet Jesu, o Jesu, son of the Virgin Mary, full of mercy and truth, a Sweet Jesu, have mercy upon me, according to thy great mercy, o benign Jesu, I beseech thee by thy most precious blood, which for us sinners thou didst deign to pour out upon the altar of the cross, to cast from thee all mine iniquities, and do not despise me, who humbly petition thee.[18]

We catch a glimpse of how the devotional ethos of such prayers fitted into a cosy domesticity from the account in the Paston letters of the death of Sir John Hevingham, who went to his parish church one fine summer's morning in 1453, and heard three masses, and came home again 'never meryer, and seyd to hys wyf that he would go sey a lytyll devocion in hese garden, and then he would dyne'.[19] Sir John dropped dead in his garden, and never got his dinner, but his pious occupation at the moment of his death will have been a comfort to his wife, as it was a matter of edification to his neighbours.

Alongside this comfortable devotional affectivity went a quite different but equally prominent development, the growth of an ever more obviously instrumental approach to prayer. The people who copied extra prayers into their books were interested in what I have called elsewhere 'Charms, pardons and promises'.[20] They wanted prayers which carried indulgences, or legends guaranteeing spiritual or material benefits, especially protection against life's troubles and the terrors of death. Thus, while many new texts were added to the standard devotions included in Books of Hours, the additions are characterised not by a reclusive interiority, but by a robust interest in measurable results. Late medieval people collected prayers as we collect recipes, and for rather similar reasons. What they put into those recipes will be the focus of the next chapter.

Part 2

SANCTIFIED WHINGEING?
THE VOICE OF PRAYER IN THE LATE MIDDLE AGES

Domine labia mea
aperies. Et os me
um annunciabit
laudem tuam.
Deus in adiutorium meum
intende. Domine ad
adiuvandum me festina. Glo
ria patri et filio et spiritui sancto.
Sicut erat in principio et nunc
et semper et in secula seculorum
amen. Alleluya. Invitatorium. Ave ma
ria gratia plena dominus tecum. Ave m
Venite exultemus dño ps.
iubilemus deo saluta
ri nostro preoccupemus faciem
eius in confessione et in psalmis
iubilemus ei. Ave maria. Quo
niam deus magnus dominus
et rex magnus super omnes deos
quoniam non repellet dominus
plebem suam quia in manu eius
sunt omnes fines terre et alti

4

A BOOK FOR AN ARISTOCRAT: THE TALBOT HOURS

In Part I we considered the intensely personal character of medieval Books of Hours. To begin with, that personal character was linked directly to their costliness. The labour-intensiveness, beauty and precious materials of most Books of Hours meant that they were sometimes the most valuable single possession a man and especially a woman might own. But their value was also spiritual, even sentimental. Their role in a devotional life which was both intimate and semi-public, for one thing, made them an obvious location for the formal exchange of intimacy. Given as gifts, they could be powerful tokens of regard or fidelity, and, as we have seen, messages written on their pages carried a solemn aura of sincerity – even when the sentiments expressed did not in fact withstand the test of time.[1] In considering that intimate character, however, we were primarily concerned with the books as objects and as surfaces on which messages could be inscribed, and we barely touched on their main function, which was to provide a script for the drama of personal religion, to be the text of the prayers which people prayed. In this chapter I want to look more closely at those prayers themselves, and to see what we can deduce from them about the inner lives of those who used them. This is a huge topic, and we can only touch the surface of it here. So in what follows I shall have relatively little to say about the routine contents of the Book of Hours, the psalms, litanies, hymns

47.
Matins in the Talbot Hours opens, as was conventional, with a miniature of the Annunciation.

Fitzwilliam Museum, Cambridge Ms 40–1950 fo. 8r, Annunciation and Matins. Page size 27 × 11 cm

and responses which made up the Hours of the Virgin and the Office of the Dead.[2] Instead I shall concentrate on the non-standard material which people added to their books to personalise them or meet particular needs, and which therefore offer us more leverage on the particularity of individual books and their users. But first we need to remind ourselves that such devotions were additions to the main contents of these books, and that it was the Bible, and above all the psalms, which provided the main framework of medieval Christian prayer.

Books of Hours were scriptural prayer-books. They were also crammed, of course, with non-biblical material – suffrages to and images of the saints, litanies, indulgenced prayers to the wounds of Jesus, to the Blessed Sacrament, to the Virgin Mary. But overwhelmingly the prayers of the Hours were drawn from the Psalter, and the illustrations in most of those books which had illustrations at all were predominantly scenes from the Bible, depicting the Infancy of Jesus, or the incidents of his Passion. The core of the book, the Little Office of the Virgin, with its constant refrain of 'Ave Maria Gratia Plena', the greeting of the Angel Gabriel, and its hymns and lessons returning again and again to the moment at which God took human flesh in the womb of the Virgin at the Annunciation, was in effect a prolonged meditation on the mystery of the Incarnation, while the psalms it contained included many of the most tender and beautiful prayers of the Psalter – 'I will lift up mine eyes to the mountains', 'I was glad when I heard them say', 'God be merciful unto us and bless us', 'When the Lord turned again the captivity of Sion'. Unsurprisingly, in those books which show most signs of wear, the pages containing the Hours themselves, rather than the auxiliary or supplementary devotions, are usually the most thumbed. The medieval user of a Book of Hours would come to know these psalms intimately from daily recitation, and indeed, many of the most often recited psalms, the fifteen so-called 'Gradual Psalms' (Psalms 119–133 Vulgate numbering) were assumed to be so familiar to the reader, that where the whole group was included as a separate item distinct from the Hours of the Virgin, as they often were, only the cue or first line might be provided, it being assumed that the user would be able to continue without the book, or at any rate turn quickly back to the part of the book in which the whole psalm was to be found.[3]

The other invariable component of the Book of Hours, the Office of the Dead, sounded deeper and more sombre notes, its psalms adding the themes of desolation and supplication to those of hope and confidence so dominant in the Hours of the Virgin – alongside 'The Lord is my shepherd', and 'I love the Lord, for he has heard the cry of my appeal', the Office of the Dead was also an urgent supplication: 'Out of the depths I have cried to thee O Lord'. The magnificent readings from the book of Job which formed the heart of Matins for the Dead probed even deeper, filled as they are with reproach and appeal to God, rooted in the sense of human fragility and suffering, the brevity of life and the bitterness of death – 'Man that is born of woman hath but a short time to live, and is full of troubles', 'Have mercy on me O God, for my days are nothing'. Even without any of the supplementary devotions often sought by lay owners, the core elements of the Book of Hours offered anyone with the basic Latin comprehension needed to grasp their content a rich and profound basis for Christian prayer.

But prayers which everybody used give us only a general grip on the interiority of medieval people. We cannot of course assume that the medieval pray-er, routinely using a psalm expressing despair or exultation or longing, felt within him- or herself the corresponding emotions, though some historians have recently insisted that this must in fact be so. We shall return to this problem in due course, but, as we shall see, it is difficult to be sure how to interpret conventional words as indicators of personal feeling. We can however get further towards a sense of the inner life of individuals by considering the non-standard material they chose to add to the stock contents of their books. That process of addition often started even as a new book was being prepared. The very earliest surviving English Book of Hours had prayers in French added for its female owner, commemorating Dominican spiritual guides, and such built-in additions remained a constant feature of such books to the end of the Middle Ages.[4] The splendid mid-fifteenth-century book commissioned by John Talbot Earl of Shrewsbury was part of a pair made for him and his second wife Margaret Beauchamp, and written in an unusual long and narrow format reminiscent of the lay-out of medieval prayer-rolls.[5] The book included in its original design, and in the series material subsequently added for Talbot, a revealing series of prayers and devotions which speak eloquently of the preoccupations of an aristocratic English soldier at war in France.[6]

Neither Talbot nor his wife would be likely to match anyone's notion of sanctity.[7] Margaret Beauchamp, whom the widowed John Talbot married as his second wife in 1422, was, it is true, in some respects sternly puritanical. She ran a strict household, and, reputedly, any member of it overheard swearing was instantly put on a penitential diet of bread and water. But she was grasping and ambitious, devoting much of her life to the vexatious pursuit of land and titles for her family. In this she was well-matched with her husband. John Talbot was idealised by Shakespeare as 'Warlike and martial Talbot' the fearless and valiant scourge of the French, and flower of English chivalry.[8] All of which was true enough, but courage came at a price, and Talbot was also one of the most violent and quarrelsome men in a violent and quarrelsome century, an aggressive and litigious neighbour, a disastrously divisive Lord Lieutenant of Ireland, and a field commander in France whose stupendous success and reputation as 'the English Achilles' was directly proportionate to his willingness to employ extreme violence and the tactics of terror. He was, as Shakespeare himself has him declare, attended by three furies, 'lean famine, quartering steel, and climbing fire'.[9]

Yet he was undoubtedly also a pious man. His Book of Hours was manifestly for use as well as ostentation: the many prayers and devotions added to it in Talbot's lifetime closely reflect the preoccupations of a soldier whose activities put him in daily danger not only of death, but of damnation. Among the less usual items in it are the texts of privileged masses to be said, almost certainly in the field, on the portable altar for which he had a special licence. On his release from almost a year as a hostage after his surrender at Rouen, in the summer of 1450, Talbot delayed what must have been a longed for return home to make the pilgrimage to Rome, to gain the great Jubilee indulgence proclaimed that year by Pope Nicholas V. And the subsequent fate of his Book of Hours itself confirms that real if conventional piety. At his death it fell into French hands, as a series of late fifteenth-century French devotional additions, and of more profane scribbles in French, make clear. The likeliest explanation for this alienation of the book from the Talbot family was that he had it with him at the siege of Chantilly at which he was killed in July 1453, and that one of his assailants took it as booty, just as Henry Tudor would take Richard III's Hours from his tent on Bosworth Field.[10]

Talbot's book of Hours is an unmistakably personal construct, from its very shape, a peculiar long thin format which is replicated in his wife's book and which seems to have been specially associated with the Talbot family. Certainly the iconography of the book begins with a resounding claim to proprietorship, for the calendar with which the book opens is immediately followed by a full-page dedication illumination containing a joint portrait of John and Margaret Talbot kneeling in prayer before the enthroned Virgin and Child, forming a frontispiece to the Hours of the Virgin which follow on immediately. In the portrait page, their patron saints stand behind them, in the husband's case not St John, his name saint, but St George, as patron of England, of soldiers and, especially, of the Order of the Garter.[11] Behind Margaret stands her name-saint, St Margaret with her dragon. Below them are two banners with the Talbot and Beauchamp arms, and below the banners, two garters, that below Talbot enclosing the Talbot dog, the one below Margaret Beauchamp enclosing her family's bear and ragged staff: at the bottom of the page is a medallion with a crowned monogram formed by the initials of the couple.

The bulk of Talbot's book is made up of standard fifteenth-century items – Hours of the Virgin, Penitential and Gradual Psalms, Litany, Office of the Dead, and a range of devotions on such conventional themes as the joys of the Virgin, the wounds of Christ, the Image of Pity (the dead Christ displaying his wounds above the tomb) and the emblems of the Passion [Pls. 48, 49].

They include the prayers on the seven last words of Jesus known as the Fifteen Oes of St Bridget, a favourite on fifteenth- and early sixteenth-century Books of Hours for English owners. The book was first compiled and decorated for Talbot in France, and though the bulk of this conventional material is of course in Latin, it includes a few vernacular devotions in French and English. The French scribes evidently could not cope very well with Talbot's barbaric native tongue, and there are comic or confusing mis-spellings and mistranscriptions in the English prayers and rubrics.[12] Most of these prayers included as part of the original design of the book reflect conventional fifteenth-century religious concern with safety and salvation,

48.
John Talbot's Book of Hours included many of the devotional images popular with lay people of every level of society in the fifteenth century, intended for devout contemplation. Here the Image of Pity has an indulgence rubric in French; below is the 'measure' of the side-wound of Jesus [cf. Pls 15, 17, 27, 28].

Fitzwilliam Museum, Cambridge Ms 40–1950 fo. 47. Page size 27 × 11 cm

ng philosophe estoit + disoit
en ce iour en ceste maniere.
e monde define en ce iour
ou le dieu de nature a souf
fert mort. Lequel philosophe
ne congnoissoit pas encore ihu
crist. puis il fu conuerti par la pre
dicacion saint pol. et dit on que
ce fu saint denis en france.
e la memoire de la souffranc
e nostre segneur ihu crist.
i blans escu signifie le corps
ihu crist. Les vermeilles ta
ches les coups des escourgies. La
memoire vest de le estache ou il fu
lies et batus. Le chapel signifie

49.
The Talbot Hours contains extensive supplements of vernacular material in English and French. Here the 'arms of Christ's passion' are 'moralised' or expounded in French.

Fitzwilliam Museum, Cambridge Ms 40–1950 fo. 58r

petitions for material and spiritual protection against temptation and the assaults of the devil, for pardon for sin, and for a 'good' death fortified by the sacraments of the Church [Pls. 49, 50]. Two English prayers, one in prose and one in verse, convey the general drift. The prose prayer is one of a sequence arranged round images of the Cross and Passion, and images of the persons of the Trinity.

50.
Vernacular prayers in the form of a verse Litany in English addressed to the Cross and the Holy Trinity.

Fitzwilliam Museum, Cambridge Ms 40–1950 fo. 81r

51. CHURCHLY PIETY

In the upper miniature John Talbot kneels to make his confession to a seated bishop. The verse prayer begins:

Hol confession with ful repentance
Of my mysdedes right reparation
Grant Lrd wyt verey and needful penaunce

In the miniature below, John and Margaret Talbot pray to St Ursinus of Bourges, patron saint of Lisieux where Talbot had property. Note Margaret's lapdog on her train [cf. Pl. 18].

Fitzwilliam Museum, Cambridge Ms 40–1950 fo. 82r

Lorde ih[es]u crist her me and have mercy up on me to day evy day and on derstonande my prayer and out frome me all infirmities sekenesses and sorwys and all fantesies of the devyll that the have no power for the noye me nyeth ne day waking ne slepyng, but all my amys [enemies] commanded and drede me and fle forme me . . .[13]

The verse prayer is part of an English verse litany [Pls. 50, 51], most of the verses arranged round images of the persons of the Trinity, but this one following a picture of a male penitent, presumably Talbot, kneeling to make his confession at the feet of a seated bishop.

Hol confession with ful repentance
Of my mysdedes right reparation
Grant Lord wyt verey and needful penaunce
Space me to mende and from dampnation
Ever me deffende and al tribulation
And for the merite of thy saintes al
Kepe me from synne and to thi mercy call.[14]

Among the devotions addressed to particular saints, prayers and hymns to saints venerated in the French regions associated with Talbot's military campaigns or family estates are specially prominent – memoria to Sts Mellon and Romanus, canonised bishops of Rouen, which was Talbot's principal base for much of his time in France, a long French hymn and Latin devotion addressed to St Hildevert of Meaux, one of the towns which Talbot eventually lost to the French, and a Latin hymn to St Ursinus of Bourges, patron saint of Lisieux where there were traditional Talbot landholdings. This special relationship between Ursinus and Talbot's family is underlined in the miniature which accompanies the prayers, depicting Talbot and his wife Margaret, identified by arms and emblems, kneeling in intercession before the saint.[15]

Many of the devotions added to this original core of the book reflect Talbot's preoccupations as a combatant soldier. Prayers and charms for protection against enemies and dangers loom large in every late medieval prayer-collection[16], but they take on a special urgency in a book commissioned by so battle-scarred a veteran as Talbot. An especially popular type of prayer-charm against danger was the so-called 'Charlemagne prayer', a solemn invocation of the Cross and the names of God, variations on which occur in many late medieval Books of Hours and devotional compilations, to which there was usually attached a rubric promising miraculous protections to the devout user. It was and would remain popular with soldiers, and versions of it were carried into battle by both French and German troops as late as the First World War.[17] Talbot had a version of the Charlemagne prayer added to the book, with a Latin rubric well adapted to his own circumstances.

> This is the letter of our Holy Saviour which Pope Leo sent on to Charles the king, saying that whoever carried it with them or in the day on which they heard or read it, that day they would not be killed by a weapon of iron, nor killed nor burned by fire, nor drowned by water, nor wicked men nor devils nor any other creature would have power to harm them, by day or by night.

And these are the words:

> + The Cross of Christ is an invincible weapon + the Cross is always with me + the Cross of Christ is what I ever adore + the Cross of Christ is true salvation + the Cross of Christ overcomes the sword + the Cross of Christ loosens the bonds of death + the Cross of Christ alone is truth . . .[18]

This is a comprehensive range of prayers, but it evidently did not meet all Talbot's religious needs, for on at least two subsequent occasions he had substantial bodies of further devotions added by English scribes. The most extensive and probably the first of these included a supplementary office of the Visitation of the Virgin, the text of the 'Ordinary' (non-varying part) of the Mass, and the 'Proper' (varying) texts for a series of votive masses – of the Holy Name of Jesus, of the Visitation, of St Gabriel, St George, the Trinity, the Holy Spirit, and a mass for the dead, with rubrics promising various indulgences and miraculous benefits.[19] The rubric before the Mass of the Holy Name of Jesus declares, for example, that 'Whoever celebrates this mass or causes it to be celebrated on thirty consecutive Fridays will not die without true contrition and worthy works of satisfaction [for sin] and oral confession and anointing with holy oil and within thirty days will come to eternal joy.'[20] These English prayers also included a long penitential address to Christ, beginning 'My sovereign Lord Jhesu the veray Son of almighty God and of the most clene and glorious virgine Mary'. In a characteristic late medieval combination of penitential abasement and confidence in salvation, it emphasised the unworthiness of the suppliant while appealing to Christ's love and mercy – 'I beseche the lorde have mercy on me a wreche and a synnere, but yet Lord I am thy creature and for thy precious passion save me and kepe me from all perell bodily and gostely.' Talbot was not alone in liking this prayer: it recurs as an addition to many late medieval Books of Hours, and we shall shortly encounter it again in a very different sort of book, and another social context. Aristocratic and more plebeian devotional tastes here coincide, and, as we shall see, in the era of the printed Book of Hours this prayer was to be a regular item in books printed for England.[21]

A second scribe subsequently added a second batch of prayers and poems in English and Latin,[22] addressed to Christ and a range of saints, including the Virgin and St Mary Magdalene, to whom the Talbots had a special devotion as the archetypal penitent. But these new additions were dominated by emphatically English material. This included six verses of the well-known devotional poem by the Norwich priest Richard of Caistor, 'Jesu Lord that madest me'. There was a Latin hymn to saint George, with an initial carefully decorated with three penwork scrolls bearing Talbot's name [Pl. 52].

The decoration of the opening of the hymn with his name confirms Talbot's special attachment to the cult of St George, which is indicated earlier in the book by the prominence of the saint in the double portrait frontispiece, and elsewhere by his gift of ornaments decorated with the Garter to be used on St George's day in the Church of the Holy Sepulchre in Rouen, and by his bequest for the foundation of a collegiate chapel dedicated to our Lady and St George at Whitchurch, where he wished to be buried. The additions to the book conclude with an English hymn addressed to St Alban by John Lydgate, with a refrain invoking the saint as 'protomartire of Brutys Albion', a vivid piece of sanctified patriotism, with a particular Lancastrian resonance.[23]

Though its tall narrow format is distinctive, Talbot's prayer-book has otherwise little originality. Its decorative scheme is essentially conventional – miniatures of the Annunciation, birth and infancy of

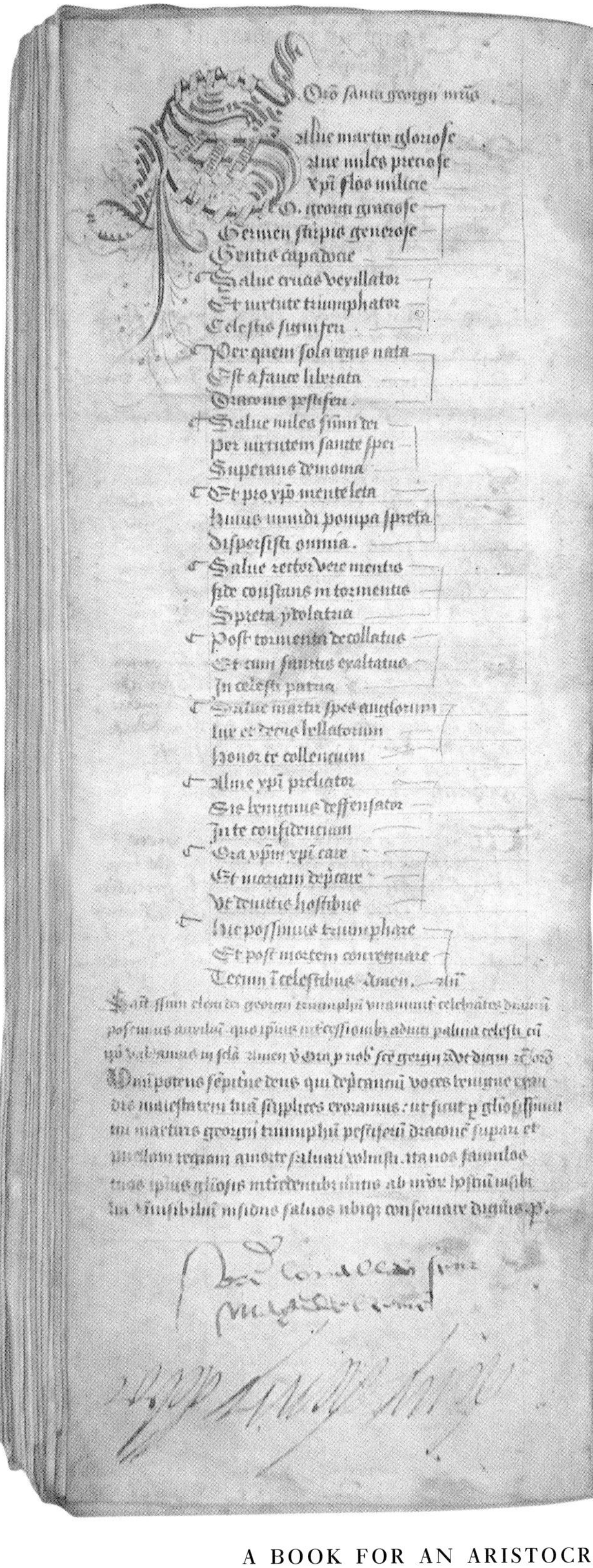

52. 'FOR ENGLAND, HARRY AND ST GEORGE'

Talbot continued to add material to his Book of Hours as his circumstances and devotional needs changed. Among the latest material in the book an English scribe has added this hymn to St George, patron saint of the Order of the Garter and protector of England. Talbot's name has been worked into the pen-work of the decorated Initial three times, a calligraphic reminder to the saint of his client's devotion.

Fitzwilliam Museum, Cambridge Ms 40–1950 fo. 135v

Christ in the Hours, devotional images of the side-wound of Christ, the arms of the Passion, the Trinity, saints. Only one image, a striking representation of the Virgin and Child enfolded in a lily, is iconographically unusual.[24] The choice of prayers added to the book can be paralleled in many late medieval prayer-books, and drew on a common pool of such devotions, circulating in pious compilations promoted by clergy and religious orders, and copied by lay people from book to book, not least within families and affinities.[25] Indeed, the verse litany from Talbot's book, together with some of the other English prayers included there, were subsequently incorporated by Caxton into a collection of English and Latin prayers published in 1491 and jointly commissioned by the Queen, Elizabeth of York, and the Queen Mother Lady Margaret Beaufort, and headed by an English translation of the Fifteen Oes of St Brigid.[26] They were thence incorporated into the influential Book of Hours printed by Wynkyn de Worde in 1494 under the patronage of Lady Margaret,[27] (a copy of which Maud and Catherine Parr inscribed for Sir William Parr)[28] and from there passed into the devotional mainstream, being reprinted subsequently in other *Horae*.[29]

Nevertheless the distinctive mix of all these conventional items is unmistakably Talbot's own, focused as it is on his French involvements, family and military, his understandably heightened concern with physical and spiritual protection, his patriotism, and the importance he attached to chivalric cult of St George and the order of the Garter. One of the English devotional rhymes he had inserted into his book at a late stage sums all this up:

Iesu whom ye serve dayly
Uppon your enemys gyff you victory.
Off the holy Crosse the vertu
Youre gode fortune alwey renew.
Oure lady and saynt gabryell
Geve you long lyffe and gode hele.
And seynt George the gode knight
Over your ffoemen geve you might.
And holy saynt kateryne
To youre begynnung send gode fine.
Saynt christophre botefull on see and lond
Joyfully make you see Englond.[30]

5

THE ROBERTS HOURS: PIETY OFF THE PEG

The Talbot Hours bears the marks of a single sensibility, preserving vividly its owner's characteristic spiritual and material preoccupations, and in it his dynastic pride is conspicuous. Ironically it became spoils of war, and passed, at the hands of the enemies he so often prayed as well as fought against, out of his family's control. But even without the dramas and reverses of the Hundred Years' War, Books of Hours were liable often to change hands, as they passed down the generations, or as they were dispersed with other belongings after the death of their owner. The Book of Hours (now Ms 43 in Ushaw College, Durham) commissioned by Richard of York (Richard III's father) and decorated with his arms, was bought second-hand by one Edmund Asheton in the early sixteenth century for a mere three shillings. And as books moved from hand to hand, many of them accumulated permanent traces of that new ownership. These were sometimes no more than a signature or a brief memorandum, like Edmund Asheton's careful note of the price he had paid for his acquisition. But they might include in many cases extensive family notes, prayers or devotional additions and enclosures even more various than those in the Talbot Hours, all of which offer us precious glimpses of the inmost preoccupations of the new users, or at any rate of what they felt was lacking in the standard contents of their book. This additional material is very varied, even though some items recur again and again.

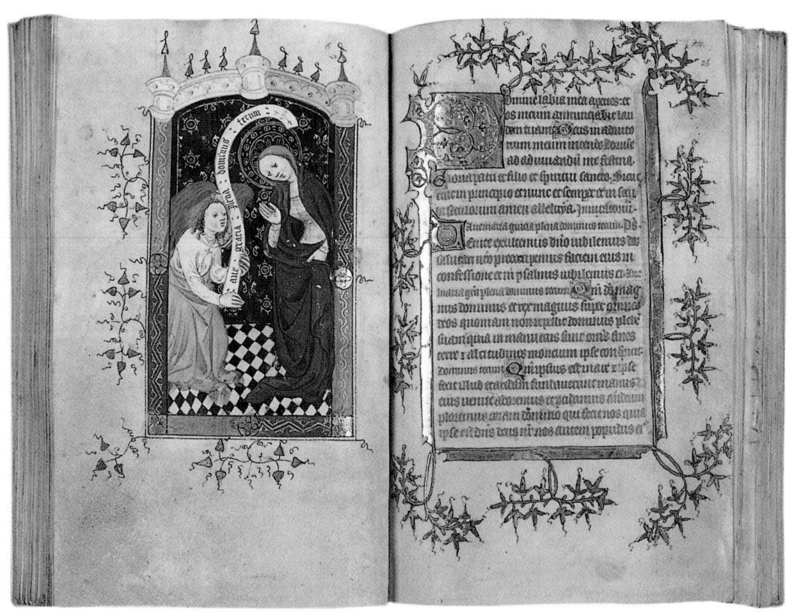

Rather than attempt a bogus synthesis or statistical analysis, we can gain a sense of the general character of this process of long-term devotional accretion by considering in some detail another single book.[1] I offer as an example, Cambridge University Library Ii.6.2, a cheapish manuscript Book of Hours produced for the English market in Bruges around 1400 or a little earlier, a date which makes it one of the first surviving examples of the wave of mass-produced works for an expanding literate class imported into England. It is brightly illustrated, with whole page miniatures of the nativity and infancy subjects before each of the Hours of the Virgin, and with a handful of other images – the Trinity, and a few major saints [Pl. 53]. But the pictures are mediocre, of a type bought in job lots by the stationer, to be bound into production-line manuscripts as required, in order to dress them up. Other examples from the same workshop also survive [Pl. 54].

This process left many blank pages in each Book of Hours, and successive owners of this particular book added their own material on the blanks. The calendar provides us with the original locality and social provenance of the book, for it contains obits for members of gentry families at Badingham and Hevingham in Suffolk.[2] One of them, indeed, commemorates Margaret Hevingham née Redisham, wife of the Sir John Hevingham whom we encountered in chapter three, reported in the Paston Letters as having dropped dead suddenly as he was saying a little devotion in his orchard: perhaps he was using this very book.[3] However that may be, by the early sixteenth century the book had passed into the hands of the Roberts family of Middlesex. The Roberts had been prosperous people in Willesden and Neasden since the thirteenth century, latterly acting as bailiffs for the Dean and Chapter of St Paul's, who had a great deal of land in the area. In the course of the fifteenth and sixteenth centuries the family steadily amassed land, both freehold and rented, so that by Elizabeth's reign they would be among the most substantial landowners in Middlesex. Much of this land had been church property, so I suppose we should include the Roberts among the hard-faced men who did well out of the Reformation.[4] Their manuscript additions to the book, some of them signed or in the same hand as Roberts family entries, offer an unusually copious but otherwise representative cross-section of the sort of material with which late medieval people made their own voice heard in their Books of Hours.

53.
Produced in Flanders for the English market at the end of the fourteenth or beginning of the fifteenth century, this is an early example of production-line Books of Hours for a middle market, and more than two hundred Sarum Books of Hours of this kind and quality survive. Its first owners were minor Suffolk gentry, and though it changed hands several times, it appears to have been in more or less continuous use for a century and a half. The Hours of the Virgin here open with the usual Annunciation scene.

Cambridge University Library Ii 6 2 fos. 33v–34r. Page size 19 × 13 cm

54.
Another early Flemish Book of Hours for England with pictures from the same workshop (note the decorative canopy in this and the previous plate; cf. Pls. 14, 15).

British Library Sloane 2683 fos. 25v–26. Page size 19 × 12 cm

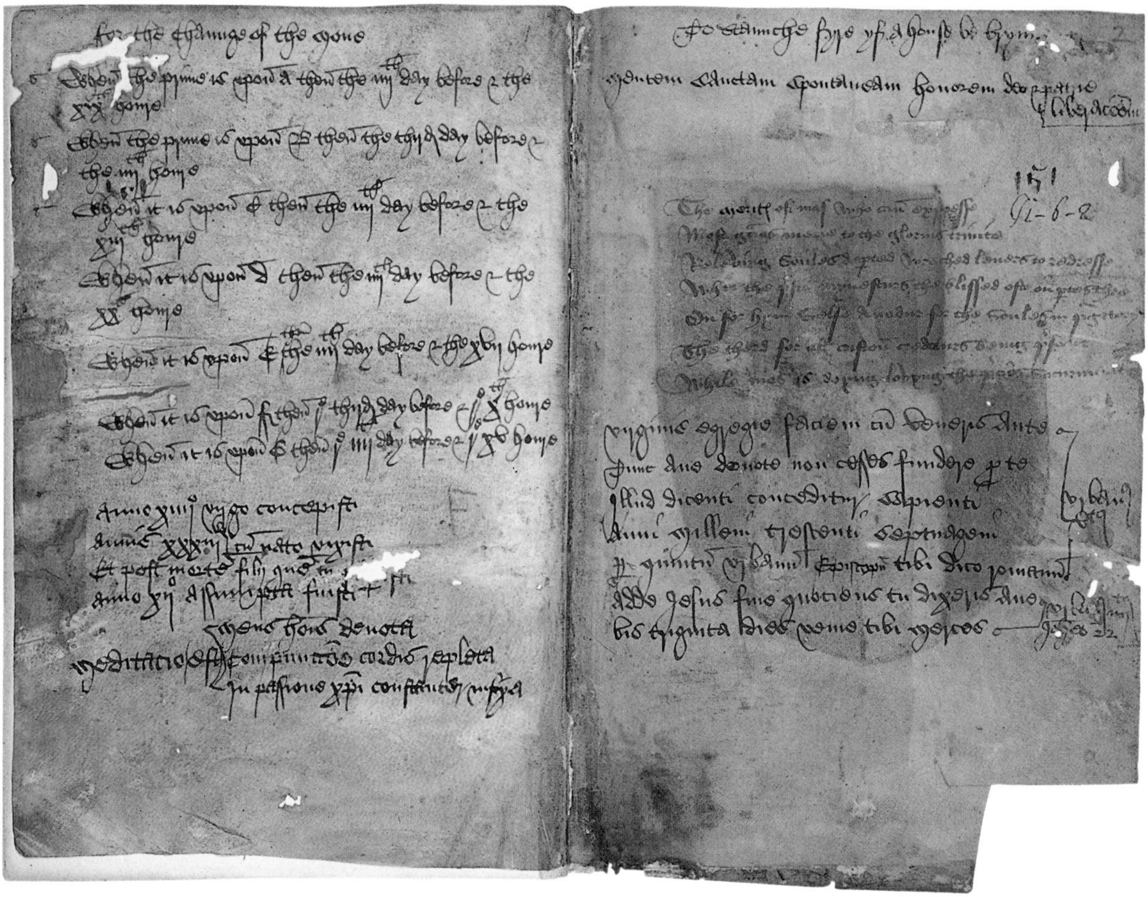

55.
The front flyleaves of the Roberts family Book of Hours has an assortment of calendrical notes, points for meditation on the Passion, a charm to quench a fire, part of a poem by the Suffolk monk-poet Lydgate on the Merit of the Mass, and a Latin devotion to the Virgin. Though in different hands, all these additions appear to date from the late fifteenth and early sixteenth century.

Cambridge University Library Ii 6 2, fos. 1v–2r. Page size 19 × 13 cm

These additions include the following: a table to calculate the conjunctions of the moon, a Latin rhyme on the life of the Virgin, and a Latin distych on the Passion of Christ (fol. 1v–2), a short spell in English to quench the flames if your house should happen to catch light, a rhyme royal stanza on the merits of the mass, and a seven line Latin rhyme about the Virgin [Pl. 55]. Turning the page (fos. 2v–3), there is a coat of arms, with the arms of the Sutton family impaling those of Tilney of Ashwellthorpe [Pl. 56].

Opposite has been written, in a late fifteenth-century hand, a long devotional instruction on the need to prepare against sudden death by constantly renewed acts of contrition and resolutions of amendment, and by undertaking to make a sacramental confession at the first opportunity 'accordyng to the commandments of all holy church', and to give alms and do good deeds. On subsequent pages

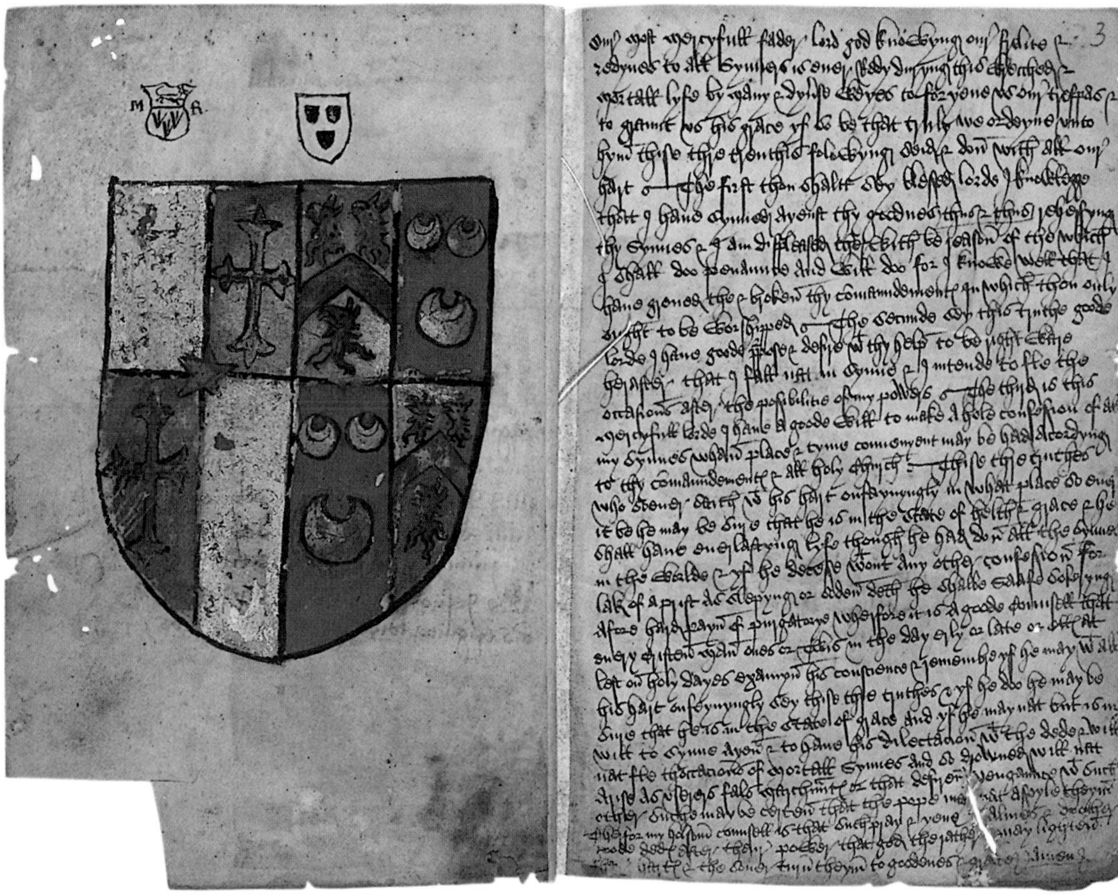

there has been added (3v) a Latin prayer to St Dorothy and a Latin rubric on the benefits of keeping an image of the saint in your house (Dorothy was a recurrent Roberts family name), a prayer (fo. 10) 'for women to conceyve a childe', a version of the Charlemagne prayer using the names of God, attributed here to Joseph of Arimathea (fo. 14), prayers to St Cornelius, St John the Baptist, St John the Evangelist, St George, St Erasmus, St Frideswide, a prayer to St Michael the Archangel attributed to Richard Fitzjames, Bishop of London, another to St Peter as 'Janitor of heaven', and more prayers to St Dorothy (fos. 15v, 17–18, 22, 24, 25v, 31v), a Latin prayer to the Virgin as Empress of hell for help at the hour of death, with a version of the English prayer to Jesus and Mary for forgiveness of sins, beginning 'O my sovereign Lord Jesu', which we have already encountered in the Talbot Hours (23v) [Pl. 57] an act of adoration in

56.
The original East Anglian provenance of the Roberts family book is represented by Suffolk obits in the calendar and by the clumsy heraldic shield on the left, on which the arms of Sutton impale those of Tilney of Ashwellthorpe. On the right is a long added instruction on a penitential regime, designed to prepare the user against sudden death.

Cambridge University Library Ii 6 2, fos. 2v–3r. Page size 19 × 13 cm

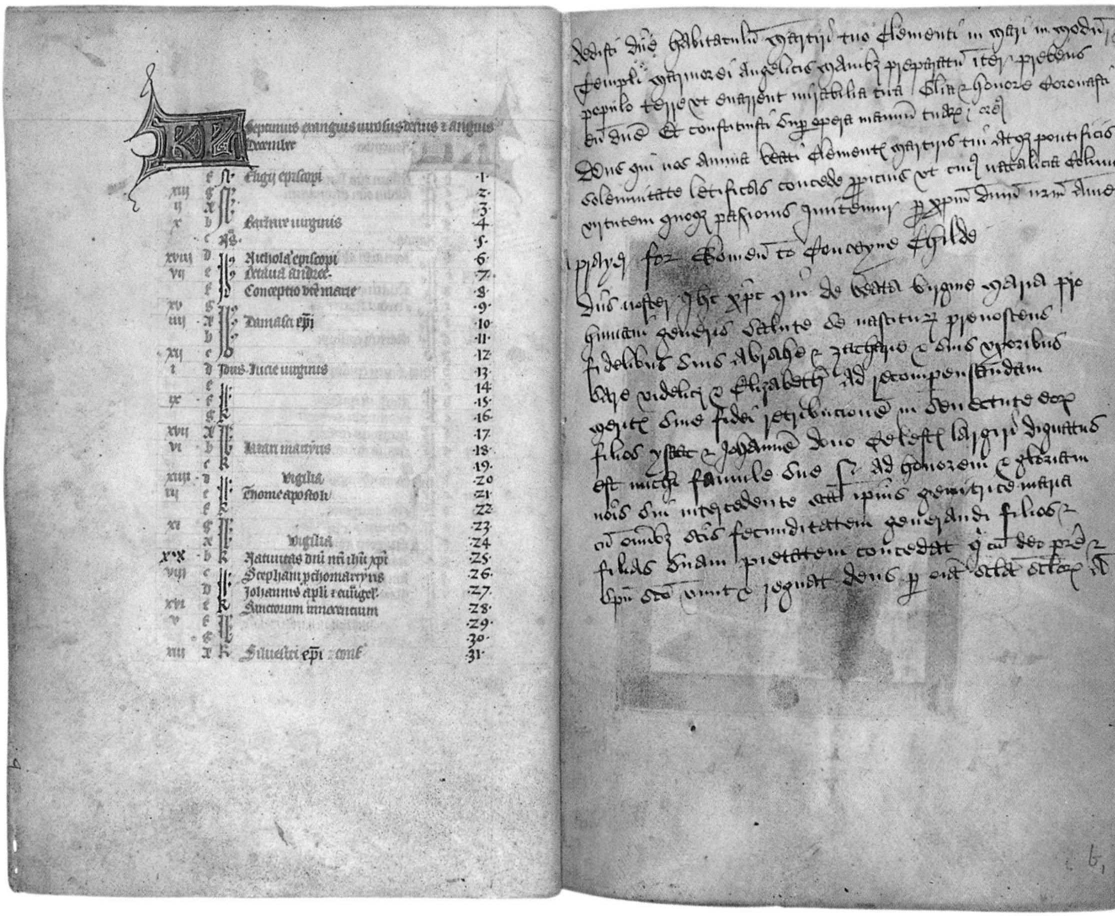

57·
On the back of the first full-page miniature in the book (the Holy Trinity, for which see Pl. 14), a member of the Roberts family has added a prayer to St Clement, and a Latin prayer 'for women to conceive chylder'. The impact of the Henrician reformation is visible in the December calendar page opposite, where the title 'Papa' (Pope) has been carefully altered to 'ep[iscopus]' (bishop) wherever it occurs, and the feast of St Thomas Becket (29 December) has been scraped out.

Cambridge University Library Ii 6 2, fos. 9v–10r

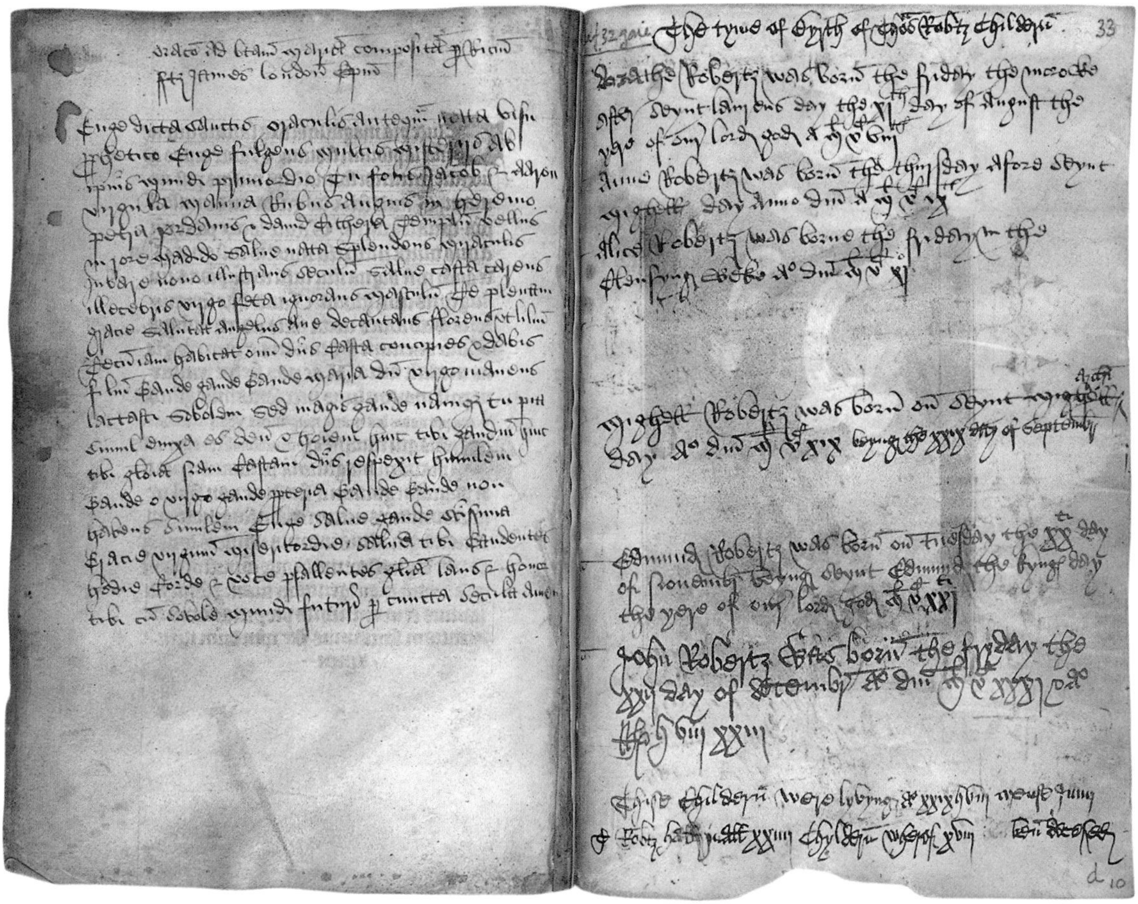

58.
On the back of the miniature of the Annunciation with which Matins of the Virgin commences are notes of the dates of birth of five of Thomas Roberts' children, probably to assist in calculating their horoscopes. Opposite is a prayer to St Michael the Archangel attributed in the heading to Richard Fitzjames, Bishop of London 1506–22.

Cambridge University Library Ii 6 2, fos. 32v–33r

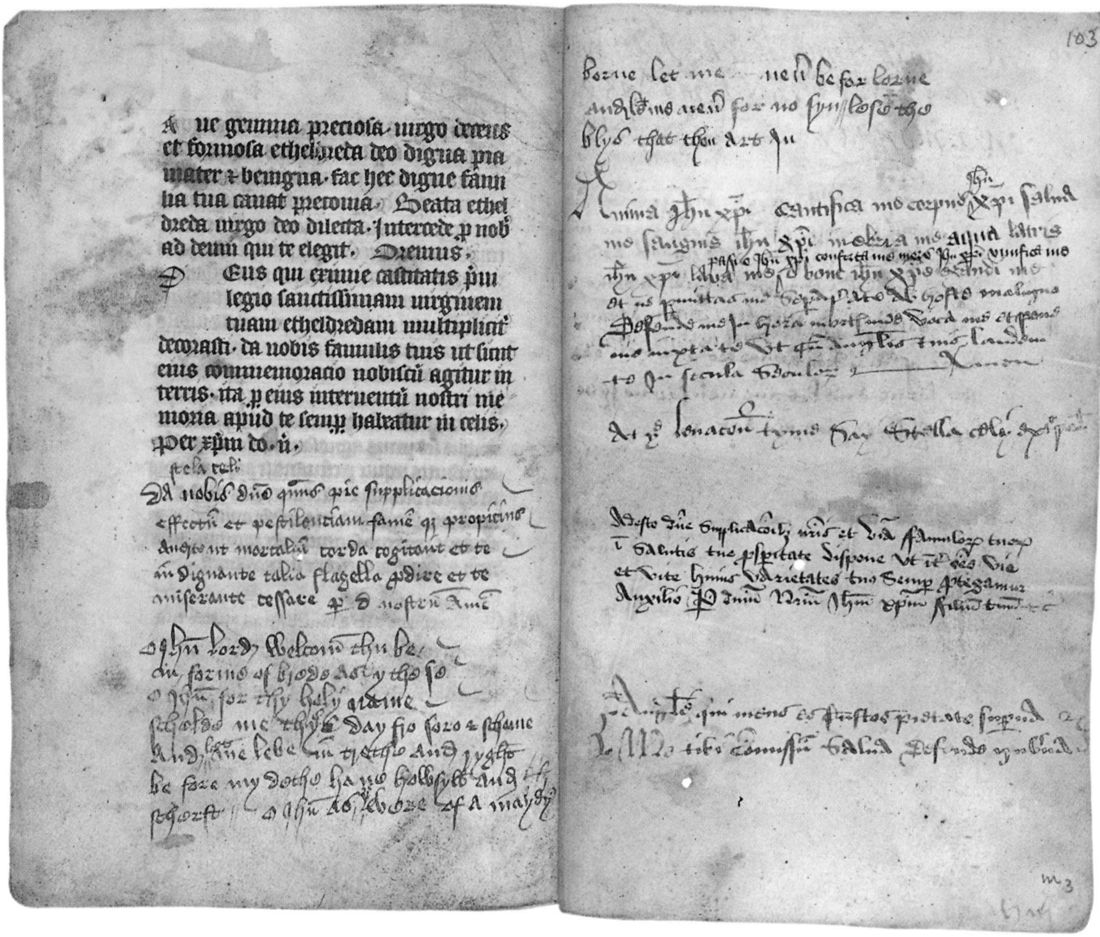

59.
The prayer to St Etheldreda of Ely (top left) is in a good scribal hand, and was probably professionally added to the book for its first East Anglian owners. The later untidier amateur additions here include a prayer to fend off the plague and a series of English and Latin devotions to be said at the Elevation in the Mass, an indication of at least one of the contexts in which the book was used.

Cambridge University Library Ii 6 2, fos. 102v–103r

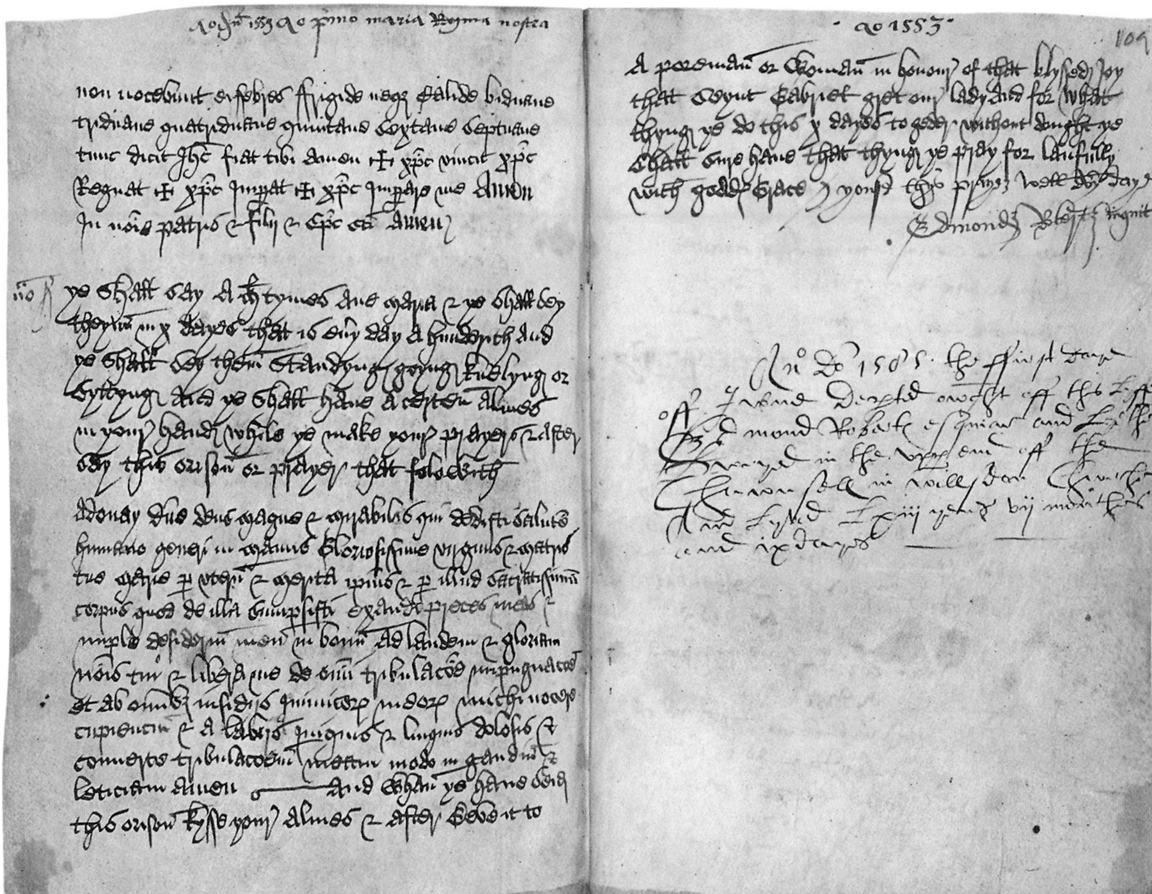

60. THE DEVOTION OF THE THOUSAND HAIL MARYS

The end of a long added instruction on the recitation over ten days of a thousand *aves*, accompanied by almsgiving, to secure a favour from God. In 1553 Edmund Roberts noted at the end of the instruction (right) that he had 'yousd thys prayer well' for ten days. In the middle of the same page is a note of Edmund's death in 1588, by which time he was a conforming protestant.

Cambridge University Library Ii 6 2 fos. 108v–109

Latin addressed to the Blessed Sacrament for use at Mass (27v). In another mode, there is a list of the times of births of five of Thomas Roberts' twenty-four children (fo. 33) [Pl. 58], a short scheme of meditation, probably late Elizabethan, in Latin, on sin and the brevity of life lamenting, among other ills, *malum commissum, bonum omissum, tempus amissum* (73v), another version of the Latin rhyme on the life of the Virgin which we have already encountered on the fly-leaf, with a note on the foundation of the shrine of Our Lady of Walsingham (fo. 75), a Latin prayer against the pestilence involving the recitation of the *Stella Coeli extirpavit* plague-hymn at the elevation of the Mass (fo. 102v) [Pl. 59], two versions of the very common elevation prayer:

O Jhesu Lorde, welcom thu be,
in forme of brede as Y the se,
Jhesu for they holy name,
schelde me thys day fro soro and shame . . .

a slightly expanded version of the Latin prayer to the blessed sacrament, *Anima Christi*, the Latin collect *Adesto Domine supplicationibus nostris*, which asks for God's guidance and protection in all the changes and chances of life (it was often included in printed Books of Hours, where it sometimes has a heading indicating that it is to be recited 'for travellers') (fo. 103), a Latin charm using the sign of the cross, the titles of Jesus and an anecdote about the Apostle Peter to banish the plague, headed *Oratio bona pro febribus* [Pl. 60]. This extraordinary prayer was followed by another charm with an English rubric which explained that the devotee must say the Hail Mary one hundred times a day for ten days, holding an alms for the poor in your hand. You then kissed the money and gave it to a poor man or woman in honour of the Annunciation, and then 'without doubt ye shall have that thynge ye pray for lawfully with Goddes grace'. This rubric, incidentally, was signed by Edmund Roberts, who left his signature in half a dozen other places in the book, usually at the beginning of one of the minor hours, opposite or on the illuminations, in a way that we would think of as spoiling the book – more about this later. The two charms are so remarkable that it is worth including a complete translation of them here.

A GOOD PRAYER FOR FEVERS THROUGH THE THOUSAND NAMES OF THE LORD

Theobal quith et quth Kanai[5]

*Through the truth of our Lord Jesus Christ may all malignant spirits flee from me. In the name of my Lord Jesus Christ sign me + with this sign +**AO** In the name of the Father and of the Son + and of the Holy Spirit + Amen + whatsoever the Father is, Azlpha and Omega, that also + is the Son + and that also is the Holy Spirit.*

Remedium, Tetragrammaton, Hosyon.[6]

The truth of Christ, the peace of Christ, the labours of Christ[7]*: Christ have mercy through the thousand names of the Lord.*

In the name of the Father and of the Son and of the Holy Ghost Amen.

Before the gates of Jerusalem Saint Peter lay oppressed with fever. Jesus came and said to him, Peter, what is the matter that you lie here? Peter said, 'Lord I lie here pierced and oppressed with fever' and the Lord said to him, 'Peter, arise, nevertheless, [autem] and receive your health'. And he was freed [from the fever]. And Peter said to him, 'I beseech you, Lord, that whoever carries this written upon them may be strengthened against troublesome or harmful fevers.' And he said to Peter, 'Let it be done according to your word.'

Amen Tetragrammaton

In the name of the Father and of the Son and of the Holy Spirit.

Saint Peter lay upon a marble stone and, coming upon him, Jesus said, 'Peter, why are you lying here?' and Peter said, 'Lord I lie here because of evil fevers.' Then Jesus said, 'Arise and scatter them' and at once he rose and scattered them. Then said Peter, 'Lord I wish that if anyone carries about them this written in your name, no fevers may harm them, whether cold or hot, whether double, or tertian, or quartain, or quintain, or sextain, or septain [fevers]. Then Jesus said, 'Let it be [so] to you. Amen'.

> *+ Christ conquers, + Christ reigns + Christ rules + Christ rule me, Amen.*
>
> *In the name of the Father and of the Son and of the Holy Spirit Amen.*

This is followed without a break by the second prayer-charm, which begins with an English rubric:

> Ye shall say M [a thousand] tyme Ave Maria [Hail Mary] and ye shall sey them in X days, that is every day a hundreth, and ye shall say them standyn and goyng and knelyng or syttynge and ye shall have a certen almys in your hande while ye make your prayer, and after, say thys orison or prayer that followeth.
>
> *O Adonai, Lord, great and wonderful God, who gave the salvation of human kind into the hands of the most glorious Virgin, your Mother Mary: through her womb and merits, and through that most holy body which you took from her, in your goodness hear my prayers and fulfil my desires for [my] good, to the praise and glory of your name. Liberate me from every tribulation and assailant, and from all the snares of my enemies who seek to harm me, and from lying lips and sharpened tongues, and change all my tribulation into rejoicing and gladness. Amen.*
>
> And when ye have seide thys orison kysse your almos, and after, geve it to a pore man or woman in honour of that blyssed joy that seynt Gabryel greeted our Lady[with], and for what thyng ye do thys ten days together, without doubt ye shall have that thynge ye pray for lawfully, with Goddes Grace.
>
> [Added in English in a later hand, 'I used this prayer well ten days, Edmund Roberts *inquit* (says)'.]

This extraordinary addition, written in the same hand as a single continuous text, is really two separate Latin charms. The first uses the sign of the cross, the titles of Jesus and an anecdote about two episodes of the healing from fever by Christ of the Apostle Peter, to protect the user against various types of fever. It was presumably run together with the second charm because both mention the number one thousand. Prayers of this kind, straddling the dividing line between magic spell and petitionary prayer, were very popular in the later Middle Ages. Theologians and bishops repeatedly condemned them as superstitious, and they were regularly denounced in sermons and pastoral textbooks, in itself a sign of their widespread popularity. It was routine for the authorities to represent such prayers as products of lay ignorance, and to associate them in particular with the lower orders, 'ignorant of simplesse'.[8] In fact, they were popular with lay people of all classes, as is indicated, for example, by the presence of a number of such prayer-charms in the prayer-book of Henry VII's mother, Lady Margaret Beaufort.[9] Other versions of the thousand Aves charm have been added to a number of surviving fifteenth-century Books of Hours.[10]

The first and apparently more bizarre of the prayers employs a number of religious strategies found also in the official liturgy of the church, including invocation of holy names, and the use of the sign of the cross. It was believed that the use of good names and holy gestures and objects (holy water, blessed candles) drove away evil and protected the user from harm: such sacred signs and words were known as 'sacramentals', and were used in the Church's official liturgy of exorcism, in baptism, and many other official ceremonies. Made by the clergy in the course of the liturgy, such sacramentals could then be deployed by lay people, without clerical supervision. The opportunities this offered for unauthorised and unorthodox elaboration worried some churchmen, and in any case theologians disagreed over whether sacramentals were simply elaborate prayers of petition, or whether they in fact carried some divine guarantee of benefit. In general, however, the church authorities encouraged such material symbolism so long as it was not imagined to be essential for the success of a prayer, or was not believed to coerce God or his angels or saints into granting the user's requests.[11]

The charm against the fever falls into two halves. The first part opens with the solemn invocation of the holy names of God, and the repeated use of the sign of the Cross: it then continues with a form of sympathetic magic, in which two apocryphal stories (i.e. not found in the New Testament), about the healing of St Peter from fever, are said to protect from fever anyone who carries around with them a paper on which the stories have been written. The stories were perhaps suggested by the incident in the Synoptic Gospels in which Jesus heals Peter's mother-in-law from a fever (Mark 1:30–31; Matthew 8:14–15; Luke 4:38–41). The injunction to Peter to 'rise up and scatter them' perhaps echoes Psalm 68 verse 1', 'Let God arise, let his foes be scattered'.

In the pre-modern world the possession of a person's true name was held to give one power over them: hence the devils in the Gospels call out Jesus' name. The invocation of the various names of God, above all the Tetragrammaton, the Hebrew name of God which Jews were forbidden to utter or to write down, was specially powerful, and was sometimes employed in the liturgy itself, while aspects of these sorts of beliefs were embodied in the growing devotion in the late Middle Ages to the holy name 'Jesus'. In medieval magical practice also, the use of the names of God, of angels, and of other supernatural figures was a regular part of the making of spells, and magical and protective names and words, like 'Anazapta' are found both in magical and in more conventionally religious texts, jewellery and amulets. The prayer here mixes real biblical names for God (Adonai, the Tetragrammaton) with names adapted from pagan sources (the Greek word 'Hosion'). Linked to this use of the holy names of God, is the repeated use of the sign of the Cross, which the medieval Church believed banished evil.

Though often condemned, the use of appropriate texts or stories in sympathetic magic also had some official connivance. It was commonly believed, for example, that the recitation of or allusion to the account of Christ's miraculous escape at Capernaum from an attempt by a hostile crowd to lynch him, would protect the believer from danger. The concluding verse of the story in St Luke's Gospel – 'Jesus however, passing through the midst of them, went on his way' (Luke 4:30) – was often inscribed on amulets,[12] and is found in some very elite contexts. It is embroidered, for example, on the halo and cuff of the robe of God in the Judgement scene in the magnificent (and theologically sophisticated) Rohan Hours.[13] Similar anecdotes, with a promise of blessing for anyone who wrote the story down and carried the writing around or kept it in their house, were attached to the legends of a number of late medieval saints, including the Roberts family favourite, St Dorothy.[14]

The second prayer-charm takes us away from protection from fever, to more universal benefits. This charm focuses on the story of the Annunciation, when the Angel Gabriel greeted Mary, the precise moment when Christ took human flesh and became an embryo in the Virgin's womb. The most popular prayer to Mary, the Hail Mary, begins with the Angel's greeting, 'Hail Mary, full of grace, the Lord is with thee'. The devotee is to recite a hundred of these Hail Maries (the equivalent of two rosaries) every day – the prayers can be recited while the devotee goes about their ordinary business, 'standing, going, kneeling or sitting', but is linked to the late medieval preoccupation with the works of mercy listed by Christ in the parable of the sheep and the goats (Matthew 25) as a means of salvation. It was believed that everyone would be judged at the Last Judgement not by words of faith or homage, but by whether or not they had concretely helped the poor and suffering. The success of the prayer is said to depend on its being accompanied by the relief of the poor, in honour of the Annunciation. But this edifying link is made in a quasi-magical way, which the church authorities would certainly have condemned – holding money in the hand while the thousand Aves are recited, then kissing it before giving it to the poor recipient. To the thousand Aves is added a Latin prayer which emphasizes the centrality in the salvation of mankind of the physical reality of the Incarnation at the Annunciation – Christ is invoked by his Mother's womb and by the flesh he himself took on in that womb. That flesh is declared to protect the user of the prayer especially from their enemies. Prayers against enemies – corporeal and incorporeal – were, as we have seen, a very prominent feature of late medieval piety. Characteristically, the English instructions attached to the prayer display some awareness of the precarious line being trod between 'legitimate' prayer and forbidden 'magic': success is guaranteed if the prayer is rightly used (a guarantee theologians rejected as magical) but that guarantee is softened by the reference to praying 'lawfully, with God's grace'. Another version of this charm included in a Book of Hours now in Ushaw College Durham declares that 'withoutttyn doute ye may noght fayle of that ye pray for and your desire be resonabyll'.[15]

The manuscript additions to the Roberts Hours conclude with some further family notes from the 1580s (including the death notice of Edmund Roberts, who 'used this prayer well' in 1553, a recipe for a plaster for sores, a prayer to St Erasmus, and a characteristic Tudor moralising rhyme:

Joy in God whose grace is beste
Obeye thy prince and live in awe
Helpe the poor to lyve in reste
And never synne against the lawe (fo. 117v)

The flourishing of the Roberts family under the Tudors suggests that they followed these injunctions very closely.

It will be evident from these predominantly early Tudor additions to the Roberts family book that no more than in the case of John Talbot are we dealing here with amateur mystics or men and women in flight from the world, the reclusive frame of mind which some historians think Books of Hours encouraged. The added prayers range from devotions to name saints or prayer to be said at the elevation of the host at Mass, to elaborate penitential prayers to be used as a temporary substitute for the sacrament of penance, and several prayers which are in fact apotropaic charms, designed to fend off evil or procure material good. They are thus very Catholic indeed, as the late Middle Ages imagined Catholicism, and as the reformers would come to detest. The prayers are churchly, sacramental, attentive to the saints, concerned with meritorious acts of charity: they are highly supernatural, but in no sense otherworldly. There are prayers here to stop your house burning down or to help a woman to conceive a baby, and it is quite clear that some of these prayers are thought of as instrumental rather than merely supplicatory: done properly, they are guaranteed to work. Yet these are not the prayers of ignorance. They were written into the book made for and used by wealthy and influential men and women: Thomas Roberts, who died in 1543, and whose surviving children are listed in the book, was clerk of the Peace and Coroner of Middlesex, a man of weight and education. The prayers come from a repertoire of such things which was appreciated at the very top of the social ladder: one of the additional prayers here, the English invocation to Jesus and Mary, 'O my sovereign Lord Jesus', is a favourite addition in Books of Hours, and we encountered it earlier, copied for the use of the first Earl of Shrewsbury into the Talbot Hours.

6

SANCTIFIED WHINGEING?

We can now ask ourselves what light this analysis throws on wider questions about the direction of late medieval religion. In chapter three I considered Professor Colin Richmond's suggestion that the Book of Hours was an instrument and symptom of a regrettable privatising of religion, the retreat of landowners and urban elites away from their neighbours, and the creation of a private sphere of religiosity which, by distancing them from the wider community, laid the ground for the reformation. Professor Richmond's verdict was in fact a qualified one, for he himself pointed to material in these Books of Hours which provided bridges to the religion of the population at large. Much more emphatically, Dr Jonathan Hughes, in a study of the religion of Richard III, has maintained that the most significant thing about the spread of the Book of Hours was the 'challenge' it posed 'to institutional, parish-orientated religion'. In his opinion, the use of these books 'reinforced individuality, emphasizing the close relationship that exists between the worshipper and God, who provides a source of strength against the hostility of neighbours, the frustrations of dealing with people'.[1]

Both Professor Richmond and Dr Hughes were developing hints in a remarkable paper published by Professor John Bossy in 1991, in which, among many fertile suggestions, Bossy made a distinction between two main types of medieval prayers, social prayers, which were 'mainly something to do with one's relation to one's neighbour', and whose archetype is the Our Father, and devotional prayers 'more directly to do with one's relation to God or other objects of religion', whose archetype is the Hail Mary. Bossy considered that most of the prayers of the Books of Hours were social prayers, but often negatively so, many of them revealing a preoccupation with the pray-er's safety, and in particular, with their deliverance from their earthly enemies. These concerns were rooted of course in the fact that the fundamental core of the Books of Hours was the Psalter, and the psalms, he thought, were mainly concerned in this way with deliverance from distress and tribulation. The Books of Hours were therefore, in Bossy's words, '*me* prayer books, full of *me* prayers'. At the end of his paper he has a savagely dismissive aside on 'the dense smog of self-centredness, malice and sanctified whingeing which comes off the prayer-books'.[2]

Despite the vehemence of that phrase, Bossy's argument is a subtle and nuanced one, and he was not straightforwardly attacking the voice of late medieval prayer, which he argued was balanced and controlled by an essentially healthy liturgical piety, focused on the elevation in the Mass: by implication, the mental and moral health of medieval people was preserved from the neurosis of the Book of Hours by the shared communal experience of public worship, and especially the veneration of the Host at Mass. Nevertheless, indeed for that very reason, his paper does set up a tension between the private piety of the Books of Hours, which, despite their 'social' concerns, he considers to have been individualistic and self-centred, on the one hand, and on the other hand, the pluralistic but socially unifying piety surrounding the Elevation of the Eucharistic Host in the mass, which he sees as altogether more robustly social. Professor Richmond does not by any means accept all of Bossy's contentions. He examines a number of the prayers added to the margins of English Books of Hours by late medieval and Tudor owners, and finds many prayers there which simply do not conform to Bossy's characterisation of them as predominantly self-centred and complaining. Nevertheless, overall, Richmond too endorses the charge that the late medieval users of Books of Hours did indeed whinge when they prayed. He supplies as an example this prayer, from a devotional compendium (not a Book of Hours) assembled for George Earl of Shrewsbury, about the year 1500:

> Most dere lorde and savyour swete jesu I beseche they moost curteys goodnes and benygne favour to be to me moost wretched creature favourable lorde protectour keper and defender and in all necessytees and nedes be to my shelde and protectyon ayenst al myne enemyes bodely and goostly. Mercyfull jesu I have none other truste hope ne succour but in the allonely my dere lorde swete Jhesus the whyche of thy infynite goodness madeest me of nought lyke unto thy moost excellent ymage . . .

And so on.[3]

Professor Richmond offers a harsh and it seems to me reductionist explanation of the rhetorical style of this prayer, speculating that its cringing tone might have had crassly political overtones: 'Could the mode', he asked, 'be a particularly upper class one: the English nobility behaving towards their Lord as they wished others to behave towards them?' The answer to this rhetorical question is, quite straightforwardly, I think, 'no, it couldn't'. For we are not in fact dealing here with something peculiar to the fifteenth-century English aristocracy, but with a matter of rhetorical register which is far from new in the later Middle Ages. The elaborate penitential deference of these English prayers reproduces pretty closely the equally 'cringeing' tone, if one chooses to call it that, of many of the Latin devotions which lay people routinely found in their books, such as the famous and universally popular prayer *O Bone Jesu*, which had been a staple of devotion for centuries, with exemplars in writers like St Anselm.

> O good Jesu, o sweet Jesu, O Jesu, son of the Virgin Mary, full of mercy and truth. O Sweet Jesu, have mercy on me according to your great mercy. O benign Jesu, I beseech you by that precious blood which you deigned to pour out for us sinners on the altar of the cross, that you will cast away from you all my iniquities, and do not despise him who humbly petitions you, and calls upon your most holy name, Jesu . . .[4]

It is just not the case that such a tone of voice was the preserve or the

61.
Made *c.* 1415 probably in London, and containing prayers which indicate that it was designed for a priest, the book was later adapted for King Richard III by the addition of a long Latin prayer for protection against his enemies. After his defeat and death at Bosworth, the book passed to Lady Margaret Beaufort, who deleted Richard's name from the prayer, and added to the rear end-pages the rhyme 'For the honor of God and St Edmunde/Pray for Margaret Richmonde'.

Lambeth Palace 454 fos. 47v–48. Page size 19 × 14cm

product of overweening aristocracy, unless the whole devotional tradition of the Latin Middle Ages, most of it clerically generated, is to be read as an expression of late medieval lay upper-class social attitudes.

Jonathan Hughes's study of late medieval praying has a single focus, the prayer-life of a somewhat surprising devotee, King Richard III, Shakespeare's villainous murderer, which he attempts to reconstruct from a study of the Book of Hours which Richard used, now in Lambeth Palace Library (Ms 474) [Pl. 61].

This was in fact a secondhand book, made originally in the early fifteenth century for a priest, and containing prayers appropriate only for use by a cleric, but Richard had added to the book a long and extraordinary prayer for relief from affliction, temptation, grief, sickness, need and danger, but above all for protection from the hatred and plots of his enemies and for reconciliation with them. This prayer is written in the first person singular, and spoken explicitly by 'me your servant King Richard', but although it has one or two distinctive features, it was not specially composed by him or for him. It is in fact a variant of a standard prayer, very similar versions of which were used throughout the fifteenth century in a Book of Hours handed from generation to generation by the Valois Dukes of Burgundy. Copies were also used by Richard's contemporary Alexander Prince of Poland, by the Emperor Maximilian I, and by Frederick of Aragon.[5] Prayers containing some of the same component elements and all the same concerns circulated much more widely, and very much further down the social scale. We have already encountered the same concern with protection against enemies in John Talbot's Hours, but versions of prayers similar to Richard's are to be found in the devotional commonplace books of the early fifteenth-century Lincolnshire gentleman Robert Thornton, and the sixteenth-century London grocer Richard Hill, and were regularly included in Books of Hours, either as part of their core content or as additions, not least the Roberts family book of Hours.[6] Indeed in a slightly tidied up version, Richard III's prayer was to become one of the component elements of the post-Tridentine Roman primer, and in that printed form would become a staple of Counter-Reformation lay piety.[7]

Despite the conventional character of this prayer, however, Dr Hughes argues that it offers us a unique insight not only into Richard's 'individualistic and idiosyncratic' piety and devotional

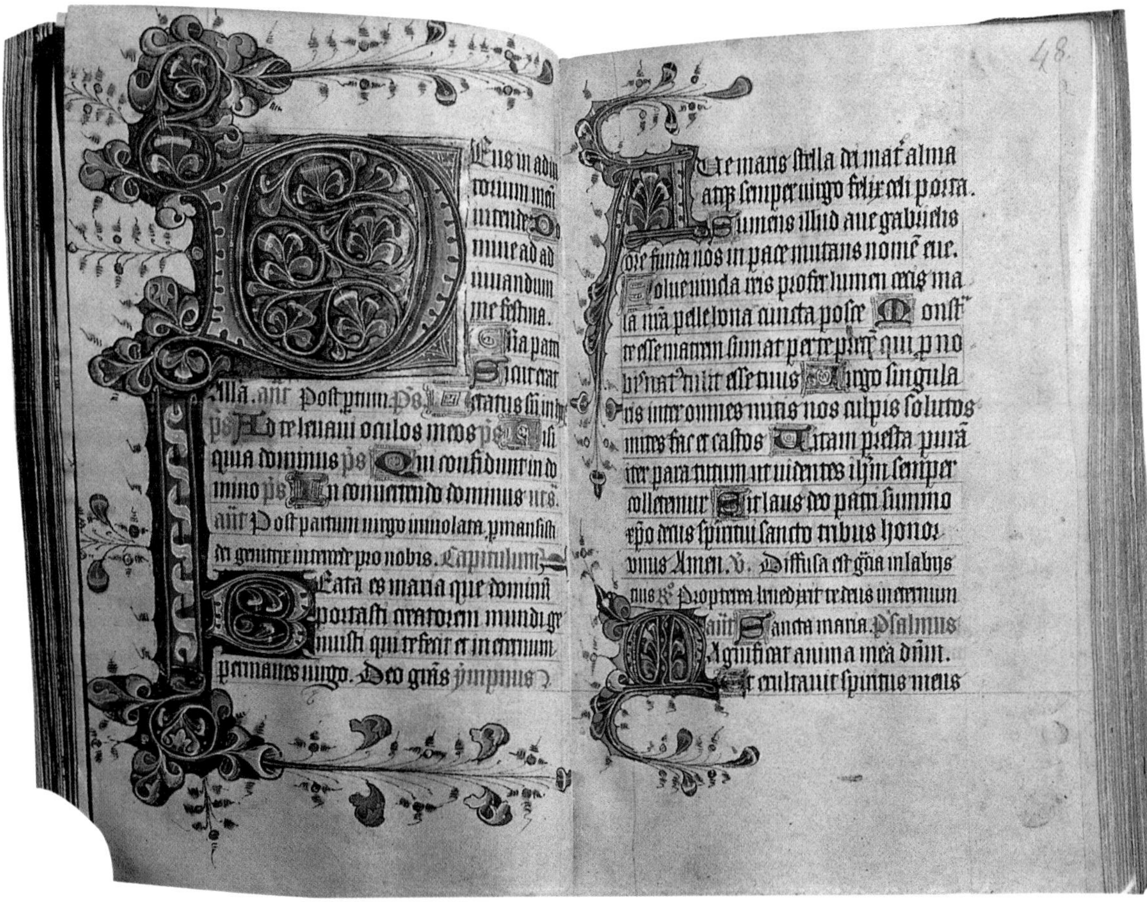

psychology, but into a drastic growth of isolated individualism and aggression in the prayer life of late medieval lay people more generally.[8] His argument turns on the fact that the complaint language of many of the psalms in the standard book of hours, including of course the one used by Richard, portrays the speaker as beleaguered by enemies, and there is a corresponding preoccupation with escape from the malice of enemies in the added prayer of Richard III.[9] People using such psalms and prayers, Hughes contends, must certainly have applied them not to spiritual forces, but to their day-to-day enemies and rivals, 'and it is likely that merchants in using such prayers had in mind their competitors, creditors and craftsmen'.[10] Richard in particular, whose prayer has a unique reference to the political rebellion of Absolom and Achitophel against King David, must have had political enemies in mind. Hughes works through a selection of the vengeful and aggressive verses of the psalms and prayers included in any Book of Hours, and takes them as revealing the attitudes medieval users of these prayers must have directed against their neighbours, business-rivals, enemies.

Medieval society, like all human societies, was of course riven with internal tensions and animosities, but if Hughes's analysis is accepted, Richard's prayer, and the Books of Hours generally, offer a horrifying picture of late medieval society as radically dysfunctional, red in tooth and claw, populated by isolated individualists constantly praying against their neighbours. Hughes considers that 'prayers in the [Books of Hours] reinforced individuality, emphasizing the close relationship that exists between the worshipper and God, who provides a source of strength against the hostility of neighbours, the frustrations of dealing with people', an 'egocentric and abrasive expression of social hostility'.[11]

This lurid account of the strife-torn world of the Wars of the Roses has some plausibility, of course, and the people who used the many prayers for protection against enemies must often have had concrete adversity in this world in mind. But the argument lacks nuance. Indeed this sort of account of what I want to call the voice of prayer in the late Middle Ages seems to me in general problematic, not only in its overwhelmingly negative characterisation of the piety which the books represented as individualistic, but in what I take to be simplistic assumptions about the way in which the users of these books appropriated their meaning.

We considered the question of individualism in chapter three, but we need to remind ourselves here that the prayers of these books were not merely used privately. Major sections of them were regularly recited collectively as part of the public worship of the whole community, or of some of its constituent sub-groupings, such as the gilds. The key item in the Books of Hours here was the office for the Dead, that is Vespers, Matins and Lauds of the Dead, or *Dirige* as it was often known from the opening word of the opening antiphon of Matins. This service was an invariable and popular feature of Books of Hours, and unlike the Little Hours of the Virgin, which formed the first part of all such books, it was neither simplified nor abbreviated, but included the full text of the Church's official prayers for the dead. The inclusion of obit notices in the calendar of such books was a reminder to the user to recite this office on the appropriate anniversary. But the office was also one of the most familiar parts of the Church's formal liturgy, publicly recited as part of every funeral, and often subsequently on weekly, monthly and yearly commemorations. Gilds usually required their members to attend these recitations for deceased brethren, and literate lay people were encouraged or expected to join in.

It was, incidentally, in this communally recited office for the dead that many of the psalms of complaint and pleading for deliverance from enemies which both Bossy and Hughes focus on are concentrated, a fact which must certainly have a bearing on how they were understood. In the context of a liturgy of intercession for a dead man or woman, the deliverance prayed for, and the enemies prayed against, are likely to be conceived of as spiritual, and the rescue hoped for otherworldly, from the devil, from purgatory and hell. Psalms of complaint do of course occur elsewhere in the Book of Hours, for example Psalm 53 (54) which is recited in the office of Prime in the Use of Sarum, singled out by Hughes because of its injunction *Averte malis inimicis meis* (Turn back evil upon mine enemies).[12] But we need to register the whole context of such utterances: Psalm 53 occurs in Prime immediately before Psalm 84 (85), *Benedixisti Domine*, which also speaks about deliverance, but where the deliverance is emphatically communal, not individualistic, 'Thou wilt turn again O Lord and give us life, and thy people shall rejoice in thee', and the psalm ends on a note of reconciliation and a vision of restored justice and peace, in an emphatically social image: 'Mercy and truth have met together, justice and peace have embraced . . . our land shall yield its fruit'.

The devout lay person, daily reciting the office of Prime, affirmed these hopeful and communitarian values as frequently and, one presumes, as meaningfully, as the more negative sentiments singled out as characteristic of medieval devout mentality by all the commentators I have been discussing. It will not do to construct a theory about growing medieval aggressive individualism drawing only on the negative utterances which form just a small part of the overall pattern of prayers which medieval people recited daily. Attending to the late medieval voice of prayer involves taking seriously what Bossy calls its plurality. It was a voice which sang on more than one note, and often in harmony with others.

And certainly the proud owners and users of Books of Hours did not conceive themselves to be separating from their neighbours, or the public worship of the parish. We noted in chapter one John and Joan Greneway's commission of a sculptured memorial depicting them kneeling at Tiverton with their Books of Hours before them: they placed those self-images with books not in the isolation of their private chantry chapel, but prominently above the south door, a key spot where marriages and the first part of baptism was celebrated. In this portrayal of the Greneways in the prestigious context of their architectural provision for the comfort of the parish community at large, we are worlds away from a paranoid shark pool inhabited by imagined merchants, savagely directing the lamentations and curses of the fiercer psalms against their neighbours, competitors, creditors and craftsmen. As we have seen, such images of the reading devotee at the heart of the parish's worship were common, for example on the Easter sepulchre, the principle focus for the community's veneration of the Blessed Sacrament at Easter-time: as we have already noted, it would simply not be possible to find a more communal context in which to depict the use of a Book of Hours.

This brief look at the use of the psalms in prayer brings me to the final point in this part of my argument. The voice of lay prayer in the late Middle Ages is essentially ventriloquial. By and large, medieval people did not speak for themselves when they prayed. They articulated their hopes and fears, however deeply felt, in the borrowed words of others, which they made their own in the act of recitation. This, of course, is not a fact only about medieval Christian prayer, but about the whole Christian tradition, since the fundamental Christian prayer-book is an ancient Hebrew liturgical anthology, the Psalter. And what was true of the Psalter, was true of prayer more generally: the manuscript additions to so many of the surviving Books of Hours show a magpie tendency to seize on good prayers wherever they might be found.

And by and large, prayers seem to have been judged 'good' not by the eloquence or appositeness of their content, but by their reputed utility and effectiveness: a 'good prayer' was more like a well-tested cookery recipe than an eloquent poem which exactly or profoundly articulated one's deepest feelings. As we have seen in the case of the Talbot and Roberts family books, most of the added prayers are instrumental, addressed to particular patron saints, or as specifics against particular ills – wounding or worse in battle, the fever, dangerous childbirth, above all *mors improvisa* – sudden and unprovided death. Many had miraculous promises or spectacular indulgences attached, guaranteeing a good result for proper use. Some were intended for use in public worship, as the various elevation prayers were. The picture that emerges from them, therefore, is not that of a scatter of alienated individualists, but of highly conventional people vigorously appropriating a conventional but versatile religion, seeking the assistance of God and his angels and saints in the major and minor needs of human existence, from danger of damnation to a bad case of toothache. These are the practical concerns we encounter everywhere in late medieval prayer.

A much copied prayer, *Deus Propicius esto michi*, invoking archangels, added to the manuscript Book of Hours used by the Reigny family, lords of the manor of Eggesford in Devon, in the early sixteenth century, has a rubric which promises its user 'remyssion of all his synnes and he schall never die in sodeyn deth'. Should they encounter 'prynces dukes, erles, barones or other men of worship', 'ye schall fynde worschip to yow, love and grace and plesyng'. Recited over water in a storm it will calm the tempest, worn on a paper into battle it would protect the bearer. It would guarantee safe delivery in childbirth, dry up a bloody flux, secure safe travel for voyagers, and, not least, at St Peter's direct request, it would bring a year of pardon for every recitation. A holy life and a good death, 'love grace and pleasing' from the great ones of the earth, safety in childbirth and journeying and battle, and the pardon and remission of one's sins: this is a comprehensive list, and a perennially relevant one.[13]

In Robert Thornton's devotional manuscript collection an almost identical set of benefits precedes the very popular prayer against enemies (it is included in the formal content of many Books of Hours, including the Roberts Hours), beginning '*Domine Deus omnipotens da michi N famulo tuo victoriam contra inimicos meos*'.[14] The rubric promises help in a range of extreme situations – a difficult childbirth, a bad diarrhoea, storms at sea, the dangers of battle, the need to make a good impression at court, thieves on journeys, a bloody flux – indicating that for Thornton at least the 'enemies' against which the prayer was directed were not neighbours, competitors and employees, but disaster, disease, death and the devil.[15]

7

THE PRAYERS OF THOMAS MORE

All of which suggests that we probably need to envisage the medieval pray-er leafing briskly through their book looking for the right tool for a particular job, rather than as an isolated introvert seeking in the Book of Hours words for his or her deepest insecurities and animosities. For the pious and the more than functionally literate, of course, prayer, above all the prayers of the Psalter, must often have had that function too. Access to that level of interiority is, however, for the most part denied to the historian. Where everyone who prayed at all used the same words, it is hard to isolate what was particular in any given individual's appropriation of them. We certainly cannot presume we have mastered that individuality, as Dr Hughes does in the case of Richard III, merely by relating the known difficulties of the devotee's life to words and sentences of the psalms and other prayers which seem to us specially appropriate to their case. But we can, as luck would have it, watch one notable late medieval devotee in the very act of praying with his Book of Hours [Pl. 62].

When Thomas More was arrested and sent to the Tower in May 1534 for refusing to take the Oath of Supremacy, he took with him an inexpensive printed Book of Hours published in 1530 by the Paris-based publisher François Regnault, who had effectively cornered the market for such books in England from 1529 onwards [Pl. 63].

62.
Unknown artist, after Hans Holbein the younger, *Portrait of Sir Thomas More*, National Portrait Gallery, London

Bound at the back of this Book of Hours, which miraculously survives in the Beinecke Library at Yale, is More's Latin Psalter, which he appears to have used for systematic devotional reading in the psalms, since the Book of Hours contains only about a third of the 150 psalms in the complete Psalter.[1] As More read through the psalms in his prison cell, he annotated them, drawing lines in the margin against verses which caught his attention, adding words or short phrases of interpretation against dozens of verses, and very occasionally writing extended comments in Latin which make clear the existential nature of his engagement with what he found there. These extended comments are rare, but all the more poignant for their reticence. Against Psalm 87 (88) vv. 5–10, 'I am counted as one who descends into the pit, I am made like a man without help, free among the dead as a wounded man sleeping in the tombs, they have placed me in the lowest deeps, in darkness and the shadow of death', he writes '*in tribulata vehemente et in carcere*' (in severe tribulation and in prison).[2] Against Psalm 37 (38) v. 14, part of a psalm of complaint

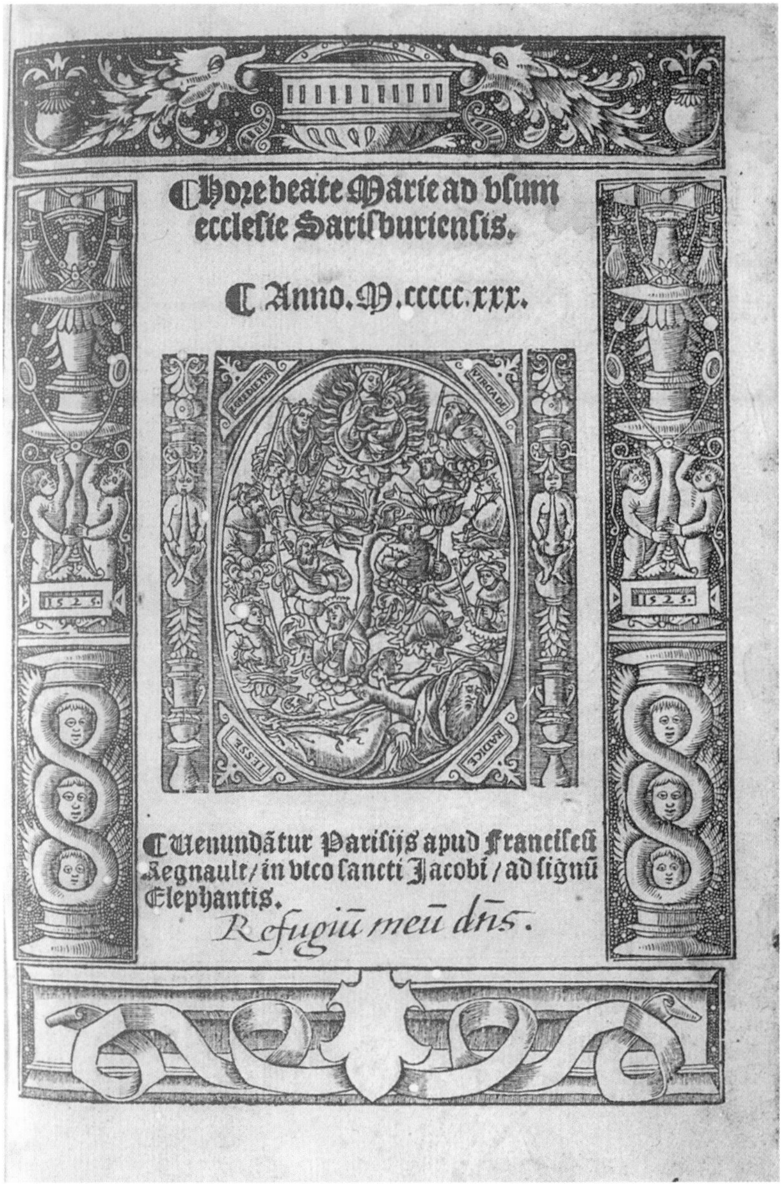

63.
Like many other London professional men, More owned and used a Book of Hours printed in Paris for the English market by François Regnault. The block for the Tree of Jesse used as a decoration here on the title-page was paired in smaller books by Regnault with an Annunciation scene and used to mark the opening of Matins of the Virgin.

RSTC 15963. Yale, Beinecke Library Ms Vault More, title-page

in which the just man is abandoned by those close to him, where the afflicted man, in the annotated verse, is said to be 'like a deaf man heard not, and as a dumb man not opening his mouth', More comments in the margin 'Thus ought the meek man to behave in tribulation: he should neither speak proudly himself nor reply to what is wickedly spoken, but he should bless the evil speakers and suffer

64.
In the tower, More annotated Psalm 83 (Vulgate numbering) 'How lovely is thy dwelling place, O Lord of Hosts' with the poignant note 'the prayer of one shut up in prison . . . longing to go to Church'.

Yale Ms Vault More, psalter, fo. lxvi

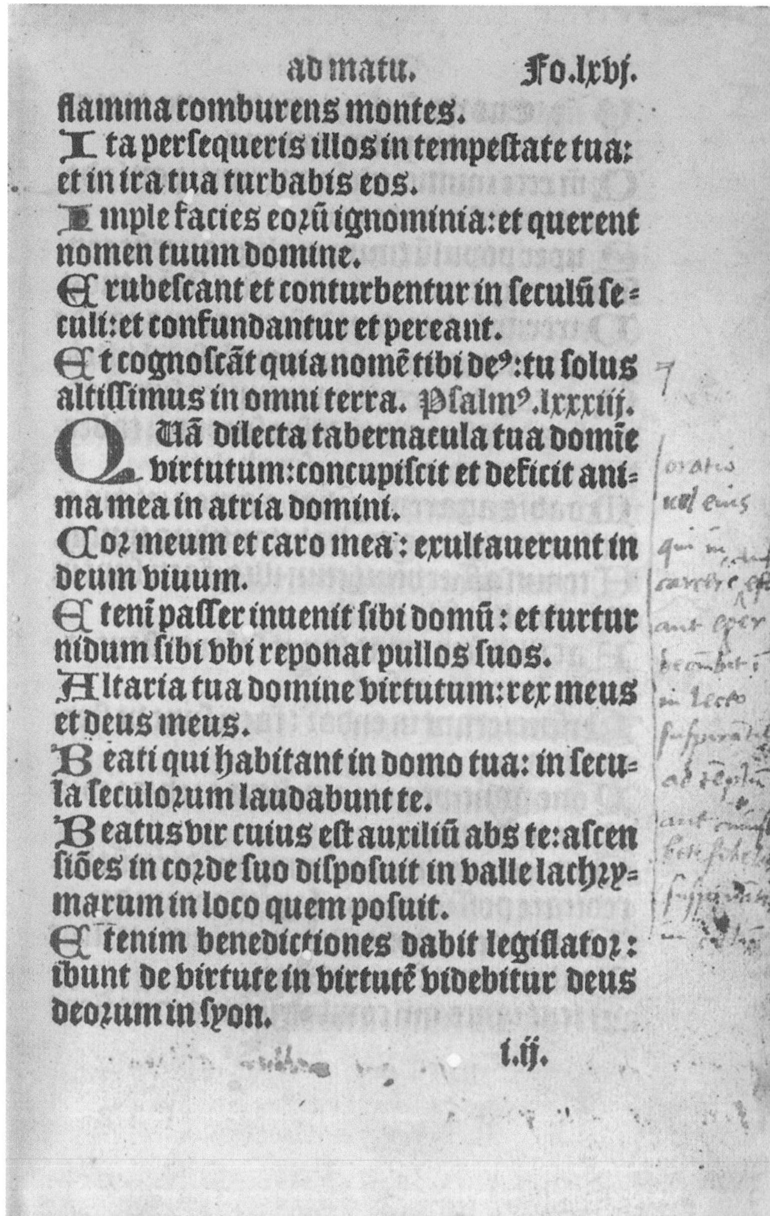

ad matu. Fo.lxvi.
flamma comburens montes.
Ita persequeris illos in tempestate tua:
et in ira tua turbabis eos.
Imple facies eorū ignominia: et querent
nomen tuum domine.
Erubescant et conturbentur in seculū seculi: et confundantur et pereant.
Et cognoscāt quia nomē tibi de⁹: tu solus
altissimus in omni terra. Psalm⁹.lxxxiij.
Quā dilecta tabernacula tua domie
virtutum: concupiscit et deficit anima mea in atria domini.
Cor meum et caro mea: exultauerunt in
deum viuum.
Etenim passer inuenit sibi domū: et turtur
nidum sibi vbi reponat pullos suos.
Altaria tua domine virtutum: rex meus
et deus meus.
Beati qui habitant in domo tua: in secula seculorum laudabunt te.
Beatus vir cuius est auxiliū abs te: ascen-
siões in corde suo disposuit in valle lachry-
marum in loco quem posuit.
Etenim benedictiones dabit legislator:
ibunt de virtute in virtutē videbitur deus
deorum in syon.
l.ij.

gladly, for the sake of justice if he has deserved it, or for the cause of God if he has deserved no evil.'[3] Against the opening of psalm 83 (84), 'How lovely are thy tabernacles O Lord of hosts, my soul longeth and fainteth for the courts of the Lord', he writes 'The prayer of one shut up in prison, or lying sick in bed, yearning to go to Church, or of any faithful soul who yearns for heaven' [Pl. 64].[4]

More, who had aspired to be a Carthusian in his youth, is often said, in Geoffrey Elton's words, to have 'found his cloister in the Tower': but that vivid glimpse of the isolated soul longing for the sociability of the parish church should give us pause, and has a direct bearing on the question of devotional individualism. The annotation recalls the prayer More wrote after he had been condemned to death, and which, despite its focus on his own approaching death, had a strong communal emphasis, articulated in petitions for 'thy grace to longe for thy holy sacraments' and that God would 'make us all lively members swete savioure Christe, of thine holy mistical body, thy catholyke church'.[5] Perhaps equally striking is More's tendency to give a broadly spiritualising interpretation to verses in the psalms which we might expect him to apply more directly autobiographically. Again and again in the complaint psalms references to triumphant or oppressive enemies are applied not to earthly misfortunes, or More's own trials, but to the assaults of demons. So, against Psalm 34 (35) v. 15 'They rejoiced against me and came together, scourges were gathered together upon me, and I knew not', he wrote ' the demons taunt us, but let us lie low, let us wear a hair shirt, let us fast and pray'. Against Psalm 7 v. 2, whose 'Lord my God, in thee have I trusted, save me from them that persecute me and deliver me' might seem perfectly appropriate to More's trial and imprisonment in the Tower, he wrote '*contra spiritales nequitas*' (against the spiritual hosts of wickedness).[6] There are over forty such references to demons, most of them in contexts where one might expect him to make a more direct application of the psalms to his own material circumstances. Indeed most of his readings are generalising or at any rate religiously conventional – notes on passages helpful in temptation or tribulation, or for a conscience overcome with scruples in confession, or offering appropriate thanksgiving for deliverance, passages urging almsgiving. Where he does apply the psalms to contemporary historical events, it is to interpret the afflictions of Jerusalem as parallel to the sufferings of Christians under the threat of Islam in Eastern Europe, writing in the margin '*contra turcas*'. His editors comment, 'can we doubt that Thomas More, as he meditates upon these psalms, is thinking of the problems of faith and infidelity in England, as well as Hungary'.[7] Well, maybe, but what is striking is the reticence and the tendency in More's notes to spiritual generality,

65. & 66.
Prime in More's book opens with a miniature of the Nativity. At the top and bottom of the page he began his famous prayer, 'Give me thy grace good Lord/to set the world at nought'. The prayer continues over the pages containing the succeeding hours, ending with Sext.

RSTC 15963. Yale, Ms Vault More, Hours, fos. xvii, xxv(v)–xxvi

rather than personal application. There is no sign here of the sort of autobiographical vehemence which, as we have seen, some historians have wanted to argue that any late medieval devotee must have brought to the reading of their Books of Hours.

As it happens, in More's Book of Hours there is in fact a manuscript prayer, certainly his own composition, added in a series of lines

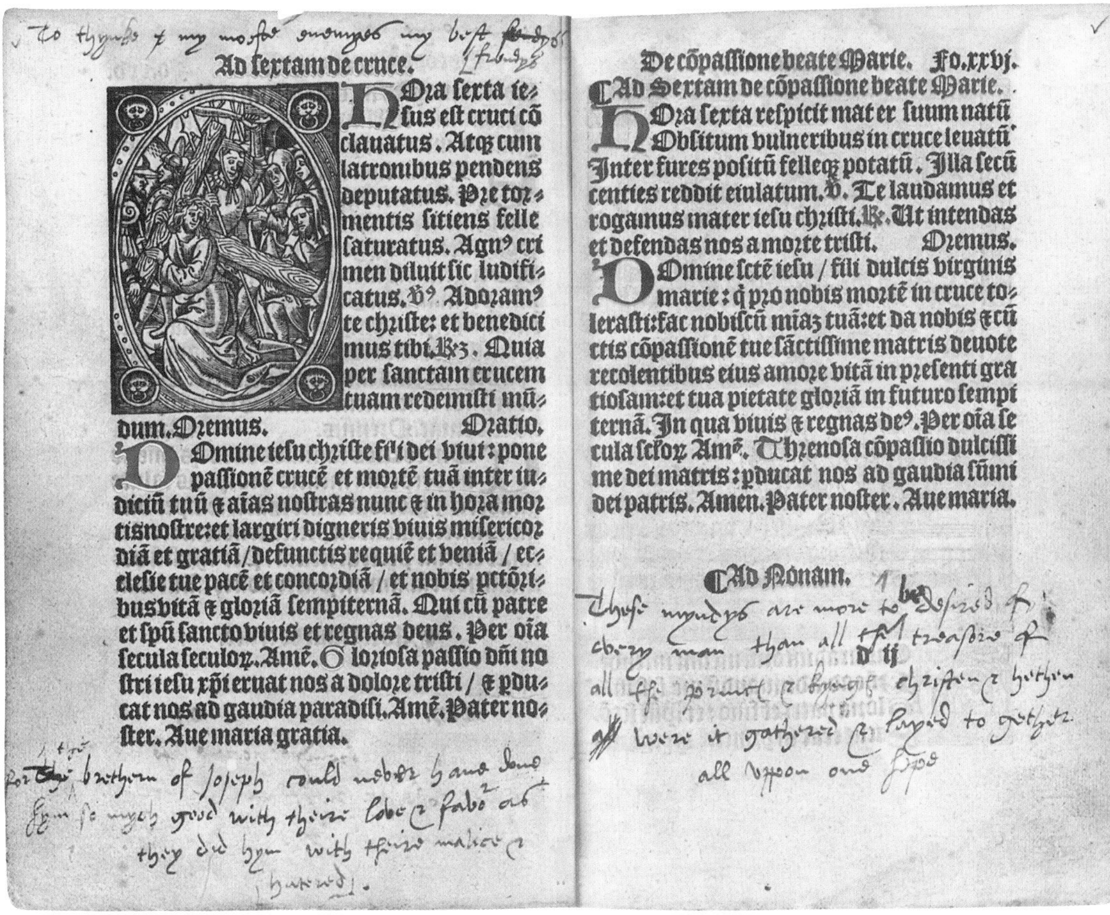

Ad sextam de cruce.

Hora sexta ie-
sus est cruci cõ
clauatus. Atq; cum
latronibus pendens
deputatus. Pre tor-
mentis sitiens felle
saturatus. Agn9 cri
men diluit sic ludifi-
catus. V9. Adoram9
te christe: et benedici
mus tibi. R3. Quia
per sanctam crucem
tuam redemisti mũ-
dum. Oremus. Oratio.

Domine iesu christe fi'i dei viui: pone
passionẽ crucẽ et mortẽ tuã inter iu-
diciũ tuũ & aĩas nostras nunc & in hora mor
tis nostre: et largiri digneris viuis misericor
diã et gratiã / defunctis requiẽ et veniã / ecclesie tue pacẽ et concordiã / et nobis pctõri-
bus vitã & gloriã sempiternã. Qui cũ patre
et spũ sancto viuis et regnas deus. Per oĩa
secula seculor. Amẽ. Gloriosa passio dñi no
stri iesu xpi eruat nos a dolore tristi / & pducat nos ad gaudia paradisi. Amẽ. Pater noster. Aue maria gratia.

De cõpassione beate Marie. Fo. xxvj.

Ad Sextam de cõpassione beate Marie.

Hora sexta respicit mater suum natũ
Oblitum vulneribus in cruce leuatũ
Inter fures positũ felleq; potatũ. Illa secũ
centies reddit eiulatum. V. Te laudamus et
rogamus mater iesu christi. R. Ut intendas
et defendas nos a morte tristi. Oremus.

Domine scte iesu / fili dulcis virginis
marie: q pro nobis mortẽ in cruce tolerasti: fac nobiscũ miaz tuã: et da nobis & cũ
ctis cõpassionẽ tue sãctissime matris deuote
recolentibus eius amore vitã in presenti gra
tiosam: et tua pietate gloriã in futuro sempi
ternã. In qua viuis & regnas de9. Per oĩa se
cula seclor. Amẽ. Threnosa cõpassio dulcissi
me dei matris: pducat nos ad gaudia sũmi
dei patris. Amen. Pater noster. Aue maria.

Ad Nonam.

spread through the Hours at the top and bottom of consecutive pages of the book, starting on the first page of Prime and ending with the last page of Sext [Pl. 65 & 66].

Attempts have been made to relate the paired lines to the printed text or illustrations of the pages on which they occur. I find none of these interpretations compelling, and they seem to me strained exercises in eisegesis rather than exegesis. More's piety was surprisingly conventional: the most heavily thumbed sections of his prayer-book were the pages containing the Fifteen Oes of St Brigid, the Penitential Psalms and the Litany, suggesting that he gravitated instinctively and most often to these prayers of penitence and ardent supplication, and shared the devotional tastes of the majority of his late medieval contemporaries.[8] And I think that More, like thousands of pious late medieval men and women before him, simply wrote his own prayer in the most convenient blank space available to him, as members of the Roberts family had done: we should not work too hard to match manuscript and print. However that may be, the prayer is certainly a noble and characteristic utterance, which gains in power and poignancy from the circumstances in which we believe it to have been composed. Read as autobiography, it seems unmistakably the prayer of an isolated man struggling to come to terms with a frightening fate.

Gyve me thy grace good lord
To sett the world at nought

To sett my mynd faste vppon the
And not to hange vppon the blaste of mennys mowthis.

To be content to be solitary
Not to long for worldely company

Lytle & litle vtterly to caste of the world
And ridde my mynd of all the bysynes therof

Not to long to here of eny worldely thyngis
But that the heryng of worldely fantesyes may be to me displesaunt

Gladly to be thinkyng of God
Pituously to call for his helpe

To lene vn to the cumfort of God
Bysyly to labor to love hym

To know myn awn vilite & wrechednesse
To humble & meken my selfe vnder the myghty hand of God

To bewayle my synnys passed
ffor the purgyng of them patiently to suffre adversite

gladly to bere my purgatory here
to be joyfull of tribulations

To walke the narrow way that ledeth to life
To bere the crosse with christ

To have the laste thing in remembraunce
To have ever a fore myne yie my deth that ys ever at hand

To make deth no straunger to me
To foresee & considre theverlastyng fyre of hell

To pray for perdon byfore the Iudge come
To have continually in myund the passion that christe suffred
for me

ffor hus benefitys vncessauntly to geve hym thankys
To by the tyme agayn that I byfore have loste

To abstayn from vayne confabulations
To estew light folysh myrth & gladnesse

Recreationys not necessary/to cutt off
of worldly substauns frendys libertie life and all
  To sett the losse at right nowght for the wynnyng of christ

To thynke my moost enemyes my best frendys
ffor the brethern of Ioseph could never have done
  hym so mych good with theire love & favor as
    they did hym with theire malice & hatered

These myndys are more to be desired of
every man than all the tresore of
all the princis & kyngis christen & hethen
  were it gathered & layed to gether
    all vppon one hepe.[9]

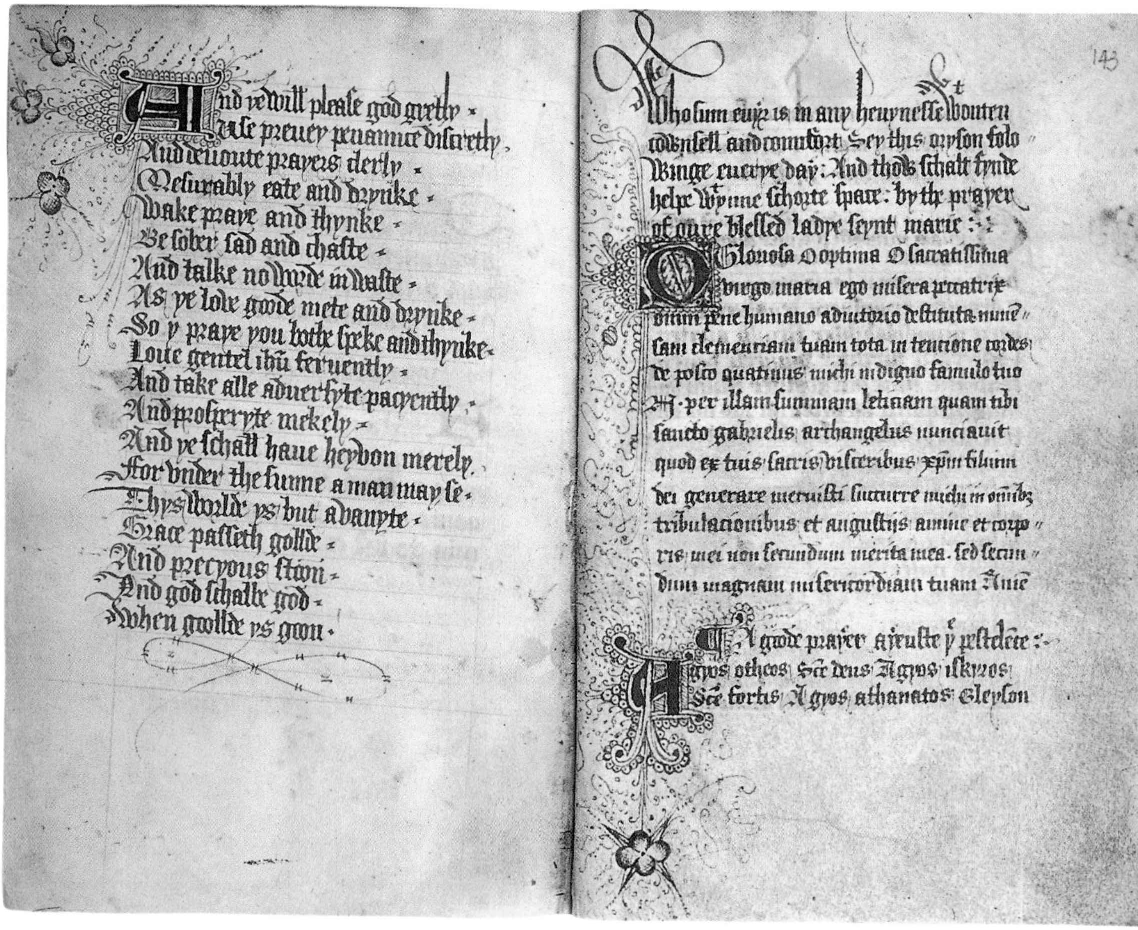

67.
This moralising rhyme is part of a supplement of Latin and English devotions added by a professional scribe to customise for a wealthy owner a Book of Hours produced in Bruges *c.* 1490 probably for use in the diocese of Lincoln.

Cambridge University Library, Dd 6 1 fols142v–143. Page size 20 × 13 cms.

This prayer, which was almost certainly composed in the Tower, picks up many of the themes of the other Tower works, and closely resembles the long prayer More composed after he had been condemned to death, not least its concluding intercession for his enemies 'make us saved soules in heaven together where we may ever live and love together with the and thy blessed saintes'. But notice that despite its special appropriateness for More in his prison, it is also an utterly conventional Tudor prayer, sections of which in fact can have had little immediate application in the Tower. Even in this extremity, More's devotional instinct moves towards the human condition in general, and to the universally applicable disciplines of the spiritual life, for in the Tower he can hardly have needed much assistance

To abstayn from vayne confabulations
To estew light folysh myrth & gladnesse
Recreationys not necessary/to cutt off

More's prayer is one of the high points of late medieval piety, but it is no isolated peak, and it contains nothing that any devout early-Tudor Christian, reflecting in their closet on their own mortality, might not have uttered. Very similar sentiments, but in the form of prose aphorisms of advice were written by the Henrician soldier-martyr, Blessed Adrian Fortescue, on the flyleaves of his Book of Hours:

Above all things love God with thy heart.
Desire his honour more than the health of thy own soul.
Take heed with all diligence to purge and cleanse thy mind with oft confession and raise thy desire or lust from earthly things.
Judge the best
Use much silence, but when thou hast necessary cause to speak.
Be solitary, as much as is convenient for thine estate
Banish from thee all grudging and detraction, and especially from thy tongue,
And pray often.[10]

Much the same sentiments occur in a manuscript addition to another Book of Hours in the Cambridge University Library [Pl. 67]. This rhymed prayer is a tin whistle to More's mighty diapason, but they are recognisably playing the same tune.

An ye will please God gretly
Use prevey penaunce discretely
And devoute prayers derly
Mesurably eate and drynke
Wake praye and thynke
Be sober sad and chaste
And talke no worde in waste
As ye love good mete and drynke
So y praye you to speke and thyncke
Love Gentel Ihesu fervently
And take all adversyte pacyently
And prosperyte merely
And ye schall have heyvon surely
For under the sunne a man may se
Thys worlde ys but a vanyte

Grace passeth golde
And precyous stoon
And god shalbe god
When goolde ys goon.[11]

From which I conclude that if we go to the prayers of the late medieval laity, we find not growing individualism, social anomie, and alienation, but the signs of individual participation in a varied but coherent public religious culture, in which private intensities are nourished by and consciously related to the public practice of religion. This was a religious culture precisely as self-centred, whingeing and individualistic as the psalms of David: which means, I take it, not notably so at all.

More's prayerbook, annotated as he waited trial in the Tower of London for his silent resistance to the Henrician reformation, has brought our consideration of the Book of Hours into the heart of the reformation crisis. In my final chapters I shall explore in more detail the fate of these most medieval and most Catholic of books in the revolutionary religious upheavals of Tudor England.

Part 3

CATHOLIC BOOKS IN A PROTESTANT WORLD

Egredietur virga de radice iesse.
Et flos de radice eius ascendet.

Domine labia mea aperies. Et os meū annunciabit laudem tuam
Deus in adiutorium meum intende. Domine ad adiuuandum

8

THE IMPACT OF PRINT

In the generation or so before the Reformation, Books of Hours were changing dramatically, but despite the expansion of the English material they contained, not in the direction of Protestantism, nor even very obviously in anticipation of reform. Indeed, if anything, they were becoming more, not less, Catholic – more sacramental, more churchly, more fortified and enhanced with indulgences and pious promises, more than ever, therefore, geared to a religious system in which the intercession of the saints, the centrality of the Mass, and the power of the priesthood to absolve and remit sin were taken as axioms. The most obvious change, of course, was the arrival of print. Mass-produced manuscript books were still being made and marketed into the last decades of the fifteenth century, and manuscript and printed Books of Hours would continue to coexist well into the sixteenth century. The wealthy and much-married merchant's wife Anne Withypole, as we have seen, owned both manuscript and printed Books of Hours, and so did Henry VII's Queen, Elizabeth, Henry VIII's first Queen, Catherine of Aragon, and members of Thomas More's family.[1] But in the long run cheap and consequently often crude manuscript books could not compete with the even cheaper but often very beautiful printed books rolling from the press. Something like one hundred and twenty separate editions of Book of Hours were printed for the English market before 1530.

68.
The opening of Matins from a sumptuous printed Book of Hours for England by the Parisian publisher Simon Vostre. The essentially Gothic design evident in the Jesse-Tree page with its elaborate borders is supplemented by a series of magnificent whole-page renaissance engravings like the Annunciation scene here. This copy has been given added status and permanence by being printed on vellum.

RSTC 15926. British Library opening of Matins C 41 e 9 (unpaginated). Page size 20 × 11 cm

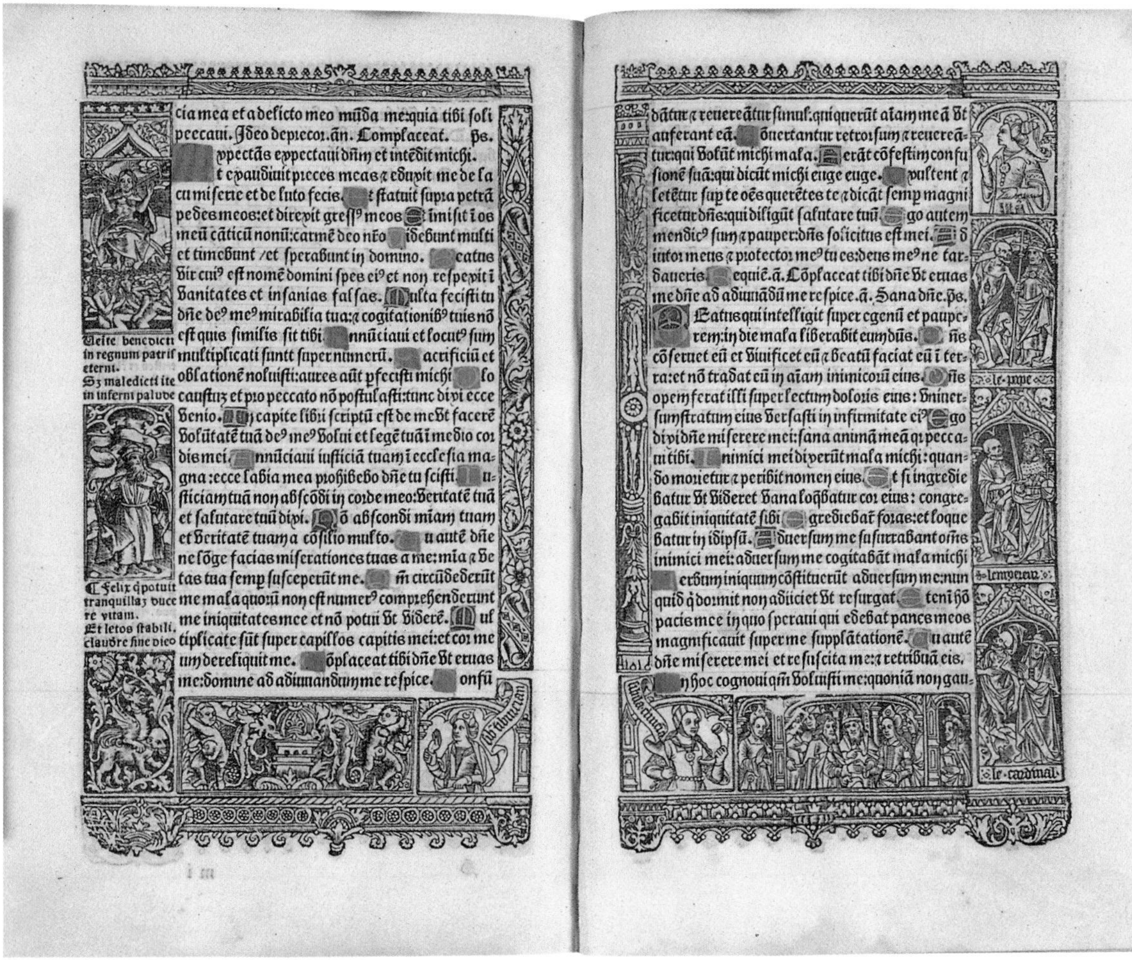

69.
The Psalms of the Passion from the same book. Hand coloured initials and elaborate border decorations make the book as elaborate as any manuscript. The borders include figures of the Sybils (a common Renaissance motif) and, on the right, the Dance of Death.

RSTC 15926. British Library C 41 e 9, Sigs M1v–M2. Page size 20 × 11 cm

These printed editions varied hugely in appearance, decoration and price, ranging from economy paper books half the size of the palm of your hand with few or no pictures, to sumptuous large quarto or octavo volumes printed on vellum, sometimes consciously passing themselves off as substitutes for manuscript, very elegantly and convincingly indeed [Pls. 68–70].

These printed Books of Hours for the English market form a fascinating and under-explored area of study in their own right.[2] I have space here to emphasize just a few points. The core content of all printed Books of Hours, considered simply as a collection of texts, was broadly similar. Though there was some material distinctive of English publishers,[3] by and large market forces led towards standardisation of

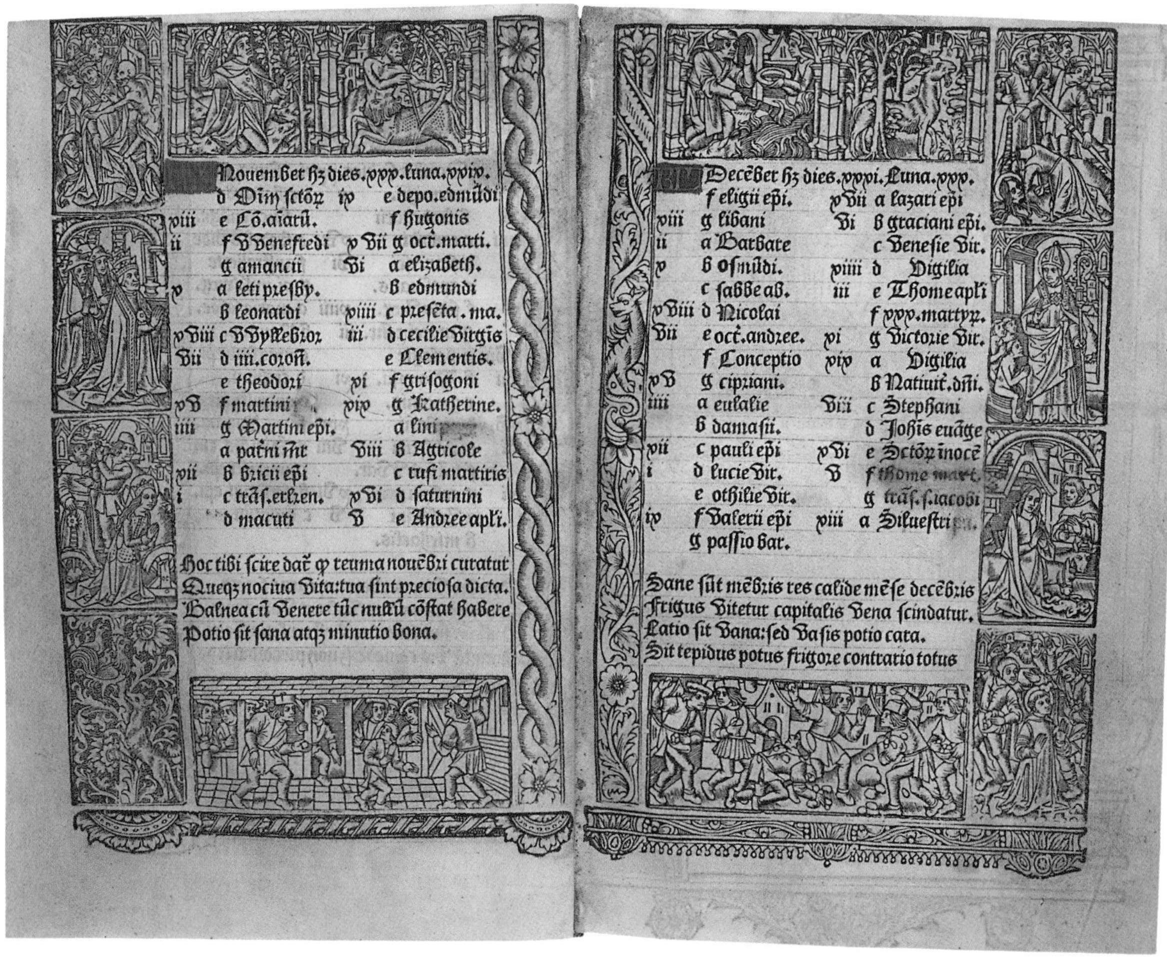
Nouember hʒ dies.xxx.Luna.xxix.
d Dim sctoꝝ xv e depo.edmũdi
xviii e Cõ.aiarũ. f hugonis
ii f Wenefredi xvii g oct.matti.
g amancii vi a elizabeth.
x a leti presby. b edmundi
b leonardi xiiii c presẽta.ma.
xviii c Wyllebroꝛ iii d cecilie virgis
vii d iiii.coꝛoñ. e Clementis.
e theodoꝛi xi f grisogoni
xv f martini xix g Katherine.
iiii g Martini epi. a lini
a patni mr viii b Agricole
xii b bricii epi c rufi martiris
i c trãs.erken. xvi d saturnini
d macuti v e Andꝛee apl'i.
Hoc tibi scire datur q̄ tenima nouẽbri curatur
Queqʒ nociua vita:tua sint preciosa dicta.
Balnea cũ venere tũc nullũ cõstat habere
Potio sit sana atqʒ minutio bona.

Decẽber hʒ dies.xxxi.Luna.xxx.
f eligii epi. xvii a lazari epi
xiiii g libani vi b graciani epi.
iii a Barbare c Venesie vir.
x b osmũdi. xiiii d Vigilia
c sabbe ab. iii e Thome apl'i
xviii d Nicolai f xxx.martyꝝ.
vii e oct.andꝛee. xi g Victoꝛie vir.
f Conceptio xix a Vigilia
xv g cipꝛiani. b Natiuit.dñi.
iiii a eulalie viii c Stephani
b damasii. d Johis euãge
xii c pauli epi xvi e Sctoꝝ inocẽ
i d lucie vir. v f thome mart.
e othilie vir. g trãs.s.iacobi
ix f Valerii epi xiii a Siluestri pa.
g passio bar.
Sane sit mẽbris res calide mẽse decẽbris
Frigus vitetur capitalis vena scindatur.
Latio sit vana:sed vasis potio cara.
Sit tepidus potus frigoꝛe contrario totus

70.
The November and December calendar from a smaller but still elaborate book by Vostre, working with the printer Philip Pigouchet, in 1507. Activities of the months fill the bottom borders, and selections of the saints with feasts in that month are represented in the right and left margins. Note the deletion of 'Papa' after the names of Sts Martin, Leo and Sylvester. Becket's name was removed (29 December) in Henry VIII's reign, but written in again in Queen Mary's reign.

RSTC 15905 (Vostre Pigouchet 1507). Calendar. Cambridge University Library Rit d 350 1. Page size 15 × 9 cm

71.
With almost forty editions to his credit between 1526 and 1538, the publisher François Regnault dominated the market for Books of Hours for England in the 1530s, producing books for every taste and pocket. Metal blocks were moved around between editions: the Seven Sorrows of the Virgin Mary, decorating Matins of the Virgin here, appears as a whole page illustration in Regnault's cheaper books.

RSTC 15968. Cambridge University Library Sss 60 19, unpaginated. Page size 22 × 14cm

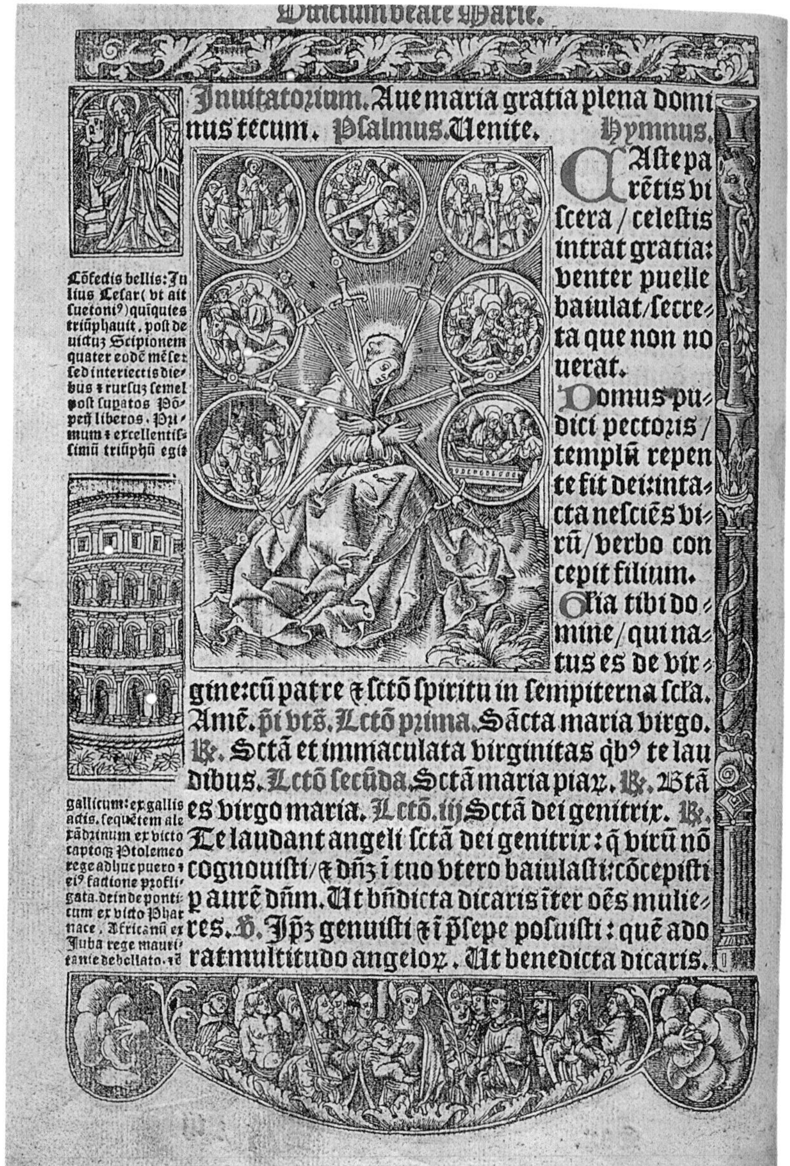

72.
Matins with the Tree of Jesse and Annunciation from one of Regnault's very successful mid-price books.

RSTC 15973 (Regnault 1531). Cambridge University Library Syn 8 53 95, fos. xxviii(v)-xxix. Page size 14 × 7 cm

73.
Matins with the Tree of Jesse and Annunciation from Regnault's cheapest range.

RSTC 15981. Cambridge University Library Syn 8 53 97 (1533) fos. xxxvii(v)–xxxviii. Page size 10 × 6 cm

74.
'Purgatory': an illustration in the Office of the Dead, from Regnault's mid-price range. Note the verses in English: Regnault's mid-price and cheap ranges had more vernacular English material than his more expensive books.

RSTC 15973 (Regnault 1531). Purgatory (fo. C and opp.), Bodleian Douce BB 89. Page size 14 × 7 cm

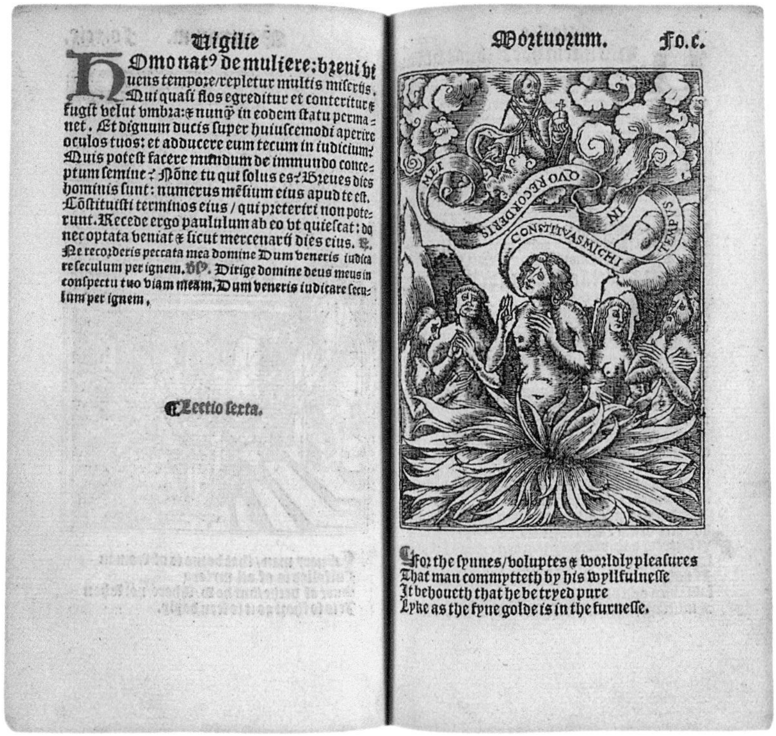
Vigilie
Homo natus de muliere: breui viuens tempore/repletur multis miseriis. Qui quasi flos egreditur et conteritur & fugit velut umbra: & nunquam in eodem statu permanet. Et dignum ducis super huiuscemodi aperire oculos tuos: et adducere eum tecum in iudicium? Quis potest facere mundum de immundo conceptum semine? Nonne tu qui solus es? Breues dies hominis sunt: numerus mensium eius apud te est. Constituisti terminos eius / qui preteriri non poterunt. Recede ergo paululum ab eo ut quiescat: donec optata veniat & sicut mercenarii dies eius. R. Ne recorderis peccata mea domine Dum veneris iudicare seculum per ignem. V. Dirige domine deus meus in conspectu tuo viam meam. Dum veneris iudicare seculum per ignem.

Lectio sexta.

Mortuorum. Fo. c.

For the synnes/voluptes & worldly pleasures
That man commytteth by his wyllfulnesse
It behoueth that he be tryed pure
Lyke as the fyne golde is in the furnesse.

contents, and the buyer was liable to get much the same basic range of prayers whatever price they paid. Price did make a difference, but in the lavishness of presentation rather than in the comprehensiveness of the text. From the 1520s the leading publishers, like François Regnault, produced up- and down-market versions of essentially the same sequence of texts, with fewer or more, cruder or more refined illustrations, according to price. From 1529 onwards at the latest Regnault introduced a range of English material into his Sarum *Horae*, which included the prayer 'God be in my head', an English verse calendar, a poem containing 'The days of the Week Moralised', an instruction on the devout life translated from the French of Jean Quentin as 'The Maner to live well devoutly and salutaryly' aimed at 'persones of mean estate', a selection of English prayers for the moment of death, and for the elevation at Mass, and an elaborate examination of conscience and preparation for sacramental confession, 'The Form of Confession'. Interestingly, Regnault's most lavish books, in quarto with many illustrations, in fact contained somewhat less vernacular material than the smaller octavo and sextodecimo books [Pl. 71].

Vigilie

COSTITVAS MIHI TĒPVS IN
QVO RECORDERIS MEI.

For the synnes/voluptes/and worldly
pleasures.
That man cōmytteth by his wyllfulnesse.
It behoueth that he be tryed pure.
Lyke as the fyne golde is in the furnesse.

Mortuorum. Fo.cxxxix.
Quis michi hoc tribuat vt in infer-
no protegas me: et abscondas me do
nec pertranseat furor tuus: et constituas
michi tempus in quo recorderis mei? Pu-
tas ne mortuus homo rursum viuat? Cū-
ctis diebus quib9 nunc milito/expecto do
nec veniat immutatio mea. Vocabis me: et
ego respōdebo tibi. Operi manuum tua-
rum porriges dexteram. Tu quidem gressus meos dinumerasti: sed parce peccatis
meis. Domine secundum actum meum
noli me iudicare: nichil dignum in conspe
ctu tuo egi. Ideo deprecor maiestatem tuā
vt tu deus deleas iniquitatem meam. V9.
Ampli9 laua me ab iniustitia mea: et a de-
licto meo mūda me: quia tibi soli peccaui.
Ideo deprecor maiestatem tuam vt tu de9
deleas iniquitatem meam. an. Compla-
ceat. Psalmus. xxxix.
Expectans expectaui dominum: et in-
tendit michi.
Et exaudiuit preces meas: et eduxit me
de lacu miserie et de luto fecis.
Et statuit supra petrā pedes meos: et dire
xit gressus meos. Et immisit in os meum
canticum nouum: carmen deo nostro.
Videbunt multi et timebunt: et sperabūt

75.
'Purgatory' from Regnault's cheapest range.

RSTC 15981 (1533). Purgatory (fo. CXXXIX and opp.) Bodleian Gough Missals 49. Page size 10 × 6 cm

Unsurprisingly, these smaller books, cheaper and with more English material, were manifestly more popular, though there was certainly no link here to the spread of reformed opinions, for all this vernacular material was strongly traditionalist in theology. Between 1529 and 1538 Regnault printed four quarto editions of the Sarum *Horae*, as against twenty-three in smaller sizes, and these books in smaller formats became his standard product [Pls. 72–9].[4]

The Primers themselves, therefore, considered simply as physical artefacts, were strikingly varied, ranging from magnificently bound and decorated books printed on vellum, sometimes hand coloured, which must in some instances have cost just as much as one of the cheaper manuscript books, down to tiny and mostly unornamented texts printed on rough paper, which can only have cost a few pence [Pls. 80–2]. That variety overlaying a largely standardised set of contents, varying most in the extent of the English material included, meant that rich and poor inhabited distinct but interpenetrating devotional worlds.

The distinctions included those of style. Many of the French Books of Hours produced for England had a decidedly Gothic look,

76.
The 'Fifteen Oes', prayers on the Passion and Wounds of Jesus, in England universally but mistakenly ascribed to the visionary St Brigid of Sweden, were among the most popular of all additions to printed Books of Hours. A standard iconography quickly developed as frontispiece to the prayers, portraying St Brigid praying before a vision of Christ usually as the Image of Pity. In this mid-price book by Regnault, the saint prays with the hat, satchel and staff of the pilgrim before her on the ground.

RSTC 15973 (Regnault 1531). Cambridge University Library, Syn 8 53 95 fo. lciv (verso). Page size 14 × 7 cm

77.
A simpler and cruder version of the same iconography from Regnault's cheapest range.

RSTC 15981 (Regnault, 1533). Cambridge University Library, Syn 8 53 97 fo. xci (verso). Page size 10 × 6 cm

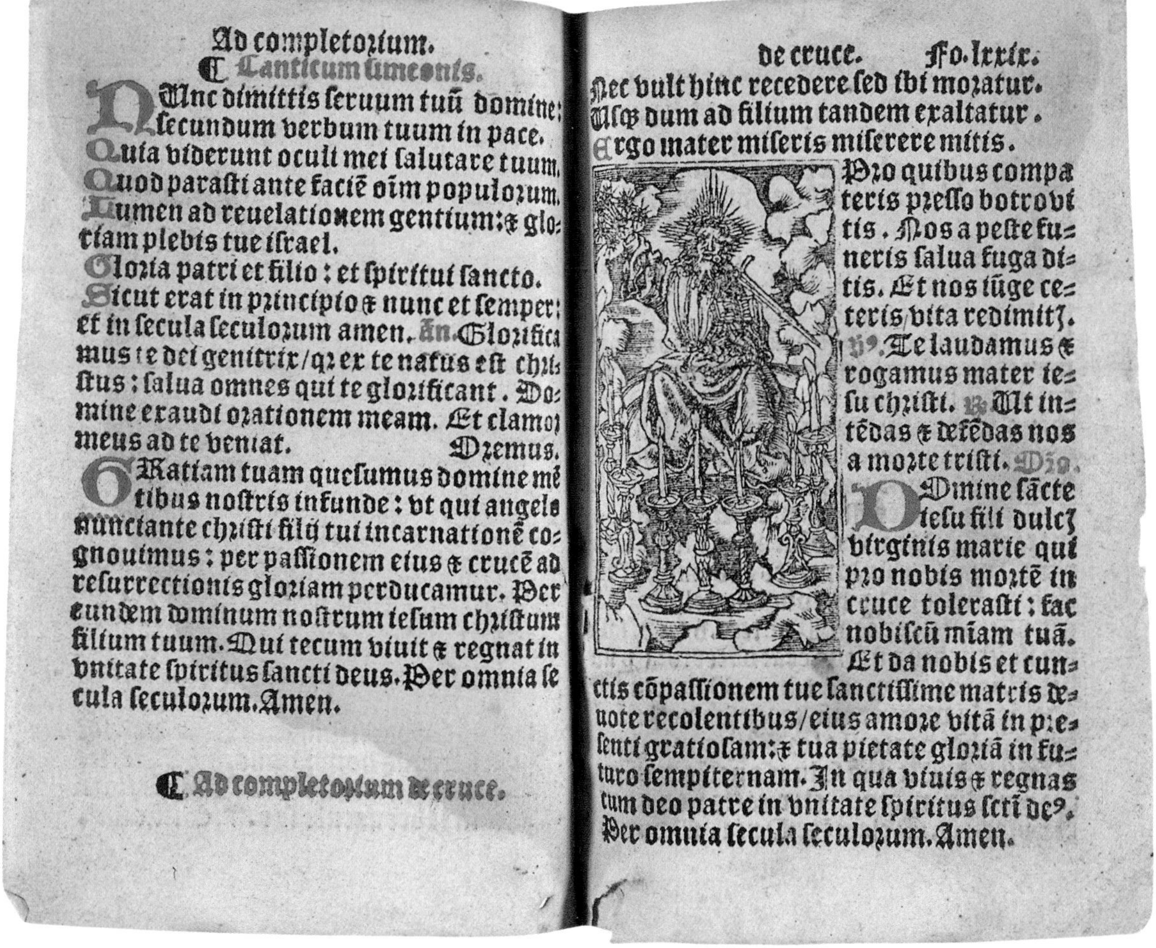

Ad completorium.
¶ Canticum simeonis.
Nunc dimittis seruum tuũ domine: secundum verbum tuum in pace.
Quia viderunt oculi mei salutare tuum.
Quod parasti ante faciẽ oĩm populorum.
Lumen ad reuelationem gentium: & gloriam plebis tue israel.
Gloria patri et filio: et spiritui sancto.
Sicut erat in principio & nunc et semper: et in secula seculorum amen. An. Glorificamus te dei genitrix/q2 ex te natus est christus: salua omnes qui te glorificant. Domine exaudi orationem meam. Et clamor meus ad te veniat. Oremus.
Gratiam tuam quesumus domine mẽtibus nostris infunde: vt qui angelo nunciante christi filij tui incarnationẽ cognouimus: per passionem eius & crucẽ ad resurrectionis gloriam perducamur. Per eundem dominum nostrum iesum christum filium tuum. Qui tecum viuit & regnat in vnitate spiritus sancti deus. Per omnia secula seculorum. Amen.

¶ Ad completorium de cruce.

de cruce. Fo. lxxix.
Nec vult hinc recedere sed ibi moratur. Usq3 dum ad filium tandem exaltatur. Ergo mater miseris miserere mitis. Pro quibus compateris presso botro vitis. Nos a peste funeris salua fuga ditis. Et nos iũge ceteris vita redimit3. V9. Te laudamus & rogamus mater iesu christi. R. Ut intẽdas & defẽdas nos a morte tristi. Oro.
Domine sãcte iesu fili dulci3 virginis marie qui pro nobis mortẽ in cruce tolerasti: fac nobiscũ miam tuã. Et da nobis et cunctis cõpassionem tue sanctissime matris deuote recolentibus/eius amore vitã in presenti graciosam: & tua pietate gloriã in futuro sempiternam. In qua viuis & regnas cum deo patre in vnitate spiritus sctĩ de9. Per omnia secula seculorum. Amen.

78.
The illustrations to printed Books of Hours were often vehicles for the transmission and popularisation of 'high' culture. In this inexpensive pocket or purse-sized Book of Hours, Compline from the Hours of the Cross is prefaced by an image of Christ among the candlesticks, copied directly from Dürer's engraving of the same scene from the Book of Revelation in his folio-sized 1498 Apocalypse.

RSTC 15970 (Regnault, 1531). Bodleian Gough Missals 49 fo. lxxix. Page size 10 × 6 cm

79. CHRIST AMONG THE CANDLESTICKS
Albrecht Dürer, *Apocalypse*, 1498

80.
Purgatory from a cheap edition of the Sarum Book of Hours by one of François Regnault's French competitors and imitators Thielman Kerver (in fact, in this case, Kerver's widow).

RSTC 15978 (Yoland Kerver 1532). Cambridge, Pepys Library, fo. clvi. Page size 10 × 5.5 cm

81.
This tiny much-thumbed book is the sole surviving copy of an edition of the Sarum *Horae* printed in England (by Wynkyn de Worde?) for the cheapest end of the market. The Oes of St Brigid are prefaced by a rubric promising lavish indulgences for daily recitation before an image of the wounded Jesus. The standard iconography has been modified in the woodcut, and the pilgrim saint kneels before a crucifix rather than the Image of Pity.

RSTC 15941. Cambridge University Library, Rit e 352 1, fo. xliiii (Oes of St Brigid). Page size 12 × 4.5 cm

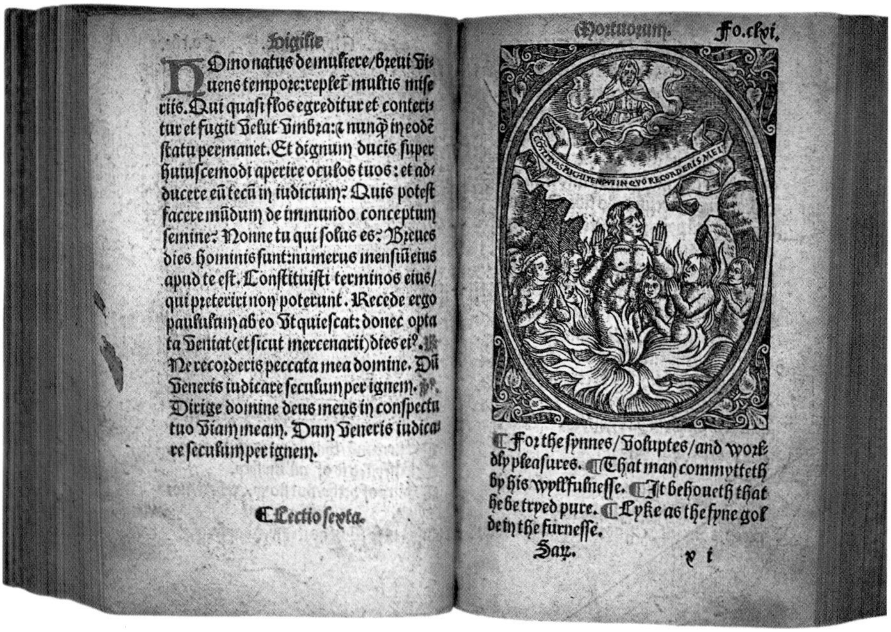
Vigilie

Lectio sexta.

Mortuorum. Fo.clvi.

For the synnes/Voluptes/and worldly pleasures. That man commytteth by his wylfulnesse. It behoueth that he be tryed pure. Lyke as the fyne golde in the furnesse.

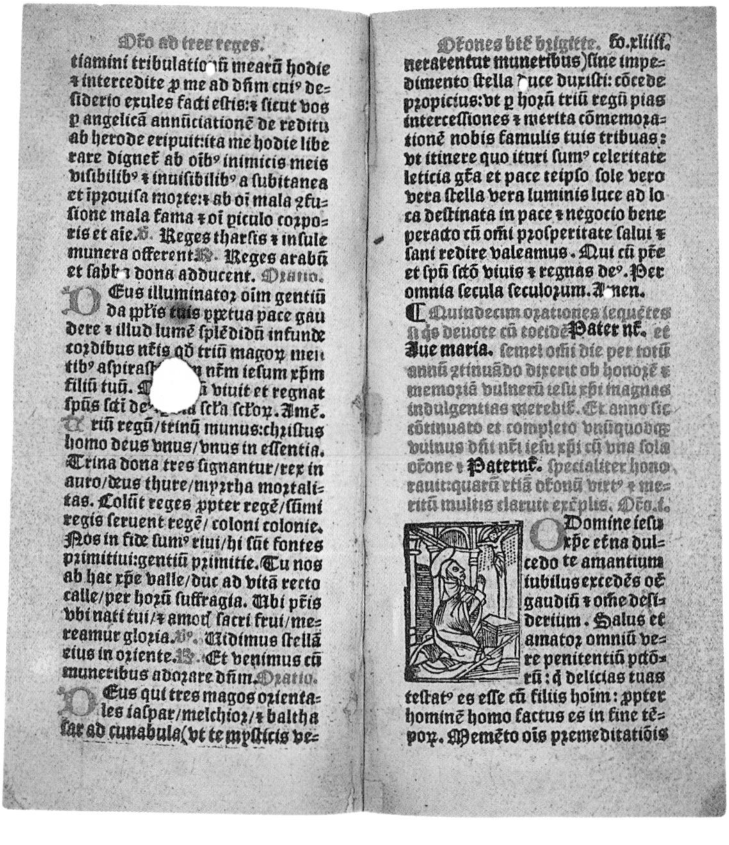
Oro ad tres reges.

fo.xliiii.

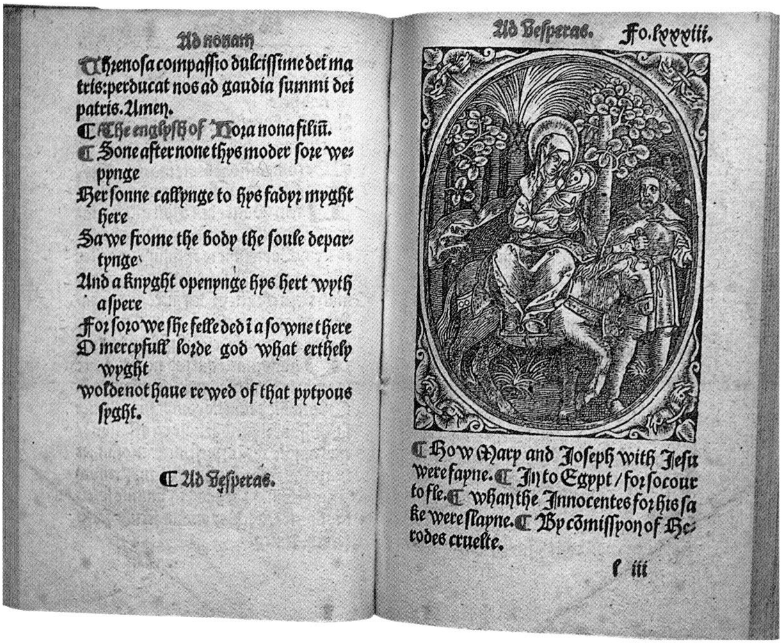
Ad nonam

Ohrenosa compassio dulcissime dei ma tris: perducat nos ad gaudia summi dei patris. Amen.

The englysshe of Hora nona filii.

Sone after none thys moder sore we- pynge
Her sonne callynge to hys fadyr myght here
Sawe frome the body the soule depar- tynge
And a knyght openynge hys hert wyth a spere
For sorowe she felle ded i a sowne there
O mercyfull lorde god what erthely wyght
wolde not haue rewed of that pytyous syght.

Ad Vesperas.

Ad Vesperas. Fo. lxxxiii.

How Mary and Joseph with Jesu were fayne. In to Egypt / for socour to fle. Whan the Innocentes for his sa ke were slayne. By cōmissyon of He rodes cruelte.

l iii

82.
Vespers of the Virgin from the same cheap edition by Kerver. Note the English rhyme, copied from Regnault.

RSTC 15978 (Yoland Kerver 1532). Cambridge, Pepys Library, fo. lxxxiii. Page size 10 × 5.5 cm

83.
English prayers (left opening) from a Paris-printed Book of Hours for the English market. This luxury copy has been printed on vellum and has hand-coloured initials.

RSTC 15905 (Vostre Pigouchet 1507). Cambridge University Library, Rit d 350.1, unpaginated.

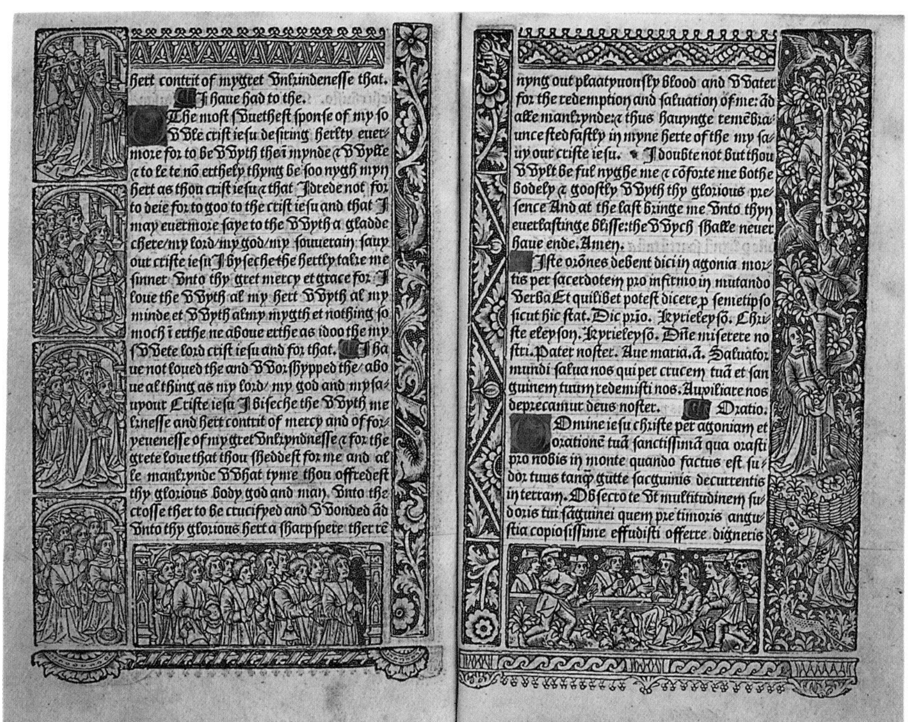
hert contrit of my gret unkindenesse that. I haue had to the.

O The most swethest sponse of my so wle crist iesu desiring hertly ever- more for to be wyth the i mynde & wylle & to lete nō erthely thyng be soo nygh myn hert as thou crist iesu & that I drede not for to deie for to goo to the crist iesu and that I may evermore saye to the wyth a gladde chere / my lord / my god / my souuerain sauy our criste iesu I byseche the hertly take me sinner unto thy gret mercy et grace for I loue the wyth al my hert wyth al my minde et wyth al my mygth et nothing so moch i erthe ne aboue erthe as i doo the my swete lord crist iesu and for that. I ha ue not loued the and worshypped the / abo ue al thing as my lord / my god and my sa- uyour Criste iesu I biseche the wyth me kenesse and hert contrit of mercy and of for- yevenesse of my gret unkyndnesse & for the grete loue that thou sheddest for me and al le mankynde what tyme thou offredest thy glorious body god and man. Unto the crosse ther to be crucifyed and wonded ād unto thy glorious hert a sharp spere ther re

nyng out plaatyuonsly blood and water for the redemption and saluation of me: ād alle mankynde: & thus hauynge remēbra- unce stedfastly in myne herte of the my sa- uyour criste iesu. I doubte not but thou wylt be ful nyghe me & cōforte me bothe bodely & goostly wyth thy glorious pre- sence And at the last bringe me unto thyn everlastinge blisse: the wych shalle never haue ende. Amen.

Iste orōnes debent dici in agonia mor- tis per sacerdotem pro infirmo in mutando verba Et quilibet potest dicere p semetipso sicut hic stat. Dic pmo. Kyrieleysō. Chri- ste eleyson. Kyrieleysō. Dn̄e miserere no stri. Pater noster. Aue maria. ā. Saluator mundi salua nos qui per crucem tuā et san guinem tuum redemisti nos. Auxiliare nos deprecamur deus noster. Oratio.

Domine iesu christe per agoniam et oratione tuā sanctissimā qua orasti pro nobis in monte quando factus est su- dor tuus tanq̄ gutte sanguinis decurrentis in terram. Obsecro te ut multitudinem su- doris tui sāguinei quem pre timoris angu- stia copiosissime effudisti offerre digneris

84.
In this handsome but plainly designed book printed in Paris for the London market, the Oes of St Brigid are prefaced by the *Ecce Homo* ('Behold the Man', the scourged Christ displayed to the crowds by Pontius Pilate). Note the deletion of references to the Pope from the rubric promising miraculous benefits, including the deliverance of fifteen souls from purgatory, for the daily recitation of the prayers for a whole year.

RSTC 15912 (Byrckman 1511). Cambridge University Library, Sss 15 20 fo. lii. Page size 16 × 10 cm

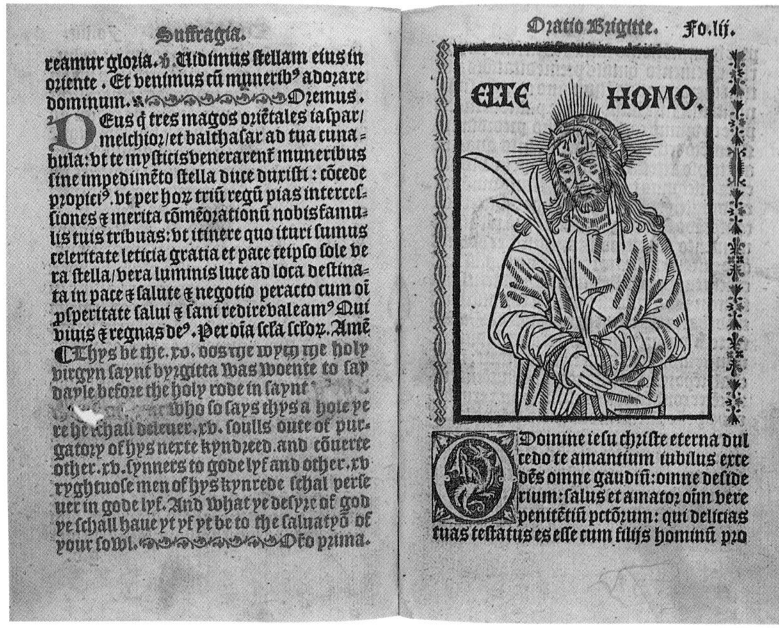
Suffragia.
reamur gloria. V. Vidimus stellam eius in oriente. Et venimus cum muneribus adorare dominum. Oremus.
Deus qui tres magos orientales iaspar/ melchior/ et balthasar ad tua cunabula: ut te mysticis venerarent muneribus sine impedimento stella duce duxisti: concede propicius. ut per horum trium regum pias intercessiones et merita commemorationum nobis famulis tuis tribuas: ut itinere quo ituri sumus celeritate leticia gratia et pace teipso sole vera stella/ vera luminis luce ad loca destinata in pace et salute et negotio peracto cum omni prosperitate salui et sani redire valeamus. Qui viuis et regnas deus. Per omnia secula seculorum. Amen.
Thys be the .xv. oos the whych the holy virgyn saynt byrgitta was woonte to say dayle before the holy rode in saynt [illegible] who so says thys a hole yere he schall deleuer .xv. soulls oute of purgatory of hys nexte kynreed. and conuerte other .xv. synners to gode lyf and other .xv. ryghtuose men of hys kynrede schal perseuer in gode lyf. And what ye desyre of god ye schall haue yt yf yt be to the saluatyon of your sowl. Deo prima.

Oratio Brigitte. Fo.lii.
ECCE HOMO.
O Domine iesu christe eterna dulcedo te amantium iubilus excedens omne gaudium: omne desiderium: salus et amator omnium vere penitentium peccatorum: qui delicias tuas testatus es esse cum filijs hominum pro

each page cut from a single metal plate, and with elaborate decorated borders. At the aristocratic end of the market, as we have seen, the Parisian partnership of the publisher Simon Vostre and printer Philip Pigouchet produced sumptuous and highly elaborate books for the English market, often on vellum, with a dense iconographic programme derived from and elaborating on the manuscript traditions of the fifteenth century [Pl. 83].[5]

Publishers in France or the Low Countries had the advantage of scale, being able to use fundamentally the same layout to cater for a Europe-wide market, customising particular editions for local or national usage by inserting variable regional elements like the calendar, and including such vernacular prayers (for England before the late 1520s, rarely as many as half a dozen) as might be required or available. In the 1520s Vostre's most beautiful books combined Gothic decorative features with spectacular renaissance full page biblical scenes at the start of each of the hours: but these were self-consciously luxurious items, and the binding of surviving copies of this edition are comparably splendid.[6]

Other books were plainer, moving away from the manuscript tradition towards books conceived not as a sequence of integrally decorated pages, but as made of pages set in movable type with only

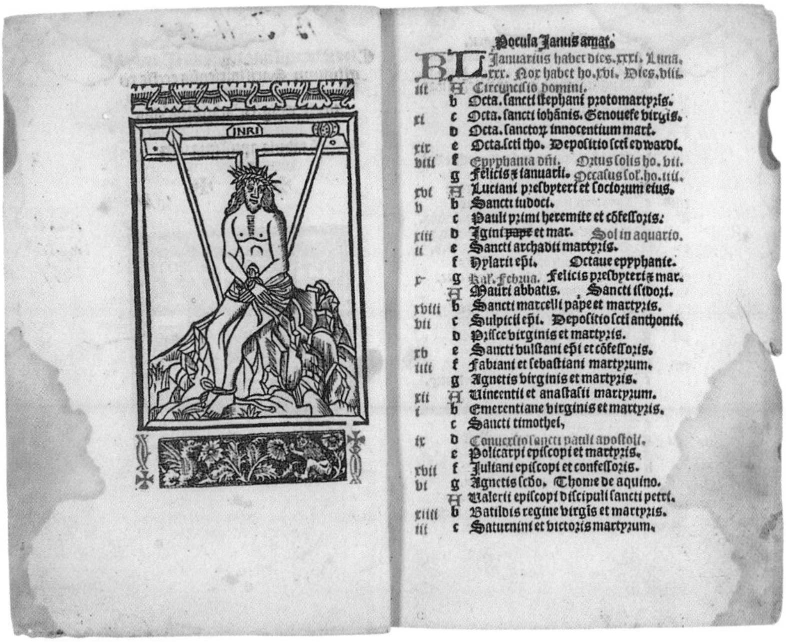
Pocula Janus amat.
Januarius habet dies.xxxi. Luna.xxx. Nox habet ho.xvi. Dies.viii.

85.
'Christ on the cold stone' or 'Christ as man of sorrows' (verso of title-page) with the calendar for January from a Book of Hours printed in London by Richard Pynson in 1522. This plainer format was popular with English publishers.

RSTC 15933 (Bodleian Gough Missals 141). TP and verso. Page size 16 × 9 cm

Gloriosa passio domini nostri iesu christi / eruat nos a dolore tristi: et perducat nos ad gaudia paradisi. Amen.

Secundum Johannem.
Initium sancti euangelii: secundu Johannem. Gloria tibi domine.
In principio erat verbu/ et verbum erat apd deum: et deus erat verbu. Hoc erat in principio apud deum. Omnia per ipsum facta sunt: et sine ipso factum est nichil. Quod factu est in ipso vita erat / et vita erat lux hominum et lux in tenebris lucet: et tenebre eam no comprehenderunt. Fuit homo missus a deo: cui nome erat iohanes. Hic venit in testimonium: vt testimoniu phiberet de lumine / vt omnes crederent p illu. Non erat ille lux: sed vt testimonium perhiberet de lumine. Erat lux vera: que illuminat omnem homine venientem in hunc mundu. In mundo erat: et mundus per

86.
The complete Passion narrative from St John's Gospel (read in the liturgy of Good Friday) was a common inclusion in printed Books of Hours. In Pynson's book it is prefaced by a whole-page engraving of the crucifixion, and a miniature of St John on Patmos.

RSTC 15933 (Bodleian Gough Missals 141). Sig A1 recto and opp. Page size 16 × 9 cm

occasional illustration. Some books of this kind were produced by continental publishers targeting the English market in the reign of Henry VIII [Pl. 84], but English printers in particular, perhaps because of their smaller market, seem often to have preferred this less lavish format [Pls. 85, 86].

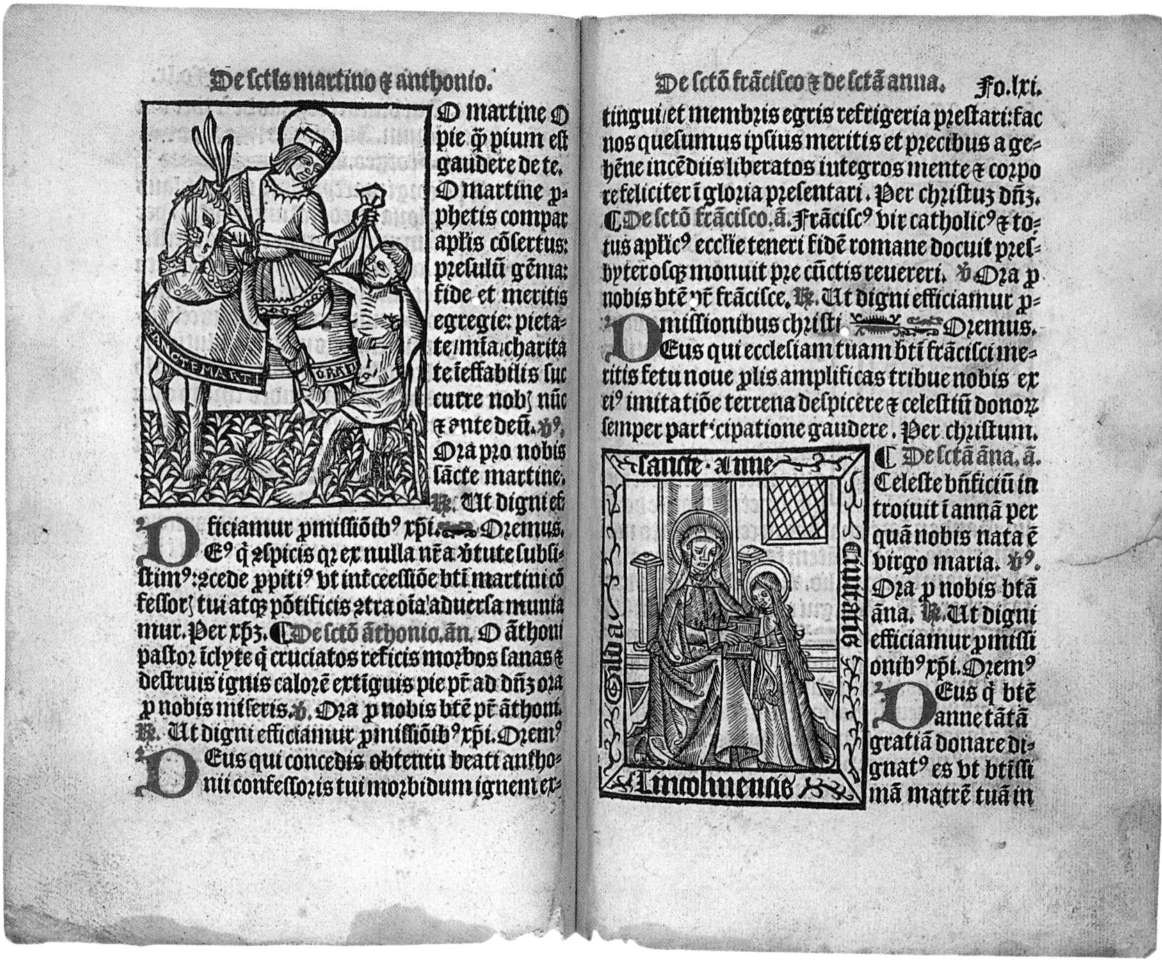

87.
The suffrages to the saints from the Hours of the Virgin in this Book of Hours by Wynkyn de Worde are illustrated with miniatures of the saints invoked. The block-print of St Anne teaching the Virgin to read (right) has a Latin inscription associating the image with the gild of St Anne in the city of Lincoln, so the block must first have been made for a gild publication, perhaps an indulgence or an edition of the gild statutes or register.

RSTC 15922 (Wynkyn de Worde 1519). Cambridge University Library, Sss 29 10 fo. lxi. Page size 17 × 10 cm

88.
The Oes of St Brigid in an English supplement of prayers first published by Caxton under the patronage of Henry VII's queen, Elizabeth, and his mother Lady Margaret Beaufort. Wynkyn de Worde has prefaced the prayers with a full-page depiction of the saint attended by a monk and nun of her order. The same block was used as frontispiece to *The Dietary of Ghostly Health*, a treatise issued from the Bridgetine house of Syon in 1520.

RSTC 15922 (Wynkyn de Worde 1519). Cambridge University Library, Sss 29 10 fo. cxxii. Page size 17 × 10 cm

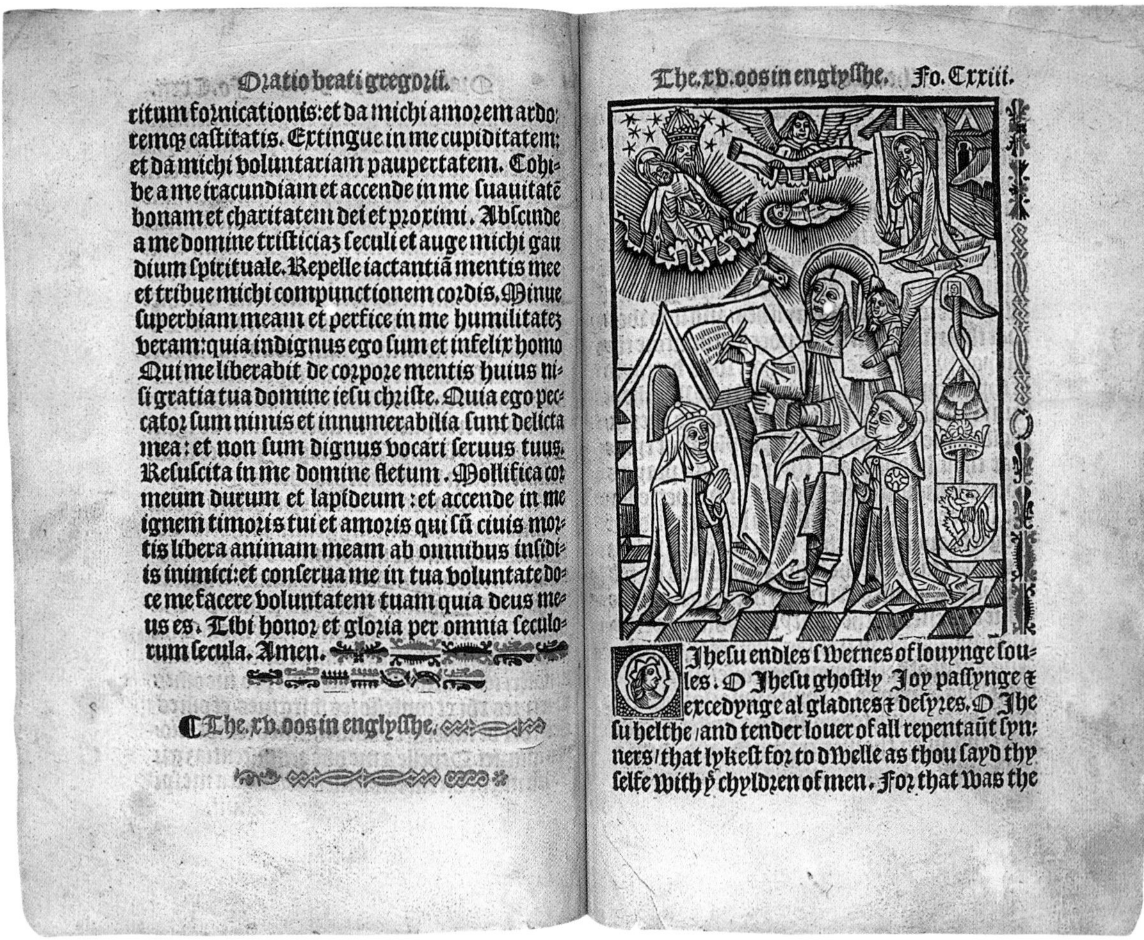
Oratio beati gregorii.
ritum fornicationis: et da michi amorem ardo-
remq castitatis. Extingue in me cupiditatem:
et da michi voluntariam paupertatem. Cohi-
be a me iracundiam et accende in me suauitatē
bonam et charitatem dei et proximi. Abscinde
a me domine tristiciaz seculi et auge michi gau
dium spirituale. Repelle iactantiā mentis mee
et tribue michi compunctionem cordis. Minue
superbiam meam et perfice in me humilitatez
veram: quia indignus ego sum et infelix homo
Qui me liberabit de corpore mentis huius ni-
si gratia tua domine iesu christe. Quia ego peccator sum nimis et innumerabilia sunt delicta
mea: et non sum dignus vocari seruus tuus.
Resuscita in me domine fletum. Mollifica cor
meum durum et lapideum: et accende in me
ignem timoris tui et amoris qui cū ciuis mortis libera animam meam ab omnibus insidi-
is inimici: et conserua me in tua voluntate do-
ce me facere voluntatem tuam quia deus meus es. Tibi honor et gloria per omnia seculorum secula. Amen.

The .xv. oos in englysshe.

The .xv. oos in englysshe. Fo. Cxxiii.

O Jhesu endles swetnes of louynge soules. O Jhesu ghostly Joy passynge &
excedynge al gladnes & desyres. O Jhe
su helthe / and tender louer of all repentaūt synners / that lykest for to dwelle as thou sayd thy
selfe with ẏ chyldren of men. For that was the

Wynken de Worde produced several very handsome books in this plainer and more modern style [Pls. 87, 88]. Characteristically, in one fine example published in 1519, he illustrated the text with blocks reused from other publications. A suffrage to St Anne, for example, is illustrated with a picture whose printed border indicates that it was derived from a document, perhaps an indulgence, printed for the Gild of St Anne at Lincoln. The presence of such a local reference in this handsome volume indicated a direct and practical link between the Book of Hours and the popular religious world of the gild, the indulgence and the local pilgrimage. This same book included the collection of English and Latin prayers made by Caxton under Royal patronage in the 1490s, beginning with a translation of the popular

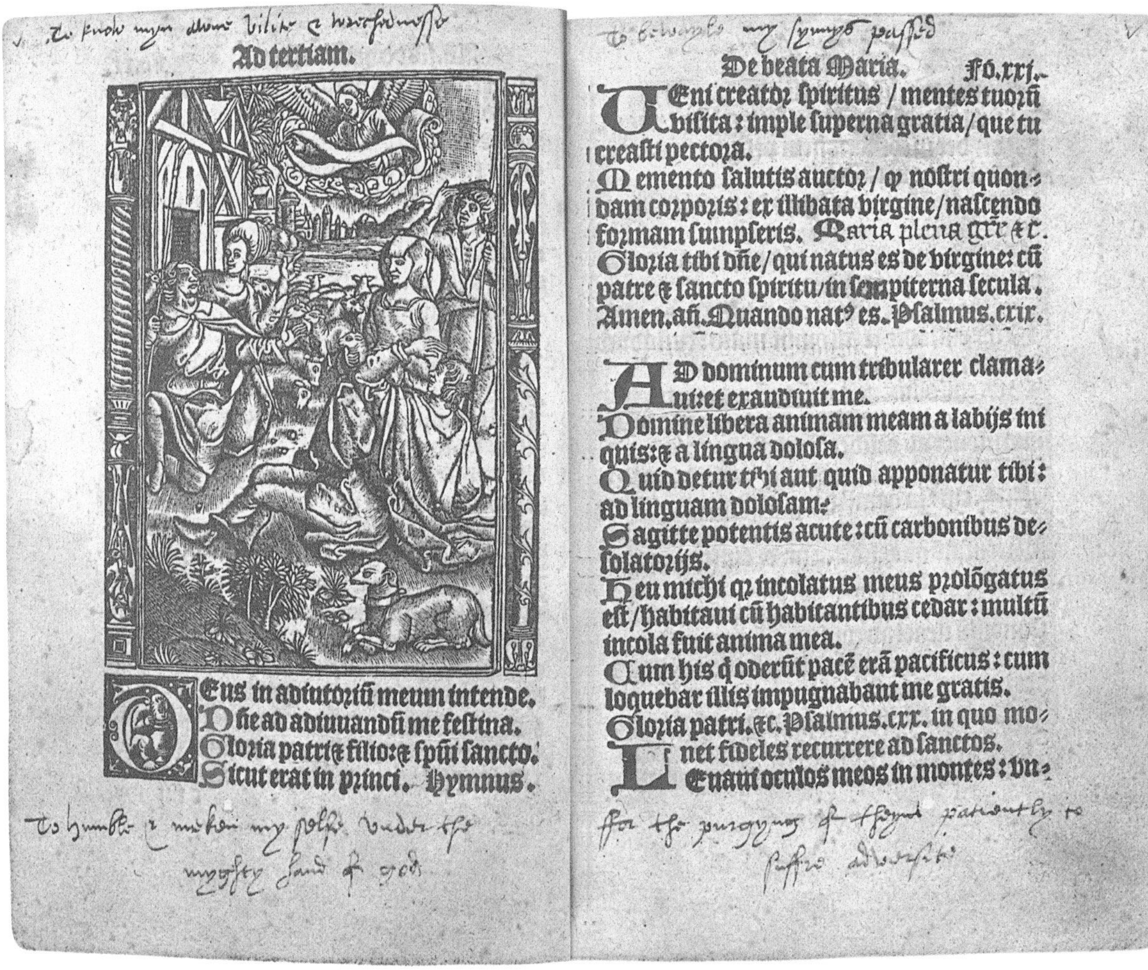

To knowe myn owne vilite & wrechednesse

Ad terciam.

Deus in adiutorium meum intende.
Domine ad adiuvandum me festina.
Gloria patri et filio: et spiritui sancto.
Sicut erat in princi. Hymnus.

To humble & meke my selfe under the myghty hand of god

To bewayle my synnys passed

De beata Maria. Fo.xxi.

Veni creator spiritus / mentes tuorum visita: imple superna gratia / que tu creasti pectora.
Memento salutis auctor / quod nostri quondam corporis: ex illibata virgine / nascendo formam sumpseris. Maria plena gratia &c.
Gloria tibi domine / qui natus es de virgine: cum patre et sancto spiritu / in sempiterna secula. Amen. an. Quando natus es. Psalmus.cxix.
Ad dominum cum tribularer clamavi: et exaudivit me.
Domine libera animam meam a labiis iniquis: et a lingua dolosa.
Quid detur tibi aut quid apponatur tibi: ad linguam dolosam.
Sagitte potentis acute: cum carbonibus desolatoriis.
Heu michi quia incolatus meus prolongatus est / habitavi cum habitantibus cedar: multum incola fuit anima mea.
Cum his qui oderunt pacem eram pacificus: cum loquebar illis impugnabant me gratis.
Gloria patri. &c. Psalmus.cxx. in quo monet fideles recurrere ad sanctos.
Levavi oculos meos in montes: un-

For the purgyng of thyne patiently to suffre adversite

89.
The Annunciation to the Shepherds, prefatory miniature to Terce, from Thomas More's Book of Hours.

RSTC 15963. Beinecke Library, Yale, Ms More Vault, fos. xx verso xxi

prayers known as the Oes of St Brigid. It was prefaced by a block depicting the saint, and the same block was to reappear the following year in the Bridgetine treatise, *The Dietary of Ghostly Helth*, a link in the other direction to Syon, one of the major powerhouses of devotional writing in early Tudor England.[7]

With so much variety in appearance and layout, no one publisher or printed edition can claim to be typical, but from the late 1520s the most prolific source of the Books of Hours flooding the bookshops on the immediate eve of the reformation was the French printing-house of François Regnault [Pls. 89, 90].[8] We have already encountered the 1530 edition of the Sarum Book of Hours taken into the Tower of London and annotated in his last imprisonment

90.
The Annunciation to the Shepherds from one of Regnault's expensive quarto editions of the Sarum Hours. The same block has been embedded within an ornate border, and an English quatrain added.

RSTC 15968 (Regnault 1530). Cambridge, Pepys Library, 1848 fo. xxxi Terce. Page size 22 × 14 cm

by Sir Thomas More, which was a characteristic Regnault product.[9] More's book was a comparatively restrained and minimalist example of its kind, its text plain and largely unornamented, its pictures few and more or less conforming to the traditional iconography. The Penitential Psalms were prefaced, as was usual, by a blockprint of the not very penitent King David watching Bathsheba as she bathes, and the Hours of the Virgin by the usual sequence of scenes from the infancy of Christ. This sequence is however broken, the usual Vespers picture of the Flight into Egypt being replaced, rather mysteriously, by a picture of the Judgement of Solomon, and the traditional Compline subjects of the Entombment of Christ or Coronation of the Virgin, being replaced

91.
The September calendar, with one of the twelve 'Ages of Man' miniatures, and moralising English quatrain, from one of Regnault's popular mid-price Sarum Hours.

STC 15973. Cambridge University Library, Syn 8 53 95, sig biij, September calendar. Page size 14 × 7 cm

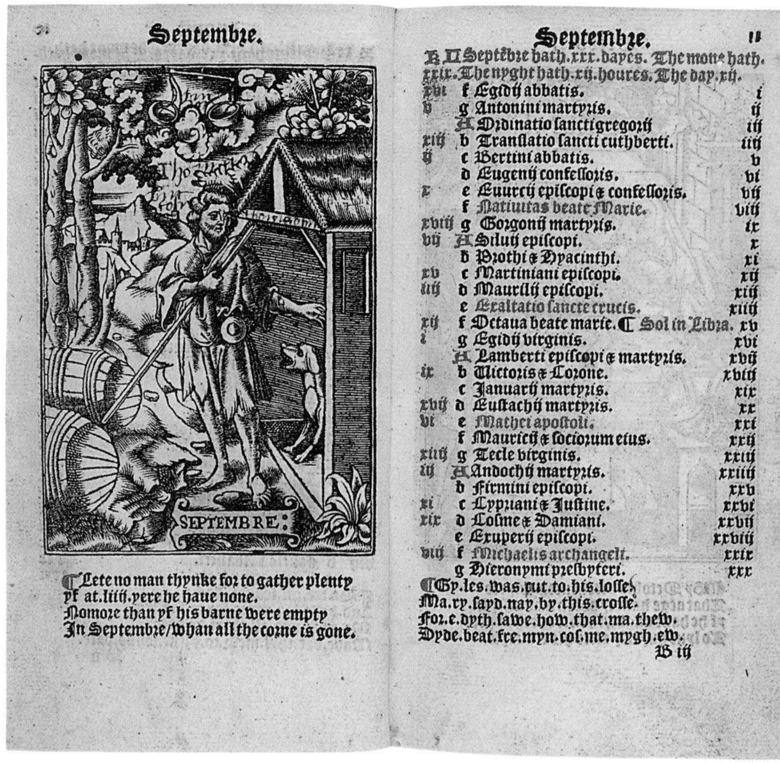

Septembre.

SEPTEMBRE:

Lete no man thynke for to gather plenty
yf at.iiii.yere he haue none.
Nomore than yf his barne were empty
In Septembre/whan all the corne is gone.

Septembre. ii

KL Septēbre hath.xxx.dayes. The mone hath.
xxix. The nyght hath.xii.houres. The day.xii.

xvi f Egidii abbatis. i
v g Antonini martyris. ii
A Ordinatio sancti gregorii iii
xiii b Translatio sancti cuthberti. iiii
ii c Bertini abbatis. v
d Eugenii confessoris. vi
x e Euurcii episcopi & confessoris. vii
f Natiuitas beate Marie. viii
xviii g Gorgonii martyris. ix
vii A Siluii episcopi. x
b Prothi & Hyacinthi. xi
xv c Martiniani episcopi. xii
iiii d Maurilii episcopi. xiii
e Exaltatio sancte crucis. xiiii
xii f Octaua beate marie. Sol in Libra. xv
i g Egidii virginis. xvi
A Lamberti episcopi & martyris. xvii
ix b Victoris & Corone. xviii
c Januarii martyris. xix
xvii d Eustachii martyris. xx
vi e Mathei apostoli. xxi
f Mauricii & sociorum eius. xxii
xiiii g Tecle virginis. xxiii
iii A Andochii martyris. xxiiii
b Firmini episcopi. xxv
xi c Cypriani & Justine. xxvi
xix d Cosme & Damiani. xxvii
e Exuperii episcopi. xxviii
viii f Michaelis archangeli. xxix
g Hieronymi presbyteri. xxx

Gy.les.was.cut.to.his.losse.
Ma.ty.sayd.nay.by.this.crosse.
For.e.dyth.sawe.how.that.ma.thew.
Dyde.beat.fre.myn.cos.me.mygh.ew.
B iii

somewhat more comprehensibly by the legendary scene of the Apostles at the funeral of the Virgin Mary.[10] This eclectic sequence is characteristic of most Regnault books of the early 1530s, with the same choice of themes, and often the same blocks, being used across the price-range.[11]

As well as being sparingly illustrated, More's book has relatively few additional prayers and devotions, with little more over and above the usual Hours, Psalms, Suffrages and Litanies, than the Fifteen Oes of St Brigid and the long English 'Form of Confession' designed to help the penitent confess his sins fully and devoutly.[12]

The compact *Horae* which Regnault produced the following year was perhaps more typical – issued in both plain and deluxe editions (the latter on vellum) it was lavishly illustrated throughout, and apart from the Oes of St Brigid, which were printed in Latin only, it contained the usual range of vernacular texts, including the doggerel verse 'Dayes of the week moralised', Jean Quentin's 'The Manner to live well', the popular summary of the faith known as 'The verytees

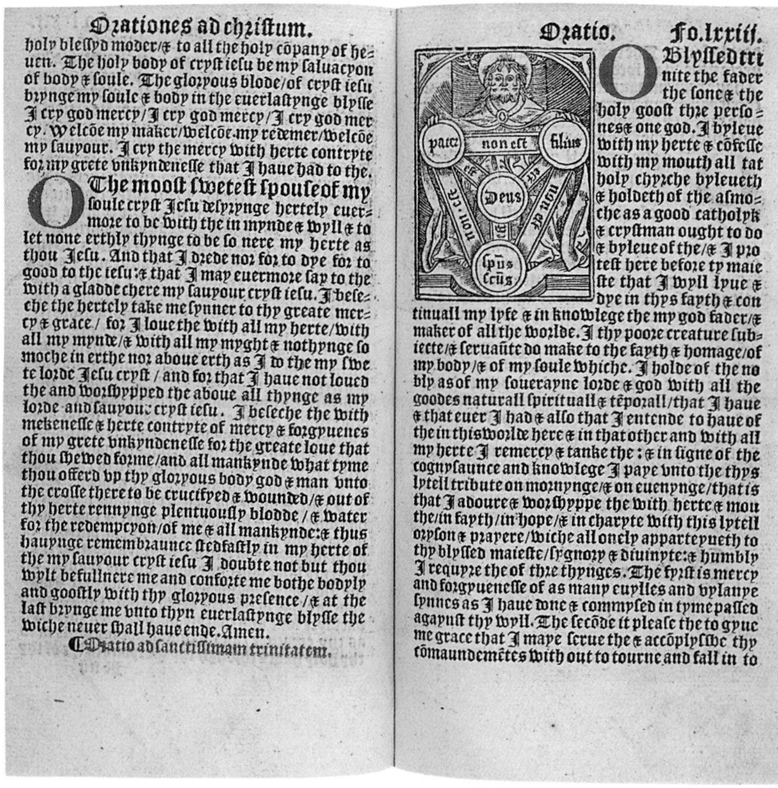

Orationes ad christum.

holy blessyd moder/& to all the holy cõpany of heuen. The holy body of cryst iesu be my saluacyon of body & soule. The gloryous blode/of cryst iesu brynge my soule & body in the euerlastynge blysse I cry god mercy/I cry god mercy/I cry god mercy. Welcõe my maker/welcõe my redemer/welcõe my sauyour. I cry the mercy with herte contryte for my grete vnkyndenesse that I haue had to the.

O The moost swetest spouse of my soule cryst Jesu desyrynge hertely euermore to be with the in mynde & wyll & to let none erthly thynge to be so nere my herte as thou Jesu. And that I drede nor for to dye for to good to the iesu: & that I may euermore say to the with a gladde chere my sauyour cryst iesu. I beseche the hertely take me synner to thy greate mercy & grace/ for I loue the with all my herte/with all my mynde/& with all my myght & nothynge so moche in erthe nor aboue erth as I do the my swete lorde Jesu cryst / and for that I haue not loued the and worshypped the aboue all thynge as my lorde and sauyour cryst iesu. I beseche the with mekenesse & herte contryte of mercy & forgyuenes of my grete vnkyndenesse for the greate loue that thou shewed for me/and all mankynde what tyme thou offerd vp thy gloryous body god & man vnto the crosse there to be crucifyed & wounded/& out of thy herte rennynge plentuously blodde / & water for the redempcyon/of me & all mankynde: & thus hauynge remembraunce stedfastly in my herte of the my sauyour cryst iesu I doubte not but thou wylt be fullnere me and conforte me bothe bodyly and goostly with thy gloryous presence / & at the last brynge me vnto thyn euerlastynge blysse the whiche neuer shall haue ende. Amen.

Oratio ad sanctissimam trinitatem.

Oratio. Fo.lxxiij.

O Blyssed trinite the fader the sone & the holy goost thre persones & one god. I byleue with my herte & cõfesse with my mouth all tat holy chyrche byleueth & holdeth of the asmoche as a good catholyk & crystman ought to do & byleue of the/& I protest here before ty maieste that I wyll lyue & dye in thys fayth & continuall my lyfe & in knowlege the my god fader/& maker of all the worlde. I thy poore creature subiecte/& seruaũte do make to the fayth & homage/of my body/& of my soule whiche. I holde of the nobly as of my soueraygne lorde & god with all the goodes naturall spirituall & tẽporall/that I haue & that euer I had & also that I entende to haue of the in this worlde here & in that other and with all my herte I remercy & tanke the: & in signe of the cognysaunce and knowlege I paye vnto the thys lytell tribute on mornynge/& on euenynge/that is that I adoure & worshyppe the with herte & mouthe/in fayth/in hope/& in charyte with this lytell oryson & prayere/wiche all onely appartenyneth to thy blyssed maieste/sygnory & diuinyte: & humbly I requyre the of thre thynges. The fyrst is mercy and forgyuenesse of as many euylles and vylanye synnes as I haue done & commysed in tyme passed agaynst thy wyll. The secõde it please the to gyue me grace that I maye serue the & accõplysshe thy cõmaundemẽtes with out to tourne and fall in to

92.
Regnault's mid-price and cheap editions were notable for the extensive vernacular material they contained. Here the usual group of prayers for a holy death are illustrated with a diagrammatic miniature of the Trinity [cf. frontispiece].

RSTC 15973 (Regnault 1531). Cambridge University Library, Syn 8 53 95, fo. lxxiij. Page size 14 × 7 cm

of Mayster John Gerson', and the ubiquitous guide to the sacrament of penance 'The Form of Confession' [Pls. 91, 92].

By 1530, therefore, those popular prayers and indulgences which owners of manuscript books had been copying into their books over the preceding century had become part of a standardised repertoire. In prayer as in other aspects of personal taste there were fashions, and the purchasers of prayer-books expected state of the art provision for their money. Market demand meant that the content of the Book of Hours had had to expand, as purchasers sought more colourful and more varied devotions, indulgences and miraculous promises, many of them now explained in English, and designed to assist and comfort in the face of life's calamities – plague, natural disaster, or the threat of sudden death. But in the early Tudor period this additional material in addition to devotions drawn from an inherited pool of medieval prayers, also routinely included moral and instructional material of the kind just noted, as well as a new feature, Latin psalm and scriptural paraphrases, adapted as prayers for various situations

93.
In this up-market book issued by Regnault, the so-called 'Charlemagne Prayer', here an exotic address to the Cross, is prefaced by a miraculous rubric promising blessings for all who simply carry the prayer around, and an indulgence of eleven years, together with preservation from sudden death, for its daily recitation. Only the title of the Pope has been defaced in this rubric.

RSTC 15968 (Regnault 1530). Cambridge Pepys Library, 1848 fo. lxv. Page size 22 × 14 cm

94.
In Regnault's mid and cheap-price range the miraculous rubrics normal before prayers of the 'Charlemagne' type, like this invocation of the names of God, have been omitted. These books also contain more vernacular material than the more expensive editions, though the English material is religiously conservative in content.

STC 15973 (Regnault 1531). Cambridge University Library, Syn 8 53 95, fo. cl. Page size 14 × 7 cm

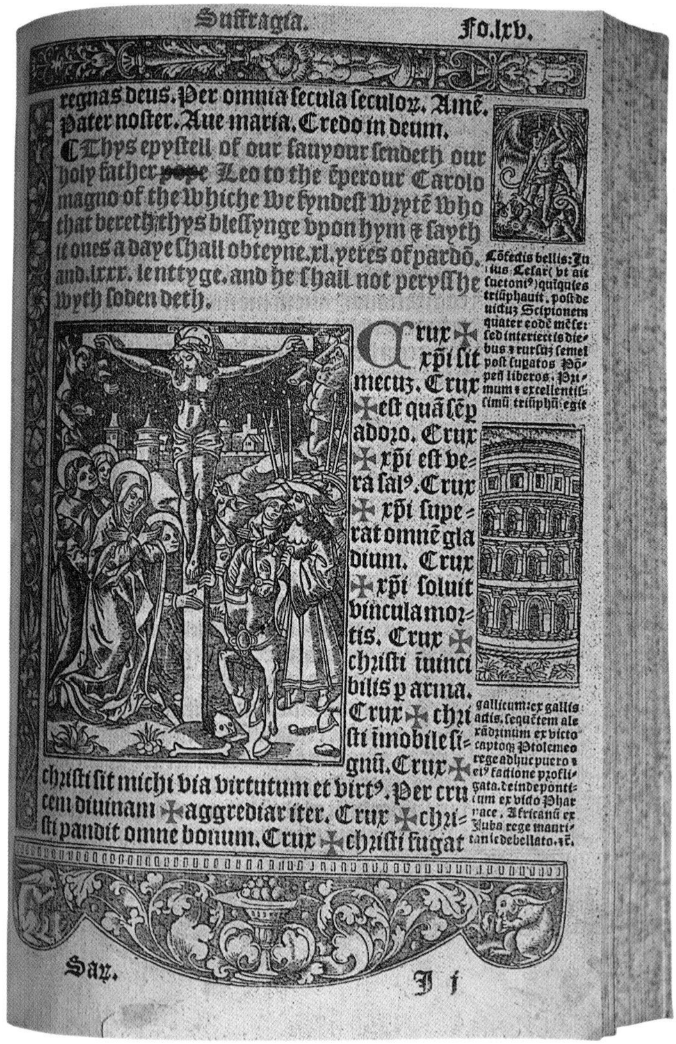
Suffragia. Fo.lxv.

regnas deus. Per omnia secula seculor. Amē. Pater noster. Aue maria. Credo in deum.

¶ Thys epystell of our sauyour sendeth our holy father ~~pope~~ Leo to the eperour Carolo magno of the whiche we fyndest wrytē who that bereth thys blessynge vpon hym & sayth it ones a daye shall obteyne .xl. yeres of pardō. and .lxxx. lenttyge. and he shall not perysshe wyth soden deth.

Crux ✠ xpi sit mecū. Crux ✠ est quā sep adoro. Crux ✠ xpi est vera sal9. Crux ✠ xpi superat omnē gladium. Crux ✠ xpi soluit vincula mortis. Crux ✠ christi inuincibilis p arma. Crux ✠ christi imobile signū. Crux ✠ christi sit michi via virtutum et virt9. Per crucem diuinam ✠ aggrediar iter. Crux ✠ christi pandit omne bonum. Crux ✠ christi fugat

Sar. I i

and problems, or more extended devotions to the Blessed Sacrament or Christ in his Passion. When, under reformed influence in the later 1530s, the Book of Hours finally moved decisively towards the vernacular, translations of these longer occasional or vocational prayers would help give the books a distinctive moralistic and discursive character, absent from their slimmer late medieval prototypes.[13] But already in the early sixteenth century the Latin versions of such prayers were often preceded by lengthy English explanatory rubrics which guided the user to the meaning of the Latin text, and which anticipated that mid-Tudor moralising devotional tone

De nominibus dei.

O Mnipotēs ✠ domin9 ✠ xps ✠ messias ✠ soter ✠ emanuel ✠ sabaoth ✠ adonai ✠ vnigenit9 ✠ via ✠ vita ✠ man9 ✠ homousion ✠ saluator ✠ alpha & oo ✠ fons ✠ origo ✠ spes ✠ fides ✠ charitas ✠ osa ✠ agn9 ✠ ouis ✠ vitul9 ✠ serpēs ✠ aries ✠ leo ✠ vmis ✠ primus ✠ nouissim9 ✠ rex ✠ pat ✠ filius ✠ spūssctūs ✠ ego sum q sum ✠ creator ✠ eternus ✠ redēptor ✠ trinitas ✠ vnitas ✠ clemēs ✠ caput ✠ o theotheos ✠ tetragrammaton ✠ Ista noīa me protegant et defendāt & ab omni aduersitate plaga & infirmitate corporis & anime plene liberēt/et assistāt michi in auxilium. Ista nomina regum videlicet/Jaspar/Melchior/Balthasar/& duodecim apostoli domini nostri Jesu christi: quorum nomina sunt hec. Petr9/Paulus/Andreas/Jacobus/Philippus/Jacobus/Simon/Thadeus/Thomas/Bartholomeus. Et quatuor euangeliste quorum nomina sunt hec. Marc9/Matheus/Lucas/Johānes: michi assistant in omnibus necessitatibus meis: ac me defendant & liberent ab omnib9 periculis tentationibus & angustijs corporis & anime: & ab vniuersis malis presentibus preteritis et futuris me custodiant nunc et in euum. Amen. Oratio.

Oratio. Fo. cl.

O Domine iesu xpe in tuam protectionem me indignū famulū tuum vel famulā tuam N. hodie & omni tēpore committo: & in protectionem angelorum & archangelorum: et in protectionem apostolorū/prophetarum/martyrū/confessorū/& virginū: & in ptectionē omnium sanctorū tuorū: tali commissione qua commisisti sanctam virginem mariā matrem tuā/sancto iohanni euangeliste in cruce. Taliter me indignū famulū tuū vel famulā tuā N. hodie & omni tempore custodire/benedicere/protegere & saluare digneris a subitanea et improuisa morte/& ab omni fantasmate diabolico/& ab omnibus hostibus malis visibilibus & inuisibilibus. Amen.

A deuout prayer to Jesu cryst.

O My soueraygne lorde Jesu/the veray sone of almyghty god/& of the moost clene & gloryous vyrgyn Mary/that suffred the bytter deth for my sake & all mankynde vpon goost fryday/& rose agayne the thyrde daye. I beseche the lorde haue mercy vpon me that am a wreched synner but yet thy creature. And for thy precyous passyon saue me & kepe me from all peryles bothe bodyly & goostly/and specyally from all tynges that myght tourne thy dyspleasure/& with all my herte I thanke the moost mercyfull lorde for thy grete mercyes that thou hast shewed me in te greate daūgers that I haue ben in/as well in my soule/as in my body. And that thy grace & endles mercy hath euer kept me/spared me & saued me fro the houre of my byrthe vnto this tyme. I beseche the lorde that thy mercy may kepe me for the alwaye/and I cry the mercy with all my hole herte for my grete offenses/for my grete vnkyndenesse/& for all my wretched and synfull lyfe/& that I can not lede my lyfe as thy seruaunt I cry the mercy. U.ij

This prayer following is the prayer of the sinful King Manasses, that shed the blood of Innocents and of Prophets, and did many other sins, as Scripture witnesseth, more than any other that was afore him or after followyng, reigning. And yet after all this, he besought God of mercy entirely, and did penance, and had mercy . . . *Oracio devota Mannasses regis filii regis Ezechie . . .*

This prayer following is for them that intend to be married, or be new married, to pray God that they

> may live together singularly, and finally to bring forth fruit betwixt them two, as the younger Thobie did and Sara his wife . . . *Oratio Thobie junioris et sara Uxor eius . . .*[14]

To turn the pages of most of these early printed Books of Hours, however, is to be struck not so much by their seriousness and moralism, as by their supernaturalism. The headings and rubrics in Latin and in English indicate the range of prayers on offer

> A prayer for carnal delectation . . . a prayer for very penance . . . against evil thoughts . . . for wayfaring men . . . for thy friend that is dead . . . Two little prayers that King Harry the sixth made . . . two short prayers taught by our Lady to St Brygytte . . . a prayer against thunder and tempest shewed by an angel to St Edward . . . a prayer against the pestilence.

And in many books these fairly restrained supernatural attributions blossom into the sort of devotional luxuriance we have already encountered in manuscript additions to Books of Hours [Pls. 93, 94]:

> This prayer showed our Lady to a devout person, saying that this golden prayer is the most sweetest and acceptablest to me, and in her appearing she had this salutation and prayer written with letters of gold in her breast: *Ave rosa sine spinis . . .*
>
> This prayer was showed unto St Augustine by revelation of the Holy Ghost, and who that devoutly say this prayer, or hear her read, or heareth about them shall not perish by fire or water, neither in battle nor in judgement. And he shall die no sudden death, and no venom shall poison him that day. And what he asketh of God he shall obtain if it be to the salvation of his soul, and when thy soul shall depart from thy body it shall not enter hell. Oratio, *Deus propitius esto mihi peccatori . . .*[15]

This supernatural sensationalism was, in print at least, a distinctively English phenomenon. European bishops seem to have ensured that 'superstitious' material of this sort, common everywhere in manuscript additions, did not find their way into printed editions of lay

This prymer of Salysbury vse is set out a long wout ony serchyng / with many prayers/and goodly pyctures in the kalēder/in the matyns of our lady/in the houres of the crosse/in the. vij. psalmes/and in the dyryge. And be newly enprynted at Parys. M.ccccc.xxxi.

God be in my hede
And in myn vnderstandynge.
God be in myn eyen
And in my lokynge
God be in my mouth
And in my spekynge.
God be in my herte
And in my thynkynge.
God be at myn ende
And at my departynge.
Sar. Ai

95. SALES TALK
The title-page of this popular mid-priced Book of Hours by Regnault advertises its simplicity of use ('set out a long without ony serchyng'), its 'many prayers and goodly pictures', and provides a sample of each for the bookshop browser, in the block-print of the Virgin and her titles, and the English prayer 'God be in my head'.

STC 15973 (Regnault 1531). Cambridge University Library, Syn 8 53 95, title-page. Page size 14 × 7 cm

prayer-books.[16] By contrast, the English hierarchy seem to have exercised little control over the publishers (unsurprisingly, since many of the books for the English market were printed in France or the Low Countries) and books printed for the English market routinely include far more of this legendary material and lavish indulgences than the corresponding books produced for French dioceses, even when issued by the same publisher, using many of the same blocks. Into the late 1520s, the title-pages and colophons of Sarum Books of Hours vie with each other to promise more, better and more beautiful prayers, more plentiful indulgences, handsomer illustrations, as well as greater ease of navigation through the rubrics [Pl. 95].

> This Prymer of Salisbury Use is set out along without any searching, with many prayers and goodly pictures in the calendar, in the matyns of our lady, in the Hours of the Cross, in the vii psalms and in the dyryge.[17]

This supernaturalism in early Tudor English piety went all the way to the top. One commonly included item in these printed books for England was an indulgence to be gained by saying three Hail Maries when the Angelus bell rang. The accompanying rubric informed the devout reader that the indulgence had been secured from Sixtus IV:

> at the instance of the high and most excellent princess Elizabeth, late Queen of England and wife to our sovereign liege lord King Harry the seventh, God have mercy on her sweet soul and all Christian souls.[18]

The printed rubric here deliberately evokes and offers wider access to the devout intimacies and courtesies which we noticed in our first chapter as a feature of the early Tudor court, and this same Elizabeth of York had been in the habit of giving or at any rate autographing Books of Hours as a token of esteem for favoured courtiers. By extension, in this printed indulgence rubric such royal devotional largesse was made available even to shopkeepers and merchants.

As this Angelus devotion suggests, devotional change on the eve of the reformation was by no means all in a sensational direction. As we have seen, there were quieter and deeper appetites to be nourished too, and the market duly catered for them. From the mid-fifteenth century we find more prayers in English being copied into manuscript primers, and by the 1490s, several of these vernacular favourites were incorporated by William Caxton in a devotional pamphlet under the patronage of the Queen and the Queen Mother.[19] This selection, which included material we have already encountered in the Talbot Hours, was subsequently incorporated into an influential printed primer issued by Wynkyn de Worde in 1494, according to the colophon at the instigation of Lady Margaret Beaufort.[20] Vernacular material used in printed *Horae*, however, was not confined to this Caxton/de Worde selection, and continental publishers in particular clearly drew on other sources. This varied vernacular material, as might be expected, often included the Fifteen Oes of St Brigid, set of prayers based on the seven last words of Christ on the Cross, popular both in Latin and English,[21] and most books also included a very popular set of deathbed prayers, and prayers of invocation to the Blessed Sacrament supplicating for the grace of a happy death.[22] Strikingly churchly in their insistence on the importance of religious orthodoxy and the indispensability of the reception of the last sacraments, these deathbed prayers were the tip of an iceberg, a body of longer English prayers copied and recopied into fifteenth century Books of Hours, now finding their way into print.

The increasing occurrence of prayers of this sort on the flyleaves and blanks of manuscript Hours, and their inclusion in the contents of printed *Horae*, certainly suggests growing lay seriousness and interiority, and it might be tempting to see them as indicators of the emergence of a proto-protestant sensibility, preparing the ground for the reformation. But this would be a mistaken conclusion. Most of these prayers are straightforward translations of Latin prayers which had long been in circulation, and most are resolutely ecclesial in their emphasis, part of the same trend which saw the inclusion or copying into books of items like the long 'Form of Confession' which leads the user through an examination of conscience based round the seven deadly sins and ten commandments. A version of this 'Form of Confession' had been copied into the fifteenth-century Bolton Hours.[23] Anne Withypole copied it into her manuscript Book of Hours,[24] and from the 1520s it became a routine item in printed books – as we have already noted, Thomas More's printed Book of Hours of 1530 contained it.[25] So we should not imagine the users of these prayers retreating into some proto-protestant retreat from institutional Christianity, but instead using the prayers to help them prepare themselves for worthy reception of the Catholic sacraments.

It is also worth recalling here that manuscript and printed Books of Hours coexisted for several generations after the advent of print, and the traffic between them was by no means all in one direction. As we have seen, printed books were often decorated to look like manuscripts, and manuscripts were expanded to include material culled from printed books, many households possessing and using both alongside each other. Anne Withypole had both a printed and a manuscript book of hours, and she added extra material to both of them. Thomas More used a printed book of hours: his son John, on the other hand used a manuscript book of the fifteenth century, now in the Bamberg diocesan museum.[26] Almost without exception, any printed Book of Hours had more prayers, devotions and indulgences than any older manuscript book: so people using manuscript books often copied material encountered in print into them, like the English prayers for a holy death mentioned earlier, or prayers to the Blessed Sacrament, or longer texts like the 'Form of Confession'. Even the seasonal doggerel rhymes which appear at the foot of the calendar illustrations in the very popular editions produced by François Regnault[27] might be considered desirable additions to the calendar of manuscript prayer-books. The owner of a manuscript Book of Hours now in the Leeds University Library duly copied these rhymes into its calendar, presumably from a printed exemplar like this one, borrowed from friends or family.[28]

9

THE BREAK WITH ROME

The expansion of the appetite and market for indulgenced prayers which I have been describing was brought to a sudden halt by the break with Rome in 1534. With the advent of Protestantism in England, it became inevitable that the Books of Hours would become a battleground. Structured round a set of offices in honour of the Virgin and the *Dirige* for the Dead, and larded with prayers to the saints and indulgenced devotions, such books were bound to become a reformed target, precisely because their use was so widespread. In 1534 the protestant propagandist and controversial writer William Marshall had produced an aggressively protestant Primer or Book of Hours under Cromwell's patronage, denouncing the 'infinite errors and perilous prayers' of the older books 'garnished with glorious titles and red letters, promising much grace and many years, days and lents of pardon'.[1] Unsurprisingly, his Primer was drastically reformed, and omitted altogether many of the traditional features of the primer, such as the Litany of the Saints and the Office for the Dead.[2] Marshall's book provoked vigorous reaction, but he called for further 'sharp reformation' of lay prayers, and in 1539 John Hilsey, Bishop of Rochester produced an official Primer in English and Latin, which, though more conservative than Marshall's, nevertheless aimed to offer an officially approved form of prayers purged of at least the worst features of popery. The calendar was drastically pruned of saints, the Litany was shortened to exclude

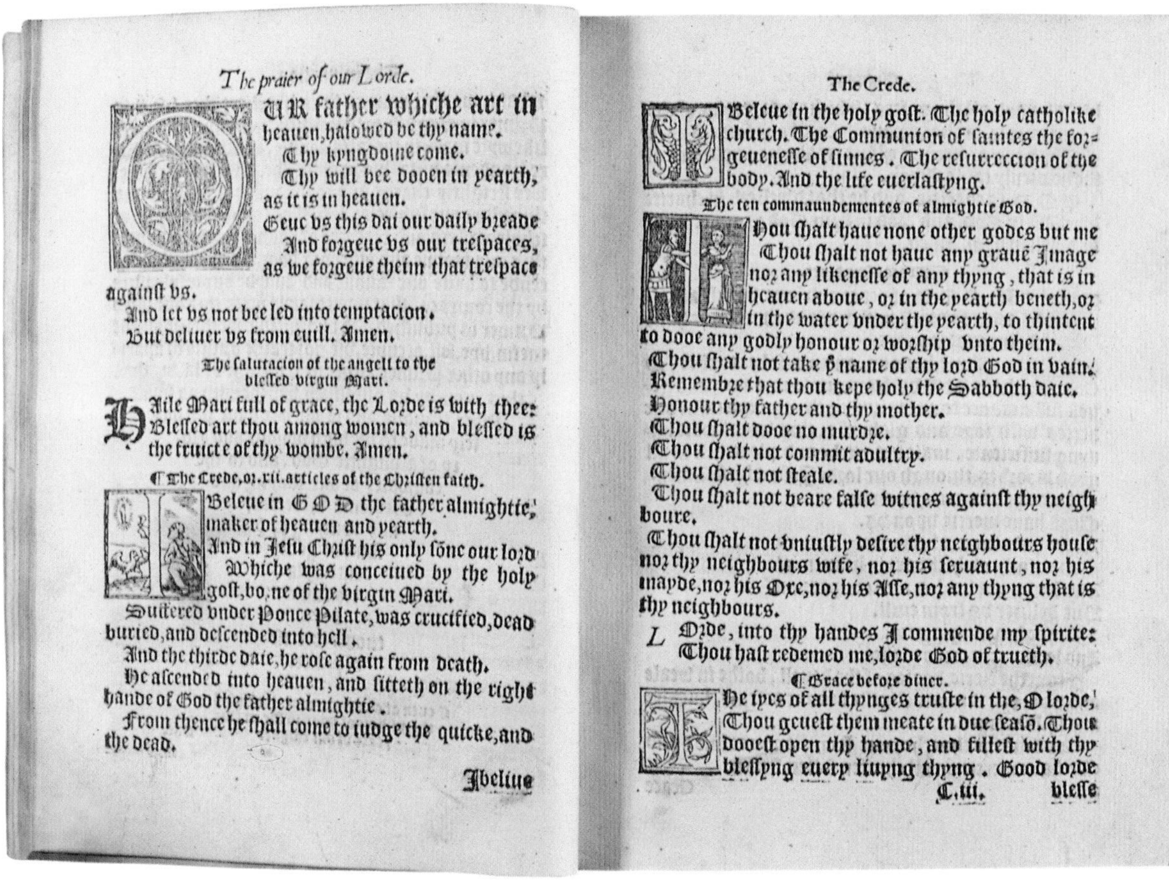
The praier of our Lorde.

OUR father whiche art in heauen, halowed be thy name.
Thy kyngdome come.
Thy will bee doen in yearth, as it is in heauen.
Geue vs this dai our daily breade
And forgeue vs our trespaces, as we forgeue theim that trespace against vs.
And let vs not bee led into temptacion.
But deliuer vs from euill. Amen.

The salutacion of the angell to the blessed virgin Mari.

HAile Mari full of grace, the Lorde is with thee: Blessed art thou among women, and blessed is the fruicte of thy wombe. Amen.

The Crede, or .xii. articles of the Christen faith.

I Beleue in GOD the father almightie, maker of heauen and yearth. And in Jesu Christ his only sone our lord Whiche was conceiued by the holy gost, borne of the virgin Mari. Suffered vnder Ponce Pilate, was crucified, dead buried, and descended into hell. And the thirde daie, he rose again from death. He ascended into heauen, and sitteth on the right hande of God the father almightie. From thence he shall come to iudge the quicke, and the dead.

Ibeliue

The Crede.

I Beleue in the holy gost. The holy catholike church. The Communion of saintes the forgeuenesse of sinnes. The resurreccion of the body. And the life euerlastyng.

The ten commaundementes of almightie God.

Thou shalt haue none other godes but me
Thou shalt not haue any grauē Image nor any likenesse of any thyng, that is in heauen aboue, or in the yearth beneth, or in the water vnder the yearth, to thintent to doe any godly honour or worship vnto theim.
Thou shalt not take ỹ name of thy lord God in vain.
Remembre that thou kepe holy the Sabboth daie.
Honour thy father and thy mother.
Thou shalt doe no murdre.
Thou shalt not commit adultry.
Thou shalt not steale.
Thou shalt not beare false witnes against thy neighboure.
Thou shalt not vniustly desire thy neighbours house nor thy neighbours wife, nor his seruaunt, nor his mayde, nor his Oxe, nor his Asse, nor any thyng that is thy neighbours.

L Orde, into thy handes I commende my spirite: Thou hast redemed me, lorde God of trueth.

Grace before diner.

The iyes of all thynges truste in the, O lorde, Thou geuest them meate in due seasō. Thou doest open thy hande, and fillest with thy blessyng euery liuyng thyng. Good lorde

C.iii. blesse

96.
Henry VIII's official Primer of 1545 was designed to replace all other Books of Hours. It contained reformed and shortened versions of the traditional hours, and a wide selection of vernacular material, including, as here, the Lord's Prayer, Hail Mary, Creed, commandments (in a protestant version emphasising the evils of image-worship) and Grace before and after meals.

King's Primer 1545 (Magdalene College Old Library, this copy not in RSTC) sigs cii(verso)–ciii

non-biblical saints, while the invocations of Mary herself were all but suppressed: even the famous Marian prayer *Salve Regina Mater Misericordiae* became 'Hail Holy King Father of Mercy', having been rewritten to address Christ rather than the Virgin. Hilsey also added a good deal of instructional and hortatory material, including a lengthy exposition of the Ten Commandments.[3] This reforming impulse would culminate in 1545 in the issue of an official Royal Primer, designed to replace all others, and much more markedly protestant than Hilsey's in character [Pls. 96, 97].[4]

The development of these reformed primers has been thoroughly studied, and is not our concern here.[5] What has received less attention is the impact of these changes on the users of more traditional Books of Hours, and the traces they left in those books themselves,

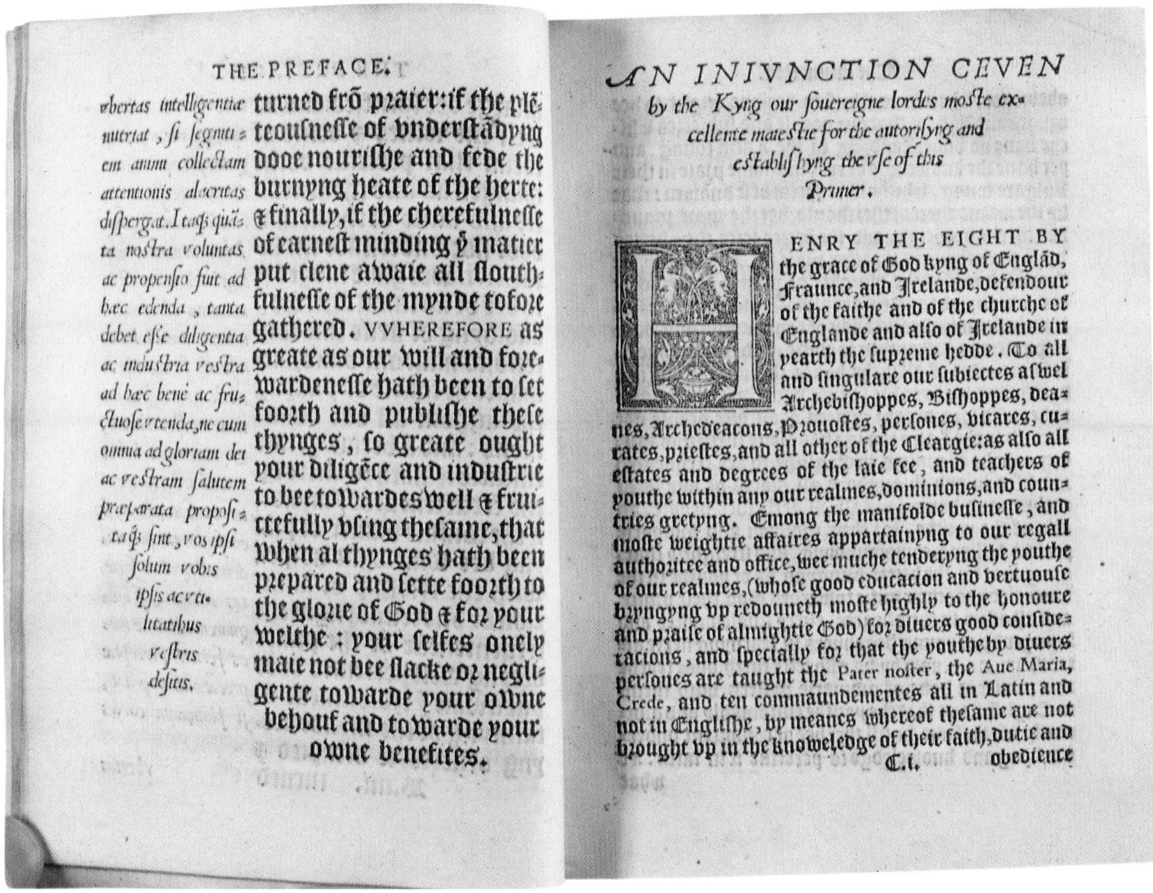
THE PREFACE.

vbertas intelligentiae nutriat, si segnitiem animi collectam attentionis alacritas dispergat. Itaque quanta nostra voluntas ac propensio fuit ad haec edenda, tanta debet esse diligentia ac industria vestra ad haec bene ac fructuose vertenda, ne cum omnia ad gloriam dei ac vestram salutem praeparata proposita sint, vos ipsi solum vobis ipsis ac vtilitatibus vestris defuitis.

turned frō praier: if the plēteousnesse of vnderstādyng dooe nourishe and fede the burnyng heate of the herte: & finally, if the cherefulnesse of earnest mindyng ỳ matier put clene awaie all slouthfulnesse of the mynde tofore gathered. VVHEREFORE as greate as our will and forwardenesse hath been to set foorth and publishe these thynges, so greate ought your diligēce and industrie to bee towardes well & fruictefully vsing thesame, that when al thynges hath been prepared and sette foorth to the glorie of God & for your welthe: your selfes onely maie not bee slacke or negligente towarde your owne behouf and towarde your owne benefites.

AN INIVNCTION GEVEN by the Kyng our soueraigne lordes moste excellente maiestie for the autorisyng and establishyng the vse of this Primer.

HENRY THE EIGHT BY the grace of God kyng of Englād, Fraunce, and Irelande, defendour of the faithe and of the churche of Englande and also of Irelande in yearth the supreme hedde. To all and singulare our subiectes aswel Archebishoppes, Bishoppes, deanes, Archedeacons, Prouostes, persones, vicares, curates, priestes, and all other of the Cleargie: as also all estates and degrees of the laie fee, and teachers of youthe within any our realmes, dominions, and countries gretyng. Emong the manifolde businesse, and moste weightie affaires appartainyng to our regall authoritee and office, wee muche tenderyng the youthe of our realmes, (whose good educacion and vertuouse bryngyng vp redouneth moste highly to the honoure and praise of almightie God) for diuers good consideracions, and specially for that the youthe by diuers persones are taught the Pater noster, the Aue Maria, Crede, and ten commaundementes all in Latin and not in Englishe, by meanes whereof thesame are not brought vp in the knoweledge of their faith, dutie and obedience

C.i.

97.
The Royal Injunction prefixed to the 1545 Primer imposing the use of the official book and criticising the traditional use of Latin in prayer.

King's Primer 1545 (Magdalene College Old Library, this copy not in RSTC) sig ci

and it is with that impact we will be concerned in the rest of what follows. We may start with two royal proclamations: the first is of 9 June 1535, enforcing the statute abolishing Papal authority in England and calling on the ecclesiastical authorities to cause

> all manner prayers, orisons, rubrics, canons in mass-books and all other books used in churches, wherein the said bishop of Rome is named or his presumptuous and proud pomp and authority preferred, utterly to be abolished, eradicated and erased out.[6]

One immediate consequence of this proclamation was that printed Books of Hours larded with papal indulgences immediately became illegal, and the market for them therefore dried up. The book trade responded promptly to the challenge. Though the Pope's name was now a dangerous embarrassment, people still wanted traditional Books of Hours. From 1536 French publishers including François Regnault, whose handsome and very varied editions adapted to all pockets had increasingly dominated the market over the previous decade, began producing Latin and English Books of Hours with a full parallel text, in which English now predominated, yet which contained most of the favourite prayers included in Books of Hours in the 1520s. The prayers were unchanged, but were however pruned of all indulgence rubrics, and all miraculous promises. Most of these books included rationalising editorial material which reveals unease about the theological implications of traditional devotional practices such as praying for the dead, an unease made more explicit as time went on. A preface to these 'pruned' primers, first introduced by the publisher Robert Redman in 1535, criticised the application to the Virgin of texts referring properly to Christ, and versions of this preface were included in most successive editions of the Sarum *Horae*, till a Royal proclamation in November 1538 made controversial marginal annotations and prologues in devotional books illegal.[7] Between 1535 and 1538 this sort of editorial intervention was reformist but moderate in tone, and nervously shadowed royal policy. From 1537 the *Dirige* carried a preface explaining the non-apostolic origin of the custom of prayer for the dead, but asserting that the service might legitimately be used since 'all that is contained therein, the collects except, may as well be applied for the living as for the dead'. In any case, the editor continued 'I think it very charitable . . . that we use any worldly obsequies about the dead or pray for them.'[8] Considerable obscurity surrounds the precise editorship of these books.[9] It is noteworthy that François Regnault preferred to substitute non-controversial vernacular material such as the *Maner to Live Well* for this more strident editorial matter, no doubt a reflection of the largely conservative opinions of his target customers. Regnault was also the printer of a Latin and English edition of Coverdale's Bible, but he was a businessman, not a Protestant, and all these English primers were in substance Catholic books. In due course, pruned of reformist editorial intrusions, they were to be used in Queen Mary's reign as the basis for the official Catholic Books of Hours sponsored by her regime [Pl. 98].[10]

The November 1538 proclamation which banned controversial

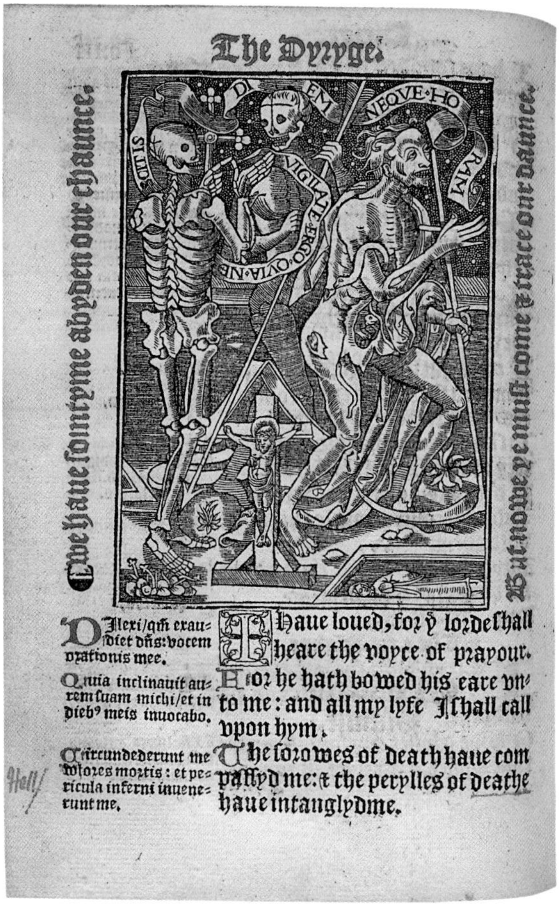

The Dyrige.

We haue somtyme abyden our chaunce,

But nowe ye must come & trace our daunce.

Dilexi/qm exaudiet dns:vocem orationis mee.

I haue loued, for ẏ lorde shall heare the voyce of prayour.

Quia inclinauit aurem suam michi/et in dieb9 meis inuocabo.

For he hath bowed his eare vnto me: and all my lyfe I shall call vpon hym.

Circumdederunt me dolores mortis: et pericula inferni inuenerunt me.

The sorowes of death haue compassyd me: & the perylles of deathe haue intanglyd me.

98.
After the break with Rome Books of Hours with traditional content went on being produced for England but with all indulgences removed. The text of the Hours was translated into English, with the Latin text relegated to the margins, and the new books carried a reforming preface criticising traditional piety, in particular excessive devotion to the Virgin Mary. This edition, printed in Rouen in 1536, has Renaissance versions of much of the traditional iconography, as here, a gruesome detail from the 'Three Living and the Three Dead', before the Office of the Dead.

RSTC 15993. Cambridge University Library, Syn 7 53 19, 'Dirige'. Page size 15 × 9 cm

marginalia and prefaces also demanded that all images of Thomas Becket should be destroyed, and that all offices, antiphons and prayers in his name should be 'erased and put out of all the books'.[11] Like the 1535 proclamation, these provisions were aimed in the first place at public service books – the breviaries, missals and antiphonaries used in church. In these public books, the royal command was observed with varying degrees of thoroughness.[12] But as we have seen, Books of Hours, though designed for private prayer, were also undoubtedly books 'used in churches', so to a quite startling extent this process of censorship was extended into the private prayer-life of the laity. The overwhelming majority of surviving manuscript and printed Books of Hours show that most Tudor devotees dutifully blotted, scraped or sliced the Pope and St Thomas Becket out of their devotions: indeed, the absence of such deletions is a reasonably safe

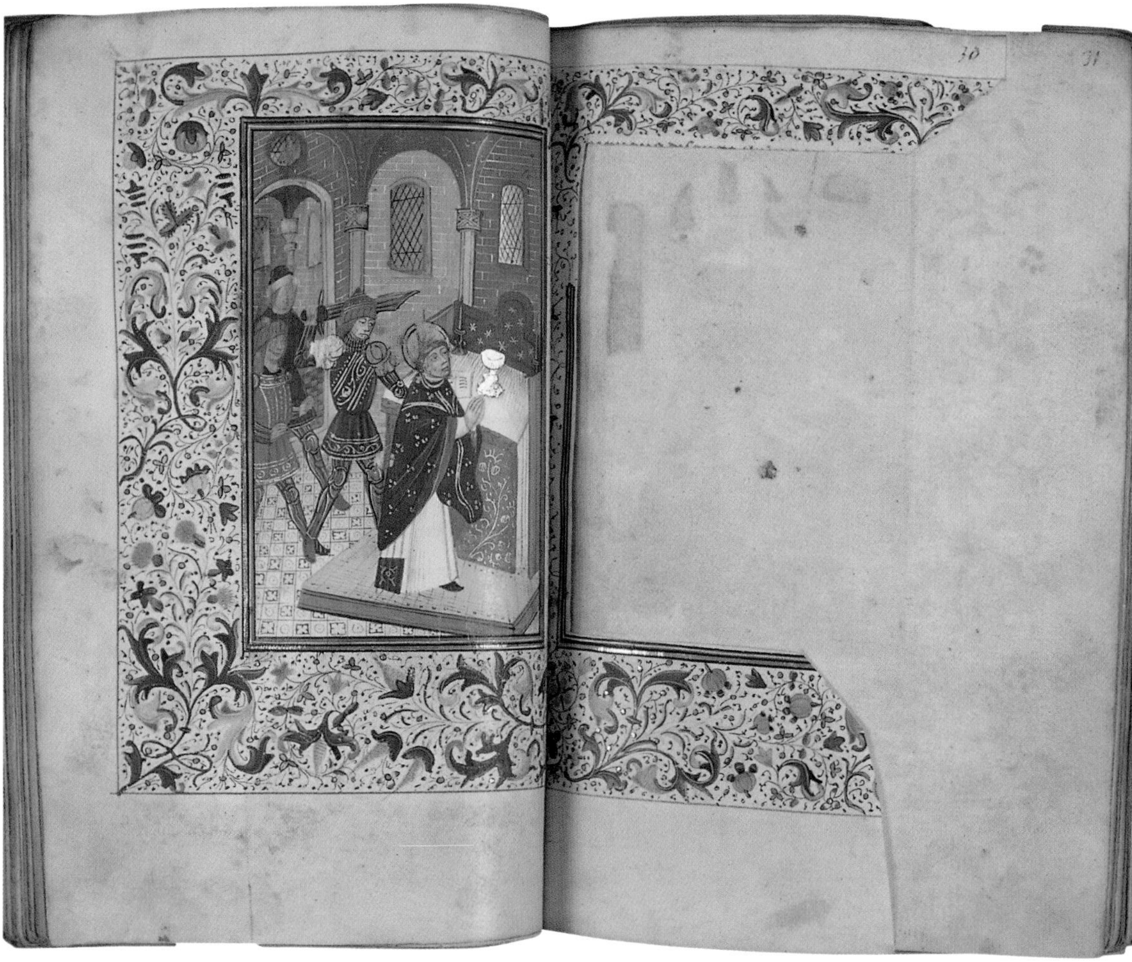

99.
In obedience to Henry VIII's proclamation of November 1538 outlawing his cult, the owner of this manuscript Book of Hours sliced out the prayers in honour of St Thomas Becket.

British Library Harley 2985 fos. 29v–30. Page size 22 × 14cm

indication that the book was not in use in England in the later part of Henry's reign. Many such deletions were quite clearly essentially a matter of form, the simple and tidy removal of the word *papa* and of Becket's name.

In the Roberts family book, St Thomas's feast has been neatly scraped out of the calendar, and the word *papa* changed to *episcopus* wherever it occurs, and this neat and minimalist conformity is fairly typical. But other owners were more drastic. The owner of the very similar book, now BL Harley 2985, left the picture of St Thomas intact, but sliced out the prayer which accompanied it [Pl. 99]. The owner of a handsome printed Book of Hours on vellum attempted to scrape and smooth away all trace of the suffrage addressed to St

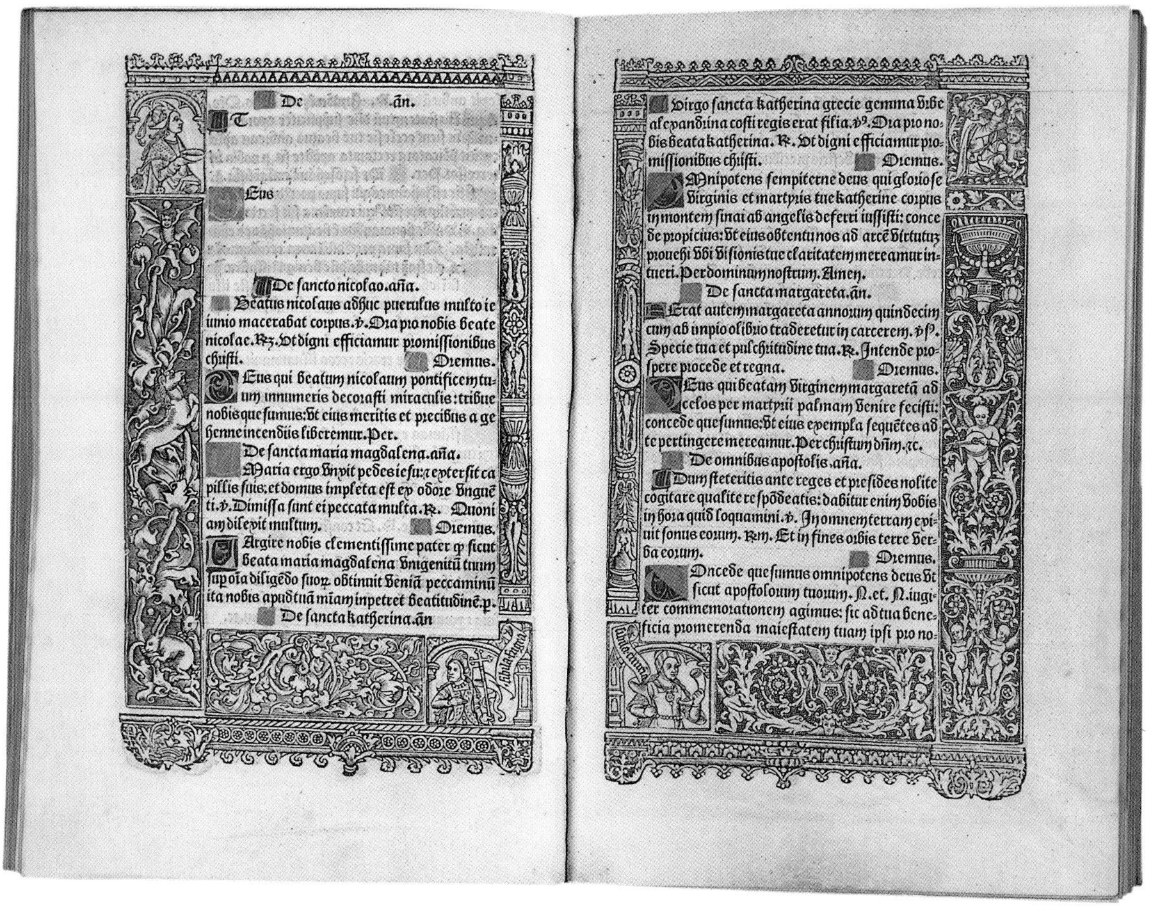
De [..] an.

De sancto nicolao.aña.
Beatus nicolaus adhuc puerulus multo ieiunio macerabat corpus.℣.Ora pro nobis beate
nicolae.℟.Ut digni efficiamur promissionibus
christi. Oremus.
Deus qui beatum nicolaum pontificem tuum innumeris decorasti miraculis: tribue
nobis que sumus:ut eius meritis et precibus a ge
henne incendiis liberemur.Per.
De sancta maria magdalena.aña.
Maria ergo unxit pedes iesu:et extersit ca
pillis suis:et domus impleta est ex odore unguē
ti.℣.Dimissa sunt ei peccata multa.℟. Quoni
am dilexit multum. Oremus.
Largire nobis clementissime pater ꝗ sicut
beata maria magdalena unigenitū tuum
super oia diligēdo suoꝝ obtinuit veniā peccaminū
ita nobis apud tuā miam impetret beatitudinē.p.
De sancta katherina.aña

Virgo sancta katherina grecie gemma urbe
alexandrina costi regis erat filia.℣.Ora pro nobis beata katherina.℟.Ut digni efficiamur promissionibus christi. Oremus.
Omnipotens sempiterne deus qui gloriose
virginis et martyris tue katherine corpus
in montem synai ab angelis deferri iussisti: conce
de propicius:ut eius obtentu nos ad arcē virtutū
provehi ubi visionis tue claritatem mereamur in-
tueri.Per dominum nostrum.Amen.
De sancta margareta.aña.
Erat autem margareta annorum quindecim
cum ab impio olibrio traderetur in carcerem.℣.Sp.
Specie tua et pulchritudine tua.℟.Intende pro-
spere procede et regna. Oremus.
Deus qui beatam virginem margaretā ad
celos per martyrii palmam venire fecisti:
concede que sumus:ut eius exempla sequētes ad
te pertingere mereamur.Per christum dnm.&c.
De omnibus apostolis.aña.
Dum steteritis ante reges et presides nolite
cogitare qualiter respōdeatis: dabitur enim vobis
in hora quid loquamini.℣.In omnem terram exi-
uit sonus eorum.℟.Et in fines orbis terre verba eorum. Oremus.
Concede que sumus omnipotens deus ut
sicut apostolorum tuorum .N.et.N.iugi-
ter commemorationem agimus: sic ad tua bene-
ficia promerenda maiestatem tuam ipsi pro no-

Thomas in Lauds of the Virgin [Pl. 100]. Indulgences, too, are scratched out, but in many cases in a selective way which suggests that it is not the idea of an indulgence in itself which is thought to be at fault, but the specific source of the indulgence, the Pope. In a 1511 book issued by the printer Byrckman, the indulgences have been left alone, provided they don't mention the Pope, or Rome. If they do, out they come [Pl. 101].

Such deletions, of course, tell us that these Catholic books are still in use in the late 1530s and early 1540s – for why bowdlerise a book you never use? But beyond that, it is hard to say how we should interpret these blots and scratches. Might we be witnessing here the traces of the spread of protestant opinion, the internalisation of the

100. OFFICIAL AMNESIA
The prayer to St Thomas has been rubbed off the surface of this luxury Book of Hours printed on vellum in 1520.

RSTC 15926 (Vostre Pigouchet 1520). British Library C 41 e 9 sig d6(v)–d7. Page size 20 × 11 cm

101.
The Henrician user of this Book of Hours was untroubled by indulgence rubrics, provided they did not mention the Pope. Those which did were scrupulously defaced, in obedience to Royal command, as in this rubric to the indulgenced prayers before the Image of Pity.

RSTC 15912. Byrckman 1511. Cambridge University Library, Sss 15 20 fo. lviij. Page size 16 × 10cm

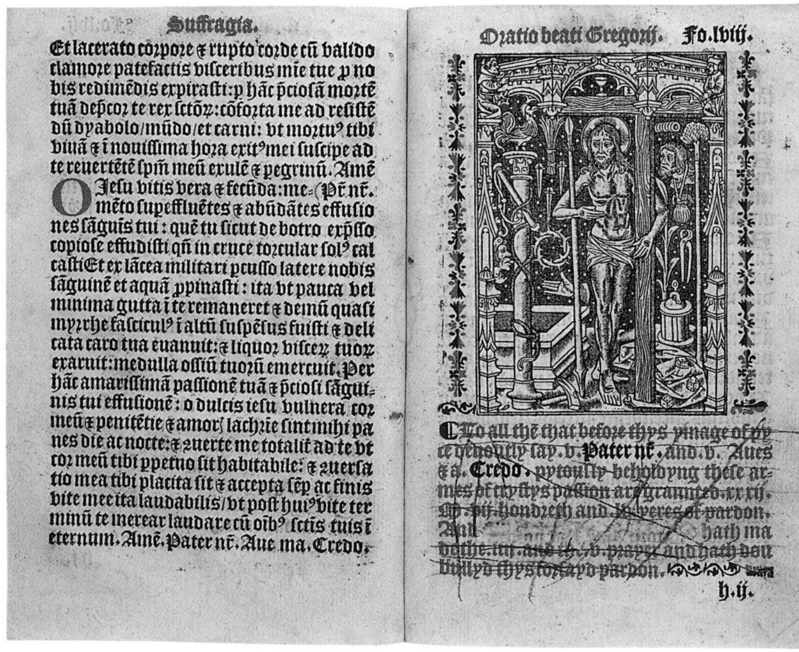

102.

RSTC 15968. Cambridge University Library, Sss 60 19 fo. xxiii(verso)–xxiiii, defaced prayers to Becket. Page size 22 × 14cm

reformed message? At the very least, the deletions suggest a remarkably widespread obedience to Henrician commands, and in some cases, maybe more. On the flyleaf of a Book of Hours now in the Bodleian someone has written in a crisp clerical hand '*Prorsus abnego et abiungo nomen Pape*' (I utterly repudiate and remove the name of the Pope), a choice of phrase which suggests something more than mere acquiescence.[13] Edmund Church, the plebeian Ipswich owner of a manuscript Book of Hours made originally for a fifteenth-century Duchess of Exeter, meticulously removed the name of St Thomas Becket from the July and December pages of the calendar, scraped out the memoria and suffrages of St Thomas from the Hours of the Virgin, and even scratched his name out of the Litany of the Saints: at the end of the book, for good measure, he wrote 'God save the kynge'.[14] The owner of a much thumbed and worn copy of one of François Regnault's cheap little sextodecimo Book of Hours now in the Bodleian not only deleted the feasts of St Thomas, and removed purgatory from a printed list of the Christian 'verytes', but carefully crossed out and overwrote the word *papa*, replacing it with *episcopus* wherever it occurred in the book's many indulgence rubrics, and even deleted the holy abbots from the Litany of the Saints, presumably in response to the suppression of the monasteries.[15] Here indeed was meticulous compliance with the spirit as well as the letter of the Royal Supremacy.

On the other hand, in many books the deletions are unsystematic and cursory – Becket's name may be removed for his December feast, but left untouched at the principle feast of his translation in July. The prayers to St Thomas in the body of the text may be defaced, but just as often they are untouched [Pl. 102].

Books which delete the Pope may retain St Thomas, or vice versa. So it would be a mistake to attribute too much significance to such obedience. For even religious conservatives placed a high value on loyalty to the regime. A manuscript book of hours which belonged to Margaret Townsend, wife of Sir Thomas Pope, conservative founder of Trinity College, Oxford, in Mary's reign, has not in fact had the Pope's name removed, but other entries in the calendar suggest a self-conscious loyalty to the Tudor regime: there are entries for the birth of Prince Edward, and one recording the outbreak of the Pilgrimage of Grace, described here as that '*detestabilis insurrectio*' in

Lincolnshire and Yorkshire.[16] A prayer-book was a place in which the obedience and affection of a good subject was appropriately displayed.

This might apply even when we know that the subject concerned almost certainly had reservations about the King's religious policies. A treasured printed Book of Hours handed on in the family of a former lady in waiting to Catherine of Aragon, 'good queen Katrin', and later given to Sir Robert Dimock by an ex-monastic prior, is a monument to the conservative opposition in Henry's reign. Nevertheless, in this book too the word *papa* is deleted wherever it occurs, and St Thomas has been removed from the December calendar.[17] In 1539 Sir Adrian Fortescue was beheaded for treason, accused of plotting against the Henrician regime. A knight of Malta and a distinguished courtier who had been at the Field of Cloth of Gold, he has since been beatified by the Roman Catholic Church. As you might expect, in the missal used in his private chapel the official bidding prayer for the King authorised in 1536 has been defaced, the sentence claiming that Henry was Supreme Head of the Church being deleted. But, as it happens, Fortescue's Book of Hours has also survived, and in it he carefully blotted out the Pope's name wherever it occurs.[18]

Some deletions are more poignant still. In the court, prayer had developed a dangerous political edge even before the break with Rome. Among the devout ladies of the court the precocious piety of the Princess Mary had become a matter of delighted comment. In 1528, at the end of the handsome courtly book belonging to Lady Guildford [Pl. 103], in which we have already seen noted the presence of affectionate messages from Catherine of Aragon and the princess Mary, Becket is almost unscathed, but there were more intimate deletions. At some stage in the 1520s the owner had copied out a long prayer attributed to St Thomas Aquinas, 'translated', as she recorded 'out of Latine into Englysse by the most excellent Princesse Mary Doghter of the moste hygh and myghty Prynce and Prynces Kyng Henry the viii and Quene Katheryn hys wyfe . . . in . . . the xi yere of her age'. The prayer was a regular item in printed Books of Hours, so the choice of this text by or for the young princess as a devout translation exercise is in itself further confirmation of the social breadth of the appeal of the Book of Hours.[19] It is not hard to imagine the context for this laborious gesture, and perhaps other cooing court

103.
Though this book was certainly publicly used by its female owner in the court of Henry VIII, only the headings to the prayers to Thomas Becket have been deleted, leaving the picture and prayers themselves untouched.

British Library Add 17012 fos. 28v–29

ladies also copied the Princess's prayer into their books and wove it into their daily round of devotions. The prayer is an extended petition for virtue and purity, and at the foot of the copy in this book Mary herself wrote 'I have red that no body lyvethe as he shulde doo but he that foloweth verttu and y reckenynge you to be one of them I pray you to remembre me in your devocyons. Mary the princesse.' The ink on this exchange of devotional politenesses can hardly have been dry, however, when the King determined to divorce Catherine, deprive her of her royal title, and bastardise their daughter. Catherine had written in this book 'I thinke the prayers of a frende the most acceptable unto God and because I take you for one of myn assured, I pray you remember me in Yours: Catherine the Quene'. But in the shark pool of Henry's court constancy and friendship were fragile commodities: Lady Guildford accordingly blotted out both Queen Catherine's titles and name, and Mary's signature. The contrast with the token gesture towards the removal of Becket's name is painful and pointed. In the shark-pool of the Tudor court, some devotions were more dangerous – and dispensable – than others [Pls 38, 39].

One of these dangerous devotions was purgatory. The Henrician Church went on praying for the dead, but the King disliked the name purgatory, and its use was prohibited by the Ten Articles of 1536.[20] The owner of a printed Books of Hours of 1527 now in the British Library, Robert Wilkes senior, was certainly a Catholic, since he copied invocations to the Virgin into one of his books, and he replaced by hand missing sections of Latin prayers on pages which had become ragged from use. He nevertheless carefully deleted the Pope's name and that of St Thomas wherever they occur, and bowdlerised any indulgence rubrics which mentioned popes. His book also contained a printed version of the Jesus Psalter, a long litany of supplication with a recurrent petition 'have mercy on the soules in purgatory for thy bitter passion I beseech thee, and for thy glorious name, Jesu.' Wilkes blotted out the word 'purgatory' wherever it recurred, even though this made a nonsense of the prayer.[21] In another well-thumbed printed Book of Hours in the British Library the indulgence and miraculous rubrics which mention purgatory have been crossed out: the others are left undisturbed.[22] This sort of selective removal of ideas outlawed by the Crown could be carried out with extraordinary literalness. In a Ms Book of Hours in the Fitzwilliam Museum in which the Pope's name and that of St Thomas have been left untouched, some earlier owner had copied an elaborate rubric into the book detailing seven masses to be said with almsgiving to secure the release from purgatory of some 'special friend': whoever owned the book in the 1530s left the rubric itself, but carefully blotted out the word purgatory.[23]

These examples could all be replicated a hundred times over, but none of them necessarily take us very far into the interiority of Tudor religion, for all of them might be explicable in terms of prudence or obedience. Nothing so far has offered us a direct clue to the extent to which the reformation had reached the hearts and minds of the users of Books of Hours. Were people's religious convictions on the move, and if so, were they moving away from the beliefs that had shaped their prayer-books, towards Protestantism? In some ways, of course, a Book of Hours is the worst possible place to look for an answer to that question. It is, after all, largely made up of prayers to the Virgin, or to other saints, or on behalf of the dead, and the prayers addressed to Christ focus on his sacramental presence and on the physical details of the passion, an emotional emphasis which by and large the reformers deplored. If the owner of a Book of Hours became a protestant, he or she was more likely to stop using the book altogether than to leave clues in its pages as to the movement of their religious opinions.

In reality, however, few religious conversions are wholesale Damascus road affairs, blinding flashes of insight or revelation which turn one round through 180 degrees. Men and women move by inches rather than leaps, and from time to time it **is** possible to see that slow movement in process. A tiny Book of Hours now in the British Library, Harleian 935, offers us an insight into the mind of one Londoner caught up in the religious flux of the 1530s and 1540s. The book in fact belonged for some part of the period to John Brygandyne, a Bachelor of Divinity of Cambridge and former fellow of St John's, who was a London clergyman and almost certainly the incumbent of St Benet Gracechurch Street between 1543 and 1559.[24] Notes in the calendar, now very hard to read, persuaded the eighteenth-century cataloguer of the Harleian Mansucripts both that Brygandyne had married late in Henry VIII's reign, and that he was a suffragan bishop.[25] He was certainly not a bishop, and since he was not deprived in Mary's reign he can hardly have been married either, though two disconcerting entries in the calendar say that on 16 September 1537 and on 21 September 1545 'uxorem duxi' first Isabellam Darrell viduam Radulph Darrell' and 'uxorem duxi' Joahanem p[ier]poynt' ('I married Isabel Darrell widow of Ralph Darrell' and 'I married Joan Pierpoynt').[26] But the handwriting is not the same throughout the book, Brygandyne may have given the book away to a parishioner whose weddings these entries record, or they may refer to his role as priest or witness. All the other entries I have been able to decipher in fact refer to the weddings and funeral of London tradesmen and merchants conducted by Brygandyne in the 1530s and 1540s, and a note that 'I byshopped william Barnes the son of John Barnes Grocer' of London on 22 October 1536 almost

104.
In the reign of Henry VIII this diminutive fifteenth-century Book of Hours belonged to a London clergyman, John Brygandyne, a Cambridge-trained theologian who added many notes, translations and vernacular devotions. He dutifully deleted these prayers to St Thomas Becket, which he first scribbled over, then covered with a glued-on sheet of paper, on which he wrote an English devotion to be recited before meals and at bed-time. This added paper has now been lost, though its outline remains, leaving only the heading, a few line endings in the margin, and the 'So be it' (translating the Greek word 'Amen') with which the English prayer ended.

British Library, Harley Mansuscript 935, fo. 70. Page size 10 × 7 cms.

105.
A few of the added devotions in Brygandyne's book suggest some inclination towards the Reformation, but most are traditional in character. In this ardent prayer for the kindling of the devout heart by the love of the heart of God the word 'heart' has been replaced throughout by a stylised drawing.

British Library Harleian 935 fo. 30 Page size 10 × 7 cms.

certainly means not that whoever wrote this was a bishop, but that he acted as confirmation sponsor.[27] I think we can discount the possibility that the book belonged to a clerical rebel.

Brygandyne's book was clearly used intensively, and it has many added vernacular prayers in the margins and blanks. Some of these are translations of Latin prayers and hymns of the Little Office from the Virgin Mary, like the supplication addressed to Mary 'Pray for the people, entreate for the clergy, make intercession for the devoute women Lett all fele thy help'. The user also translated the hymn *O Gloriosa Domina*, not a distinguished performance, though once again it suggests that he did not question the legitimacy of devotion to Mary.

> Gloriose flower of madhed,
> On the starres inthronysed
> Thy holy brestes have norished
> That lorde that hath the created . . .[28]

Whoever wrote this was almost certainly responding here to the appearance of the tidied up translations of Sarum Book of Hours produced after the proclamation of 1535 by Regnault and others. At the end of the Litany of the Saints he copied into the margin the Hail Mary in English and a version of the Lord's Prayer ending with the distinctive petition 'And let us not be led into temptacion, But delyver us from evyll. So be ytt', which had first appeared in the purged Books of Hours which first excluded all mention of Thomas Becket in 1538, an edition by Robert Redman: it would be incorporated from there into the King's Primer of 1545.[29]

But Brygandyne or his parishioner did more than modernise his Book of Hours by adding material from the new approved translations of the traditional Book of Hours. He also added a series of very distinctive English prayers of his own, some of them with clumsy illuminated initials designed to imitate the decoration of the original book, a conservative gesture of continuity suggesting that he felt no contradiction in moving between the traditional Latin prayers and these new English ones. Some of these added prayers are exercises in a devotional mode long familiar from prayers like the English translations of the Oes of St Brigid, and the type was very current in the 1530s and early 1540s in collections like the *Paradise of Souls*, a mixture of traditional and reforming material. Here is one of them:

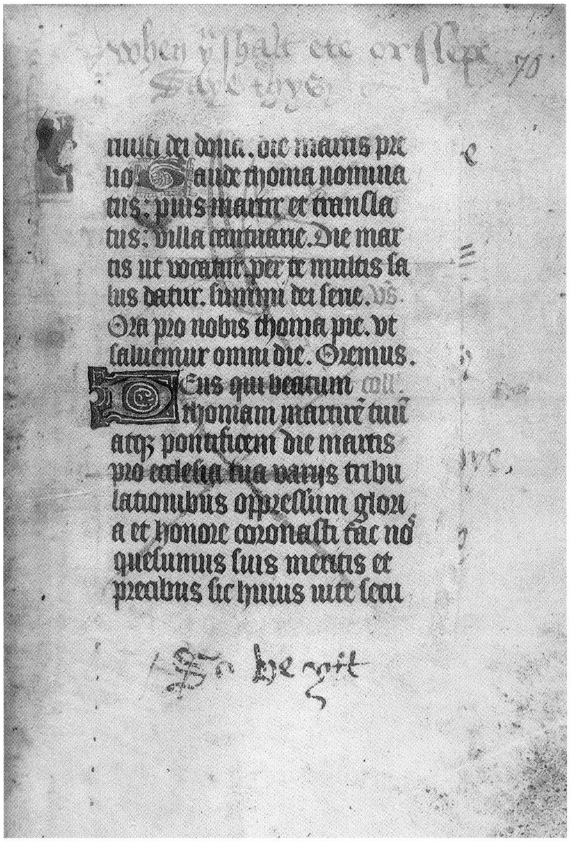
when y shalt ete or slepe Saye thys 70

nitti dei dona. die martis pre lio. Sancte thoma nomina tus: passus martir et transla tus: villa cantuarie. Die mar tis ut vocatur per te multis sa lus datur. summi dei sene. Ora pro nobis thoma pie. Ut salvemur omni die. Oremus. Deus qui beatum thomam martirem tuum atque pontificem die martis pro ecclesia tua variis tribu lationibus oppressum glori a et honore coronasti fac nos quesumus suis meritis et precibus sic huius vite secu

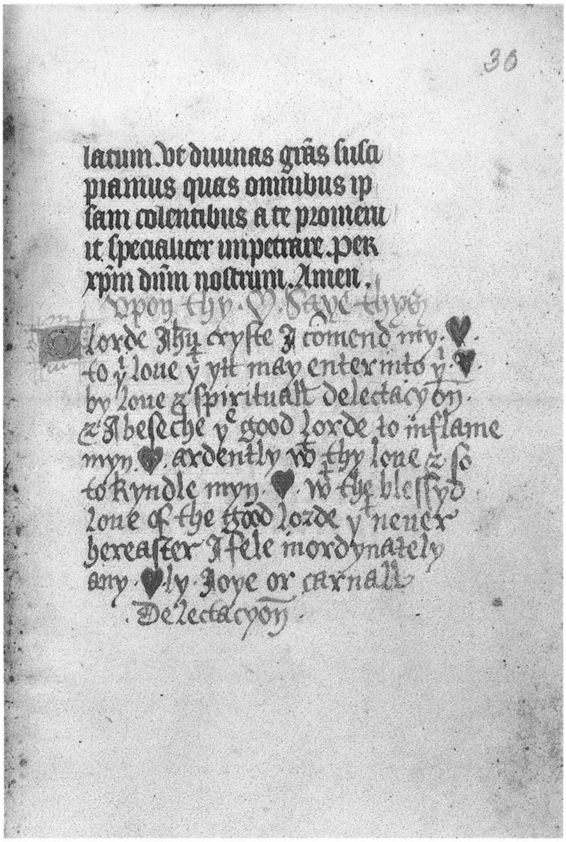
30

latum. ut divinas gratias susci piamus quas omnibus ip sam colentibus a te promeru it specialiter impetrare. per xpm dnm nostrum. Amen. upon thy ♥ saye thys Lorde Jhu cryste I comend my ♥ to thy love that yt may enter into thy ♥ by love & spirituall delectacyon & I beseche the good lorde to inflame myn ♥ ardently wt thy love & so to kyndle myn ♥ wt the blessyd love of the good lorde that never hereafter I fele inordynately any ♥ly Joye or carnall Delectacyon

> O good Lorde Jhus, remember thy inestymable love that thou beyng equall in glory with the father in hevyn wast content to take upon the all our myser wch we wer cast into by the originall offence of Adam. Thou sufferyd pacyently hungere and weryness, pensyveness of mynd, rebukes, all paynefulness and at laste, the moste shamefull dethe that cold be . . .[30]

Some of the prayers are hard to imagine even the most moderate protestant using, like the prayer to his guardian angel beginning 'O good angell which ert deputyd to kepe me in puretye of conscyence.'[31] There are prayers for the right use of the hearing and sight,[32] a prayer for the worthy saying of prayers, 'as part of my service'. But the most distinctive prayers all focus on the theme of the heart – the heart of the person praying, and the heart of Jesus [Pls. 104, 105]. There are three of these heart prayers, all of them sharing the very striking feature that whoever copied the prayer never writes the word 'heart', but instead at each occurrence draws a little heart which he carefully filled in with red ink. The second of these prayers runs like this: it is headed, 'upon thy [heart] say thys'.

> O lorde Jhu Cryste I commende my [heart] to thy love that ytt may enter into thi [heart] of love and spiritual delectacyon and I beseche the good lorde to inflame myn [heart] ardently with thy love and so to kyndle myn [heart] with the blessyd love of the good lorde that never hereafter I fele inordinately any [heart]ly joye or carnall delectacyon.[33]

All of these prayers have the mark of mid-Tudor sensibility on them, but none is in any sense protestant. But one prayer in Brygandyne's book does perhaps suggest that the user may have been moving in a definitely reformed direction, though even that is ambiguous: it is a prayer concerned with good works, and runs like this.

> When thou shalt do any good worke saye
> 'O good lorde, as thou did exersise thiselfe in labours of charite and brynyng love whilst thou lyvid emongst men and yet contynually dothe, in like manner for the love that I have to thee, I to (sic) all'.[34]

That need not be a Lutheran prayer: but its overall emphasis, that good works are done not to gain eternal life or to make amends for sin, but in imitation of the charity of Christ and out of love for him, is not a common medieval emphasis: whoever wrote this prayer had absorbed some at least of the new teachings, and in the range of these added prayers, from invocations to a guardian angel or prayers for an ardent heart, to this up-to-date little prayer on the right place of good works, we catch a glimpse of the impact on personal religion of the religious flux of mid-Tudor England.

In an earlier chapter, we took the Roberts family of Willesden as representatives of the late medieval and early Tudor users of the Book of Hours, and subjected one of their surviving Books of Hours to close scrutiny. Where do they stand in all this process of change? Like most other users of Books of Hours in Henry's reign, they certainly brought their private devotions into line with royal policy by deleting Becket and the Pope from the calendar, and by doctoring indulgence rubrics. We have no way of knowing what they thought of the religious changes of the ensuing years. But in 1553 Edmund Roberts inherited the family Book of Hours, perhaps from his elder brother Michael's wife Ursula. Edmund was almost certainly a religious conformist: he was certainly not a man to rock the boat, business came first with him – he was to go on avidly adding to the family's landholdings till his death in 1585, and certainly died a conforming member of the church of Elizabeth I. In 1553, however, as we have already seen, he established his possession of the book by writing his name five or six times in the book, proprietarily on many of the pictures [Pl. 53].[35] To a modern sensibility, this is an act of vandalism. Might it also be an act of iconoclasm, a sign that Edmund Roberts was by 1553 a protestant?

I do not think he can have been. He went on using the book as his father had done, as a place to record his children's births into the 1570s. This in itself, has little or no religious significance: many known protestants did the same. More strikingly, however, he indicated his approval of some of the most 'medieval' elements in the book. It may be recalled that one of the most uncompromisingly 'superstitious' prayers added to the Roberts family book was the devotion of the Thousand Aves, which had to be said, a hundred at a time ten days running, holding an alms in your hand, which you then kissed and gave to a poor man or woman in honour of the Annunciation, upon which 'without dought ye shall have that thyng ye pray for lawfully'. The rubric has added Edmund's signature, which almost certainly dates from 1553, and runs 'I yousd thys prayer well thys daye, *Edmund Robertes Inquit*.'[36]

It would be hard to say whether the sorts of mental and religious accommodations evident in John Brygandyne's book was more or less representative than the conservativism apparent in Edmund Roberts's use of his magical prayer in 1553. Nor do we know whether Edmund Roberts 'yousd this prayer well' before or after the accession of the Catholic Queen Mary in that year. But at any rate, it does not seem that Edmund had acquired a protestant mindset by 1553, and at the very least, reversion to earlier devotional attitudes seems to have come easily to him.

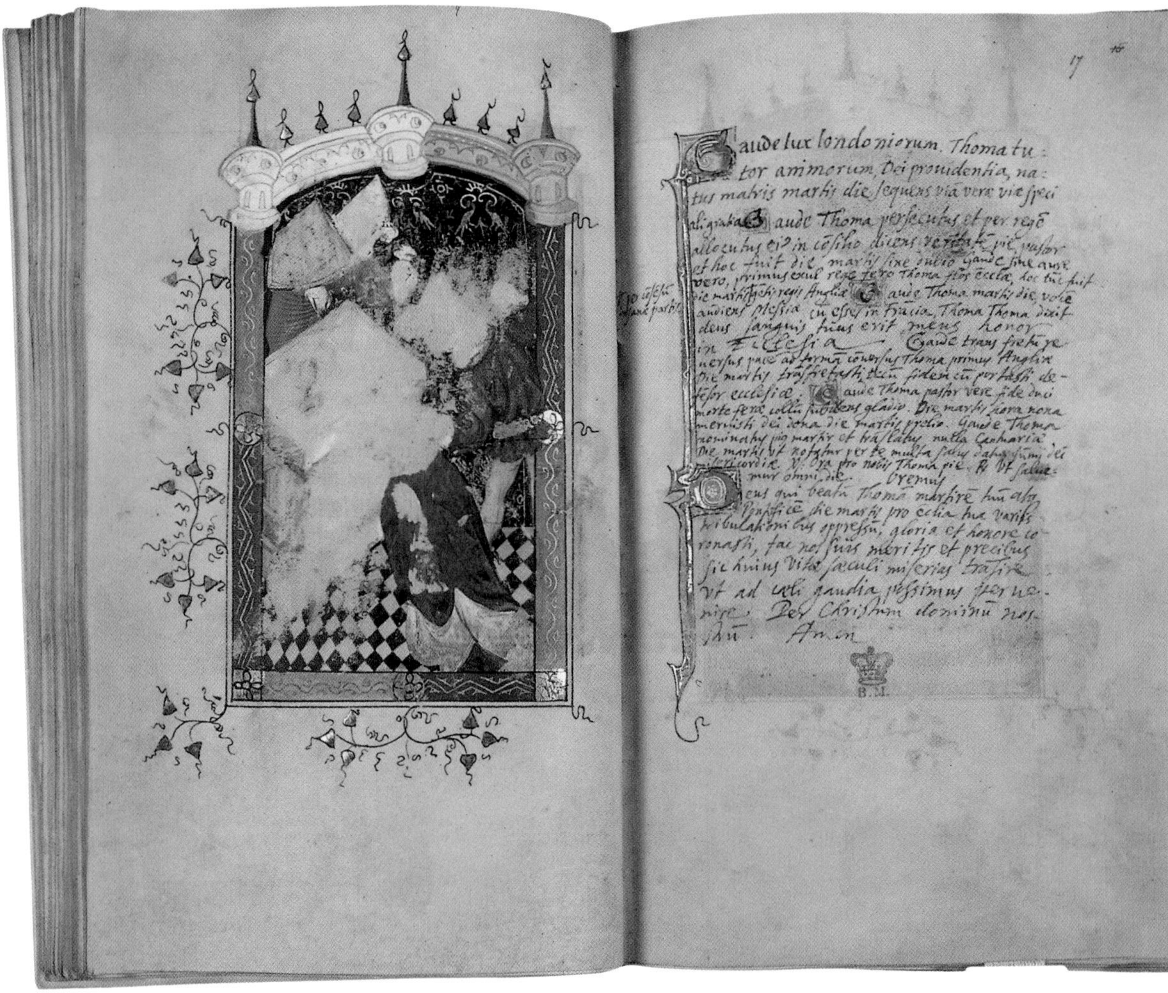

106.
In Henry's reign, the owner of this Flemish Book of Hours for the English market, still in use though more than a century old, dutifully scraped out St Thomas Becket's image and removed the prayer to St Thomas from the opposite page. In Mary's reign the prayer was restored, though no royal command required this.

British Library, Sloane 2683, fos. 16v–17. Page size 20 × 12 cm

Regimes might dictate drastic change – Henry VIII banned the import of Books of Hours printed abroad in 1538, a move incidentally that came close to ruining François Regnault, who had thousands of primers in his continental warehouses, which now became unsaleable. From 1545 there was an officially imposed Royal Primer 'to be taught, learned and read, and none other to be said throughout all his dominions': its accompanying injunction insisted that the 'diversity of primer books that are now abroad, whereof are almost innumerable sorts . . . minister occasion of contentions and vain disputations rather than to edify', and forbade booksellers to sell or anyone to use any other Book of Hours than the newly appointed book.[37]

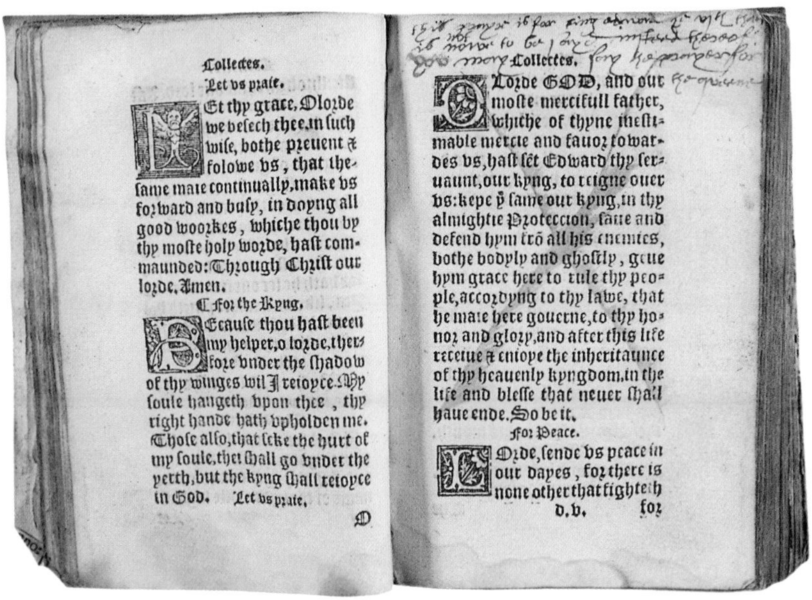

Collectes.

Let vs praie.

Et thy grace, O lorde we besech thee, in such wise, bothe preuent & folowe vs, that the same maie continually, make vs forward and busy, in doyng all good workes, whiche thou by thy moste holy worde, hast commaunded: Through Christ our lorde. Amen.

¶ For the Kyng.

Because thou hast been my helper, o lorde, therfore vnder the shadow of thy winges wil I reioyce. My soule hangeth vpon thee, thy right hande hath upholden me. Those also, that seke the hurt of my soule, they shall go vnder the yerth, but the kyng shall reioyce in God. Let vs praie.

D

Collectes.

O Lorde GOD, and our moste mercifull father, whiche of thyne inestimable mercie and fauor towardes vs, hast set Edward thy seruaunt, our kyng, to reigne ouer vs: kepe þ same our kyng, in thy almightie protection, saue and defend hym frō all his enemies, bothe bodyly and ghostly, geue hym grace here to rule thy people, accordyng to thy lawe, that he maie here gouerne, to thy honor and glory, and after this life receiue & enioye the inheritaunce of thy heauenly kyngdom, in the life and blesse that neuer shall haue ende. So be it.

For Peace.

Lorde, sende vs peace in our dayes, for there is none other that fighteth

D.v. for

107.
Still using this emphatically protestant official Primer of Edward VI in the reign of his Catholic sister Mary, the owner drew a cross through the prayer for Edward, and directed prayer for Queen Mary instead. Since there is no mention of Philip of Spain, the alteration must have been made before the Queen's marriage.

RSTC 16054. (1551). Magdalene College Old Library. Sig D.v. Page size 12 × 6 cm

But such an injunction was aspirational rather than real. As we have seen, Books of Hours were family books, and even printed ones had long lives, and several consecutive users. Such books, handed on from parent to child, were bound to survive changes of rulers, and therefore to straddle and slow the impact of the religious reversals which disturbed mid-Tudor England. 'Protestantising' changes like the removal of prayers to St Thomas or the Pope's name, however drastically performed, might be reversed in Mary's reign [Pl. 106].

And the prayer-life of the laity certainly must often have lagged behind shifts in royal religious policy. Even dutiful alterations made to prayer-books indicate a process of adjustment within an overarching continuity of habit and use. In a 1551 copy of the very protestant Edwardine Royal Primer, now in Magdalene College library, less a Book of Hours than a slimmed down version of the Book of Common Prayer, the prayer for the boy King has been crossed out with a large inky cross, and above it has been written 'This prayer is for King Edward the VIth and is not now to be said. Instead thereof you may say the prayers for the Queene' [Pl. 107]. Clearly, therefore, this protestant book went on being used into the Catholic Queen's

108.
The restoration of Catholicism under Mary produced renewed demand for traditional books of Hours. This French-printed edition of 1555 reverted to Latin for the Hours of the Virgin and most other prayers, but followed the pattern of the Primers printed after 1534 in omitting all indulgences.

RSTC 16068 (Rouen 1555). Cambridge University Library, Syn 8 55 171, sig Diii. Page size 14 × 8 cm

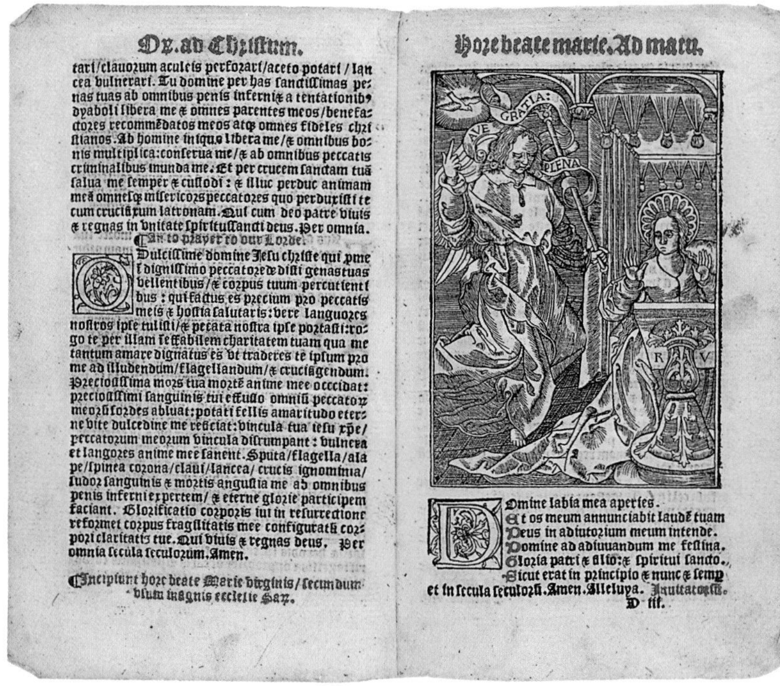
Or. ad Christum.
tari/clauorum aculeis perforari/aceto potari / lancea vulnerari. Tu domine per has sanctissimas penas tuas ab omnibus penis inferni ⁊ a tentationib⁹ dyaboli libera me ⁊ omnes parentes meos/benefactores recommendatos meos atq omnes fideles christianos. Ab homine iniquo libera me/⁊ omnibus bonis multiplica: conserua me/⁊ ab omnibus peccatis criminalibus munda me. Et per crucem sanctam tuā salua me semper ⁊ custodi: ⁊ illuc perduc animam meā omnesq misericors peccatores quo perduxisti tecum crucifixum latronem. Qui cum deo patre viuis ⁊ regnas in vnitate spiritussancti deus. Per omnia.
¶ An to prayer to our Lorde.
O Dulcissime domine Jesu christe qui pro e dignissimo peccatore dixi genas tuas bellentibus/⁊ corpus tuum percutientibus: qui factus es precium pro peccatis meis ⁊ hostia salutaris: vere languores nostros ipse tulisti/⁊ pecata nostra ipse portasti: rogo te per illam ineffabilem charitatem tuam qua me tantum amare dignatus es vt traderes te ipsum pro me ad illudendum/flagellandum/⁊ crucifigendum. Preciosissima mors tua morte anime mee occidat: preciosissimi sanguinis tui effusio omniū peccator meorū sordes abluat: potatio fellis amaritudo eterne vite dulcedine me reficiat: vincula tua iesu xpe/ peccatorum meorum vincula dirumpant: vulnera et langores anime mee sanent. Sputa/flagella/alape/spinea corona/claui/lancea/ crucis ignominia/ ludos sanguinis ⁊ mortis angustia me ab omnibus penis inferni expertem/⁊ eterne glorie participem faciant. Glorificatio corporis tui in resurrectione reformet corpus fragilitatis mee configuratū corpori claritatis tue. Qui viuis ⁊ regnas deus. Per omnia secula seculorum. Amen.
¶ Incipiunt hore beate Marie virginis/secundum vsum insignis ecclesie Sar.

Hore beate marie. Ad matu.

Domine labia mea aperies.
Et os meum annunciabit laudē tuam
Deus in adiutorium meum intende.
Domine ad adiuuandum me festina.
Gloria patri ⁊ filio: ⁊ spiritui sancto.
Sicut erat in principio ⁊ nunc ⁊ semp et in secula seculorū. Amen. Alleluya. Inuitatoriū.
D iiii.

109.
Like her father and brother, Queen Mary sponsored an 'official' Book of Hours, though unlike them, she did not ban other versions. Interestingly, these official Marian Primers, illustrated sparsely or not at all, privileged English as the main language of private worship, relegating the Latin text to the margins.

RSTC 16065 (Wayland 1555, Young 263, Matins). Cambridge University Library. Page size 17 × 11 cm

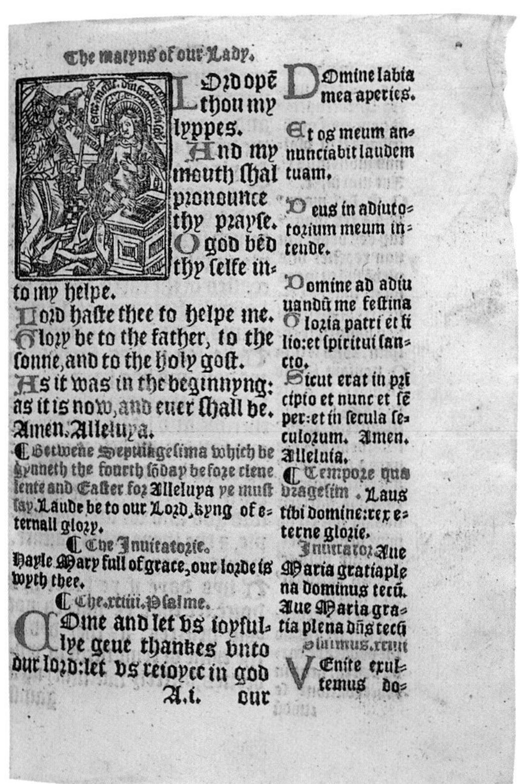
The matyns of our Lady.
LOrde opē thou my lyppes. And my mouth shal pronounce thy prayse. O god bēd thy selfe into my helpe.
Lord haste thee to helpe me.
Glory be to the father, to the sonne, and to the holy gost.
As it was in the beginnyng: as it is now, and euer shall be. Amen. Alleluya.
¶ Betwene Septuagesima which begynneth the fourth sonday before clene lente and Easter for Alleluya ye must say. Laude be to our Lorde, kyng of eternall glory.
¶ The Inuitatorie.
Hayle Mary full of grace, our lorde is wyth thee.
¶ The.xciiii. Psalme.
COme and let vs ioyfullye geue thankes vnto our lord: let vs reioyce in god our
A.i.

Domine labia mea aperies.
Et os meum annunciabit laudem tuam.
Deus in adiutorium meum intende.
Domine ad adiuuandū me festina
Gloria patri et filio: et spiritui sancto.
Sicut erat in principio et nunc et sēper: et in secula seculorum. Amen. Alleluia.
¶ Tempore quīuagesim. Laus tibi domine: rex eterne glorie.
Inuitator. Aue Maria gratia plena dominus tecū.
Aue Maria gratia plena dūs tecū.
Psalmus. xciiii
Venite exultemus do:

regime. Equally clearly, its dutiful owner was concerned to adjust it to the new situation as best he or she could.

Successive Tudor regimes themselves sought what continuities they might, if only to sugar the pill of change. Even the Catholic authorities in Mary's reign shied away from aggressive discontinuity with the primers in use in Henry and Edward's reign. Though some of the Books of Hours sold in Mary's reign made no concessions to the vernacular or the more prosy devotional ethos of the mid-century, reverting to the contents and form of earlier years [Pl. 108], the characteristic and official Book of Hours of Mary's reign was the so-called Wayland Primer, a Catholic book printed by a committed protestant publisher who had been and would be again a major contributor to the reformation propaganda effort, but who was just now, perhaps under constraint, working his passage back into royal favour.[38] These official Books of Hours were closer in appearance to Henry VIII's official Primer of 1545 than to any earlier Catholic book [Pl. 109]. The book restored the full traditional Sarum Book of Hours but it had no miraculous promises, no indulgences, few pictures, and the text of the Hours themselves was given in English, with the Latin in small type at the margin, or in some editions even omitted altogether. The latter was more radical than the layout of the Sarum books printed for England in the late 1530s, after the break with Rome, or even than the King's Primer of 1545, for both of these had retained the Latin. These official Marian primers were therefore a tacit acknowledgement of a shift in devotional sensibility achieved by the watershed of Edward's reign, and the Wayland book even included prayers by protestant authors like Cranmer and Thomas Becon, including, quite amazingly, the bowdlerised protestant version of the *Salve Regina*, 'Hail Holy King'.[39] And in due course on Mary's death, Elizabeth's regime too would seek continuity in prayer, by issuing a reformed Primer retaining some common material with the Marian books, a recognition by the Crown that English people were perhaps at their most conservative when on their knees.[40]

This official striving for continuity was of course more than matched by the conservativism of users, by family pieties, as children inherited their parents' prayer-books, and of course by the expense of replacing even moderately cheap books. As a result of all that, throughout the 1540s, 1550s and 1560s, Catholics used reformed

110.
The protestantising owner of this luxury book by Regnault has customised the 'form of confession' by removing references to the saints and to the priest acting as confessor, turning the preparation for auricular confession into an exercise addressed to God alone.

RSTC 15968. Cambridge University Library, Sss 60 19 fo. clxxxii (v). Page size 22 × 14 cm

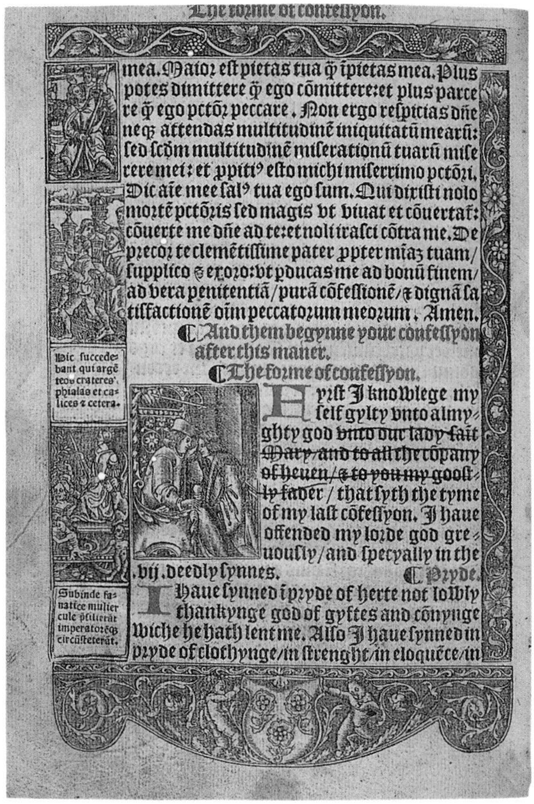
The forme of confessyon.

mea. Maior est pietas tua q̃ ipietas mea. Plus potes dimittere q̃ ego cõmittere: et plus parcere q̃ ego pctõr peccare. Non ergo respicias dñe neq; attendas multitudinẽ iniquitatũ mearũ: sed scdm multitudinẽ miserationũ tuarũ miserere mei: et ppiti⁹ esto michi miserrimo pctõri. Dic aĩe mee sal⁹ tua ego sum. Qui dixisti nolo mortẽ pctõris sed magis vt viuat et cõuertat: cõuerte me dñe ad te: et noli irasci cõtra me. Deprecor te clemẽtissime pater ppter mĩaz tuam/ supplico & exoro: vt pducas me ad bonũ finem/ ad vera penitentiã/ purã cõfessionẽ/ & dignã satisfactionẽ oĩm peccatorum meorum. Amen.

And them begynne your confessyon after this maner.

The forme of confessyon.

Fyrst I knowlege my self gylty vnto almyghty god ~~vnto our lady saint Mary/ and to all the cõpany of heuen/ & to you my goostly fader~~/ that syth the tyme of my last cõfessyon. I haue offended my lorde god greuously/ and specyally in the .vij. deedly synnes.

Pryde.

I haue synned ĩ pryde of herte not lowly thankynge god of gyftes and cõnynge wiche he hath lent me. Also I haue synned in pryde of clothynge/ in strenght/ in eloquẽce/ in

Hic succedebant qui argẽteos crateres, phialas et calices & cetera.

Subinde fanatice mulier cule psiliterãt imperatorẽq; circũsteterãt.

111. & 112.
This Marian Primer (printed in English only) went on being used by a protestant owner in Elizabeth's reign. To bring it into line with reformation teaching, the owner has deleted any prayers to the Virgin, and to the Blessed Sacrament.

RSTC 16074 (Primer by King, 1556). Cambridge University Library, Syn 8 55 157, unpaginated. Page size 12 × 7 cm

Books of Hours, and Protestants used Catholic books, and the books themselves often bear the marks of the discomforts which that involved. In some cases the changes were doubtless welcome enough. The restoration of calendar entries relating to St Thomas, and the rewriting of prayers addressed to him into books from which they had been removed was common. Since Mary's regime did not enforce the private observance of St Thomas's day, this looks like a spontaneous act of piety.

But such gestures might run in the opposite direction. An edition of a Regnault primer of 1530 now in Cambridge University Library [Pl. 110], a typically flashy example of Regnault's upmarket quarto editions, contains among other supplementary items the 'Form of Confession'. The protestant owner of this book evidently continued to use it as a devotional aid, not now as a formula for sacramental confession to a priest, however, but as an aid to private examination of conscience and confession to God alone. Accordingly, he or she has

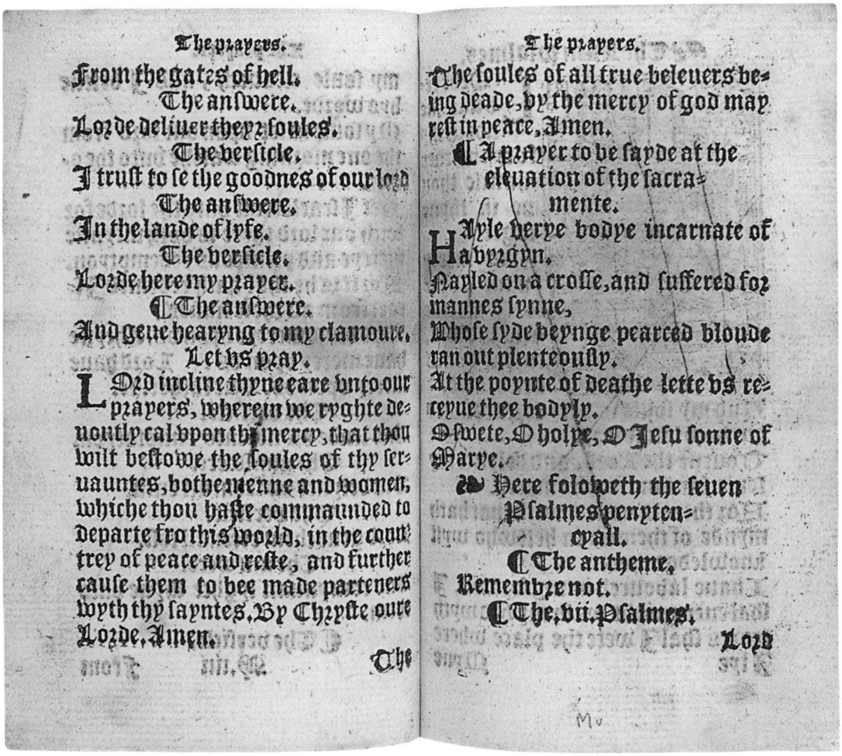
The prayers.

From the gates of hell.

The answere.

Lorde deliuer theyr soules.

The versicle.

I trust to se the goodnes of our lord

The answere.

In the lande of lyfe.

The versicle.

Lorde here my prayer.

¶ The answere.

And geue hearyng to my clamoure.

Let vs pray.

LOrd incline thyne eare vnto our prayers, wherein we ryghte deuoutly cal vpon thy mercy, that thou wilt bestowe the soules of thy seruauntes, bothe menne and women, whiche thou haste commaunded to departe fro this world, in the countrey of peace and reste, and further cause them to bee made parteners wyth thy sayntes, By Chryste oure Lorde, Amen.

The

The prayers.

The soules of all true beleuers beyng deade, by the mercy of god may rest in peace, Amen.

¶ A prayer to be sayde at the eleuation of the sacramente.

HAyle verye bodye incarnate of a vyrgyn,
Nayled on a crosse, and suffered for mannes synne,
Whose syde beynge pearced bloude ran out plenteously,
At the poynte of deathe lette vs receyue thee bodyly.
O swete, O holye, O Jesu sonne of Marye.

Here foloweth the seuen Psalmes penytencyall.

¶ The antheme.

Remembre not.

¶ The. vii. Psalmes.

Lord

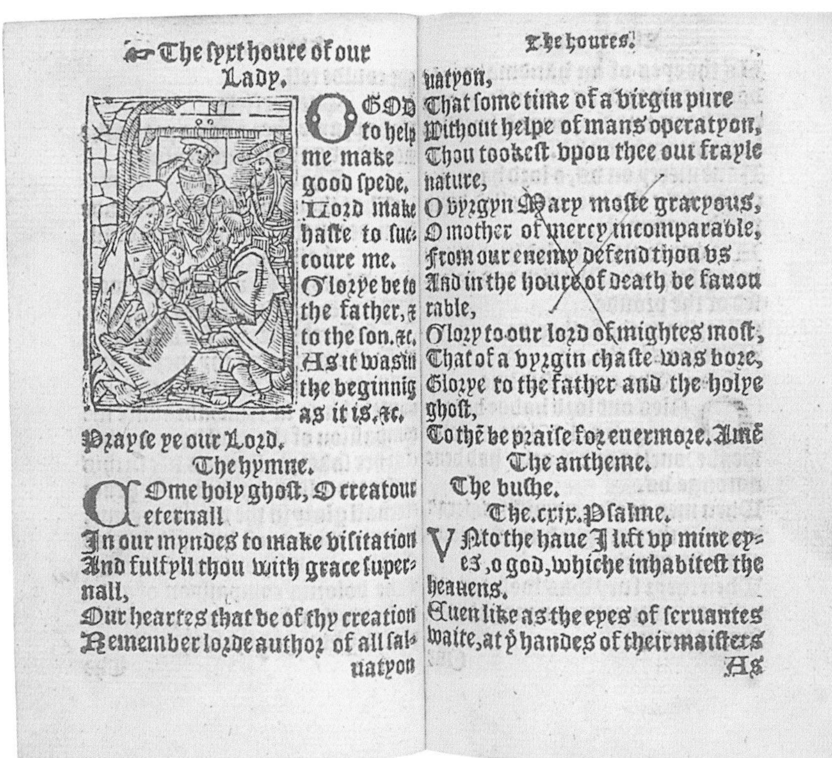
The syxt houre of our Lady.

O GOD to help me make good spede.
Lord make haste to succoure me.
Glorye be to the father, & to the son. &c.
As it was in the beginnig as it is, &c.
Prayse ye our Lord.

The hymne.

COme holy ghost, O creatour eternall
In our myndes to make visitation
And fulfyll thou with grace supernall,
Our heartes that be of thy creation
Remember lorde author of all saluatyon

The houres.

uatyon,
That some time of a virgin pure
Without helpe of mans operatyon,
Thou tookest vpon thee our frayle nature,
O vyrgyn Mary moste gracyous,
O mother of mercy incomparable,
From our enemy defend thou vs
And in the houre of death be fauourable,
Glory to our lord of mightes most,
That of a vyrgin chaste was bore,
Glorye to the father and the holye ghost,
To thē be praise for euermore. Amē

The antheme.

The bushe.

The. cxix. Psalme.

VNto the haue I lift vp mine eyes, o god, whiche inhabitest the heauens.
Euen like as the eyes of seruantes waite, at ẏ handes of their maisters

As

'corrected it' by deleting the words in which the penitent confesses to the Virgin and the priest. This is clearly not a matter of law, which had nothing to say on the matter, but of personal conviction. Protestant understanding of the sacraments and reservations about the role of Mary in salvation are here being internalised. Again, in a copy of a Marian primer from the Cambridge University Library, an Elizabethan protestant user has systematically crossed out all the doctrinally objectionable passage – prayers to Mary, prayers of adoration of the Blessed Sacrament, references to purgatory [Pls. 111, 112].

10

MARGINALITY AND ECLIPSE

But the Book of Hours could not long survive as a protestant devotional tool. The Elizabethan regime issued a Book of Hours, modelled on the protestantised form current in the early years of Edward VI, in 1560, again in 1565, and then in 1575. But by that date it was a curiosity, out of step with the evolving Protestantism of the Elizabethan church, in which the whole notion of such a book and the devotional regimes it implied was increasingly alien. There were to be no further editions, and when the idea of a Book of Hours for Protestants was again revived in 1627 by John Cosin, it would cause a storm of denunciation of popery. The continuing attraction of the old format was attested in 1578, when the publisher John Day issued a *Booke of Christian Prayers* which, though not a Book of Hours, nevertheless was decorated with borders designed to evoke the appearance of the printed Books of Hours of the early sixteenth century.[1] But the *Book of Christian Prayers* was in fact a Trojan Horse, harnessing the old forms to smuggle in the new religion. It included theologically tidied up versions of much of the material included among the additional devotions of the printed *Horae*, including the Fifteen Oes of St Brigid and affective prayers like the *O Bone Jesu*. But the prayers were carefully pruned of any hints of 'false' doctrine, and the border decorations, superficially so close to those of the pre-reformation books, were in fact carefully

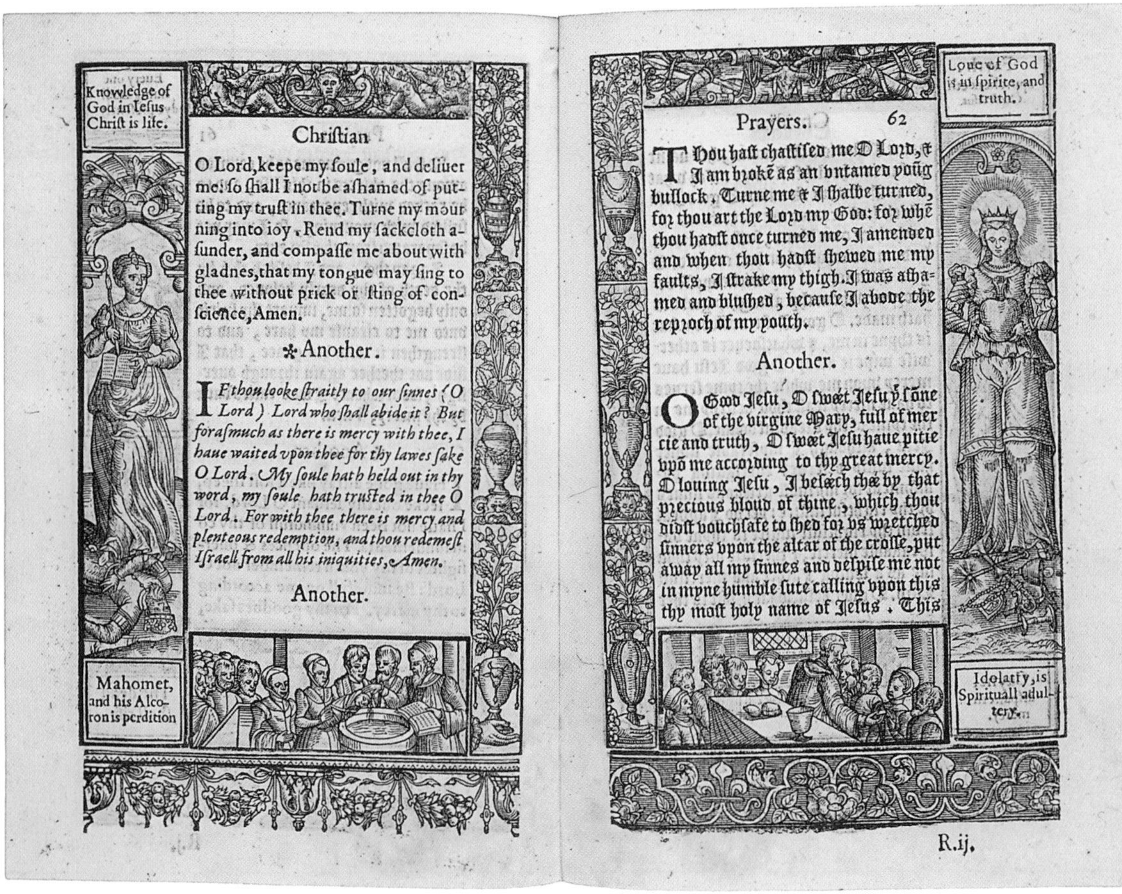
Knowledge of God in Iesus Christ is life.

Christian

O Lord, keepe my soule, and deliuer me: so shall I not be ashamed of putting my trust in thee. Turne my mourning into ioy, Rend my sackcloth asunder, and compasse me about with gladnes, that my tongue may sing to thee without prick or sting of conscience, Amen.

Another.

IF thou looke straitly to our sinnes (O Lord) Lord who shall abide it? But forasmuch as there is mercy with thee, I haue waited vpon thee for thy lawes sake O Lord. My soule hath held out in thy word, my soule hath trusted in thee O Lord. For with thee there is mercy and plenteous redemption, and thou redeemest Israell from all his iniquities, Amen.

Another.

Mahomet, and his Alcoron is perdition

Loue of God is in spirite, and truth.

Prayers. 62

THou hast chastised me O Lord, & I am broke as an vntamed young bullock. Turne me & I shalbe turned, for thou art the Lord my God: for whē thou hadst once turned me, I amended and when thou hadst shewed me my faults, I strake my thigh. I was ashamed and blushed, because I abode the reproch of my youth.

Another.

O Good Iesu, O sweet Iesu þ sone of the virgine Mary, full of mercie and truth, O sweet Iesu haue pitie vpō me according to thy great mercy. O louing Iesu, I beseech thee by that precious bloud of thine, which thou didst vouchsafe to shed for vs wretched sinners vpon the altar of the crosse, put away all my sinnes and despise me not in myne humble sute calling vpon this thy most holy name of Iesus. This

Idolatry is Spirituall adultery.

R.ij.

113. A TROJAN HORSE

In Elizabeth's reign the Book of Hours came to be associated with Catholicism. The *booke of Christian prayers*, first issued in 1578, adapted the form and layout of the discredited Book of Hours to promote protestant devotion. Here a favourite item in the older books, the prayer *O Bone Jesu*, is flanked by an image of true religion treading popish idolatry in the form of beads, candles, holy water sprinkler and the Blessed Sacrament, while at the foot of the page a protestant communion service is in progress.

RSTC 6429. A booke of Christian prayers (1578). Cambridge University Library, Sss 24 13 fo. 61v–62

114. A TROJAN HORSE

Deceptively traditional-looking border decorations, depicting the Passion of Christ and its Old Testament ante-types, here flank a prayer by John Foxe recalling the persecution of protestants under Queen Mary and denouncing the Pope.

RSTC 6429. A booke of Christian prayers (1578). Cambridge University Library, Sss 24 13 30v–31

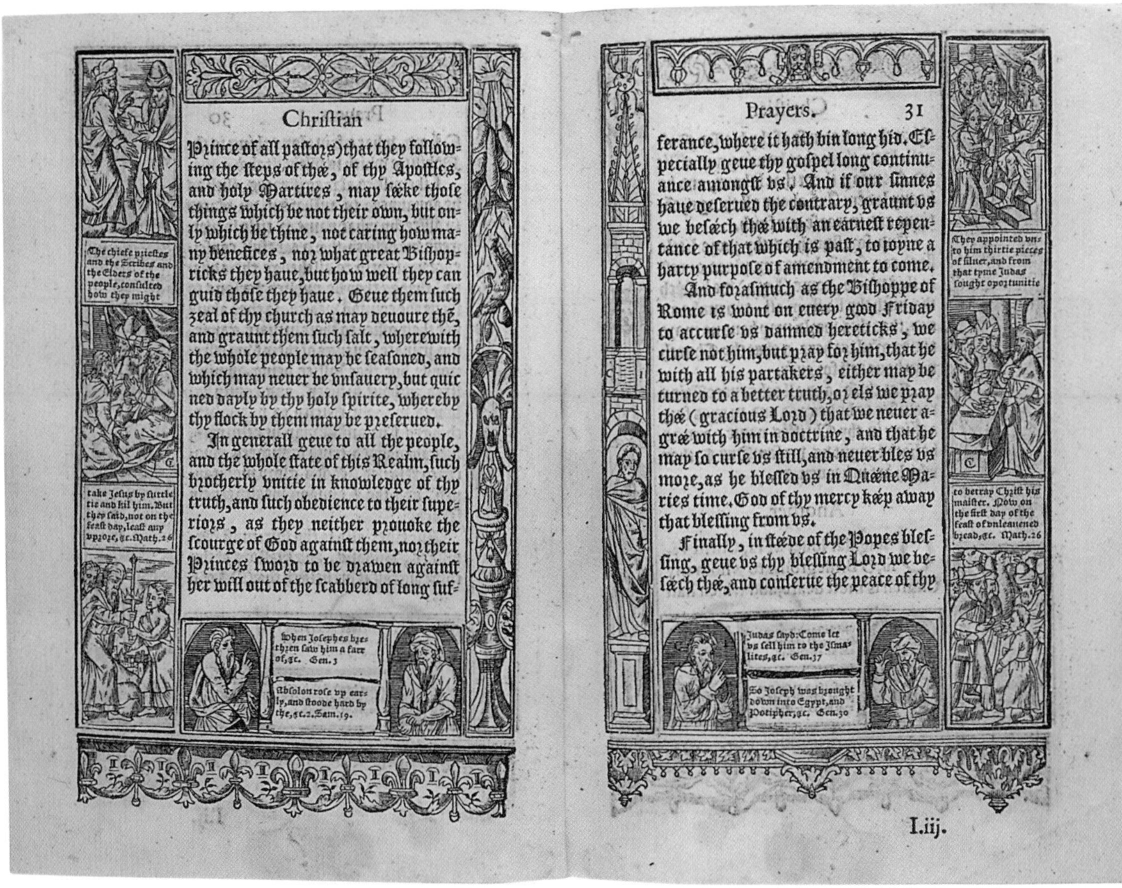
Christian

Prince of all pastors) that they following the steps of thee, of thy Apostles,
and holy Martires, may seeke those
things which be not their own, but only which be thine, not caring how many benefices, nor what great Bishop-
ricks they haue, but how well they can
guid those they haue. Geue them such
zeal of thy church as may deuoure thee,
and graunt them such salt, wherewith
the whole people may be seasoned, and
which may neuer be unsauery, but quic
ned dayly by thy holy spirite, whereby
thy flock by them may be preserued.
In generall geue to all the people,
and the whole state of this Realm, such
brotherly unitie in knowledge of thy
truth, and such obedience to their supe-
riors, as they neither prouoke the
scourge of God against them, nor their
Princes sword to be drawen against
her will out of the scabberd of long suf-

Prayers. 31

ferance, where it hath bin long hid. Especially geue thy gospel long continu-
ance amongst us. And if our sinnes
haue deserued the contrary, graunt us
we beseech thee with an earnest repentance of that which is past, to ioyne a
harty purpose of amendment to come.
And forasmuch as the Bishoppe of
Rome is wont on euery good Friday
to accurse us damned hereticks, we
curse not him, but pray for him, that he
with all his partakers, either may be
turned to a better truth, or els we pray
thee (gracious Lord) that we neuer a-
gree with him in doctrine, and that he
may so curse us still, and neuer bles us
more, as he blessed us in Queene Maries time. God of thy mercy keep away
that blessing from us.
Finally, in steede of the Popes blessing, geue us thy blessing Lord we beseech thee, and conserue the peace of thy

I.iij.

purged of papistical error and included many images of protestant religious activities. One might therefore recite an English version of the venerable catholic prayer *O Bone Jesu*, but the designs at the bottom of the page showed a protestant baptism and a protestant celebration of the Holy Communion, with a broken loaf of ordinary bread prominently placed directly on the communion table [Pl. 113].

And even in more traditional borders, portraying scenes from the Gospels, the devotee would find prayers against the Pope [Pl. 114], designed to remind him or her of the horrors of the bad old days of popery and the reign of Bloody Mary:

> And forasmuch as the Bishopp of Rome is wont every Good Friday to accurse us damned hereticks, we curse not him, but pray for him, that he with all

> his partakers, either may be turned to a better truth, or else we pray thee (gracious Lord) that we never agree with him in doctrine, and that he may so curse us still, and never bless us more, as he blessed us in Queene Maries time. God of thy mercy keep away that blessing from us.[2]

By the 1570s, then, the Book of Hours was widely taken to be the unmistakable mark of recidivists and papists, and the protestant satirist Thomas Ingelend, author of the morality play *The Disobedient Child*, could poke fun at the ignorant and ungodly 'maydecooke' boasting of her literacy: the *Disobedient Child* mocks the opening of Our Lady's Matins, in a speech which relies for its effect on the fading memory of old prayers in the minds of the Elizabethan audience:

> I dare saye she knoweth not how her Primer began
> Which of her Master she learned then.
> I trowe it began with *Domine labia aperies*
> What dyd it begyn with buttered pease
> Hoo how with my Madame laye in the peas
> Yea Mary I judged it went such wayes
> It began with Dorothe laye up the keyes.[3]

Conformist and Protestant families, it is true, often held on to manuscript Books of Hours, and occasionally copied unmistakeably protestant prayers into them, raising questions about the exact nature of their continuing use.[4] But most Books of Hours added to by protestant owners were being used essentially as family record albums. The age of the family Bible had not yet arrived, and the book of hours might retain power as a symbol of family continuities: for that reason birthdays – and much more rarely obits – continued to be entered in them. The Roberts family had certainly conformed by the 1580s, but they too went on using the book to record family births. A Book of Hours printed on vellum by Wynken de Worde in 1510 now in the British Library has a series of inscriptions which trace this persisting sentiment in a protestant family. A note across the February and March pages of the calendar records that

> Mr Roger North late of Walkringe in the countie of Nottingham deceased bestowed this boke of Mrs Syth Staunton, then the wyfe of Mr Anthonie Staunton Esq. The said Mr North then newly

> marryed unto Elizabeth daughter of the said Anthony and Syth anno 1548 wch Syth in her turne byquethyd this said boke to Wylm Staunton.

1548 is getting late for such a book to be given as a working devotional aid, but the pages of English prayers and the Office of Compline are heavily worn, and Mistress Scythe Staunton signed the book towards the end. It looks as if she used it. However that may be, the book evidently passed out of the family, and was then with some difficulty recovered. Thirty pages on is another note, in a much later hand:

> Memorandum, that I Harvey Staunton did after many dissents procure this boke again of the gift of Mr Gervase Dodsley Rector or vicar of Stretly March 9th 1692.

Sixty pages further on still are a series of names in an eighteenth-century hand – Ann Stanton, Mary Stanton, Elizabeth Stanton, Jane Stanton.[5]

So it was almost exclusively in recusant families that Books of Hours continued to be used for their original purposes. No Catholic Book of Hours was produced for English use between 1558 and 1599, when the first bilingual edition of the Tridentine Primer was printed by the Anglo-Dutch publisher and propagandist Richard Verstegen.[6] Till then, Catholics in search of a Book of Hours with which to say their prayers had to resort to inherited family books, or to buy others secondhand, and a high proportion of surviving Sarum Books of Hours have this sort of recusant provenance [cf. Frontispiece]. A fifteenth-century northern manuscript Book of Hours which had once belonged to a York vintner (now in the library of Downside Abbey), contains a long exhortation added in 1576 by Thomas Thomson, scholar, begging whoever 'to whom the keeping of this boke casually may happen' to pray that before his death he, Thomson, 'may have full contrition, confession, satisfaction and salvation, that he may swerve not from the true faythe nor renounce holly churche' and that 'he may dye with generall repentance and receive the reall sacrament'. Thomson clearly took it for granted that the possessor of such a book would be a Catholic, willing to make such prayers.[7] In the same library there is a Marian Book of Hours printed by John Wayland in 1554, the first sixteen folios of which are made up of manuscript prayers dating from the late Tudor and Stuart periods. These additions include indulgences secured for England by William Allen in the 1570s, and a long intercession that God will 'strengthen and bylde agane the walles and gates of thy Cittie the Churche Catholick. Restore the ruynes and gather to geathere the citizens thereof, now dispersed like sheepe withoute a Pastor, by lycednsyouse lyfe and perverse doctrine'.[8]

But the Catholic clergy arriving on the mission after 1574 worried about this use of pre- or non-Tridentine books. The Council of Trent had ordered the reform of the old liturgical books, targeting especially the sort of miraculous legends and bogus indulgence rubrics with which the older books teemed, and the Douai priests were instructed by their moral theology teachers that such superstitious legends must be removed from books still in use. They also worried about continued Catholic use of the books produced for England after 1536, including the Marian primers, because they had no indulgences at all in them. As one Elizabethan casuist on the seminary staff wrote 'in my judgement it is stupid to want to read those editions which carry no indulgences, and to refuse to read those books which have indulgences'.[9] Additions like those in the Downside 1554 volume clearly seek to rectify these defects. Inevitably, however, suspect alike to Protestant and Catholic clergy, the traditional Book of Hours was destined to fade.

But whatever the difficulties which over-precise seminary priests might oppose to their use, in the middle years of Elizabeth the continuing use of such prayer-books was above all a badge of non-compliance with the Reformation. Archbishop Grindal's Injunctions for the York diocese in 1571 ordered that 'no person or persons shall . . . pray either in Latin or in English upon beads or knots or any other like superstitious thing, nor shall pray upon any popish Latin or English Primer'.[10] He had in mind deviants like the church papist Sir Thomas Cornwallis who 'all service time when others on their knees are at prayers will sett contemptuously reading in a book, most likely some Lady psalter or porteus which have been found in his pew', or Arthur Chapman, a blacksmith of County Durham, who in 1570 disturbed the parishioners on St Matthew's day by his reading of an 'ynglisshe booke or prymer', or John Harely of Brompton in 1577 who comes to church but 'doth there in the time of divine service reade so loude uppon his latin popish primer (that he understandeth not) that he troubleth both the minister and people'.[11] Now indeed the Book of Hours had become the mark of the religious individualist, though it had taken fifty years of religious turmoil and a revolution in devotional sentiment to make it so.

NOTES

Chapter 1

1. For the role of the Book of Hours in the Annunciation, see below pp. 43–5: for examples of donors with Books of Hours, Pls. 1, 13, 18, 22, 42 below.
2. The estimates in Mary C. Erler, 'Devotional Literature', in L. Hellinga and J.B. Trapp (eds), *The Cambridge History of the Book in Britain*, Cambridge 1999, vol. III, 1400–1557, pp. 495–6, are certainly too conservative. My larger figure of almost 800 manuscripts (789 to be precise) is derived from a database of surviving manuscripts compiled by Professor Nigel Morgan, who kindly made the information available to me.
3. Most of the vast literature on Books of Hours is written by or for art historians. The best introductions are J. Harthan, *Books of Hours and their Owners*, London 1977; Christopher de Hamel, *A History of Illuminated Manuscripts*, London 1994, ch. 6; Roger S. Wieck, *The Book of Hours in Medieval Art and Life*, London 1988, and the same author's *Painted Prayers: the Book of Hours in Medieval and Renaissance Art*, New York 1997, both of which are however also helpful on the religious texts in Books of Hours. The standard authority on the contents of Books of Hours is V. Leroquais, *Les Livres d'heures manuscripts de la Bibliothèque nationale*, Paris 1927, with a Supplément, 1947. For early English Books of Hours, see: Janet Backhouse, *The Madresfield Hours*, Oxford 1976; Claire Donovan, *The De Brailes Hours*, London 1991; and Kathryn A. Smith, *Art, Identity and Devotion in Fourteenth-Century England: Three Women and their Books of Hours*, London and Toronto 2003. For the place of the Sarum Book of Hours, manuscript and printed, in the wider context of late medieval religious book production and circulation, see Mary C. Erler, 'Devotional Literature', pp. 495–525.
4. This is the title for the relevant chapter of de Hamel's *History of Illuminated Manuscripts*.
5. Erler, 'Devotional Literature', p. 497.
6. Edmund Bishop, 'On the origin of the prymer', *Liturgica Historica*, Oxford 1918, pp. 211–37: S. E. Ropes, *Medieval English Benedictine Liturgy. Studies in the Foundation, Structure and Content of the Monastic Votive Office c. 950–1540*. New York and London 1993.
7. For a survey of which, see Robert Swanson, *Religion and Devotion in Europe 1215–1515*, Cambridge 1993, chs. 1 and 5.
8. On lay literacy in the Middle Ages, see M. T. Clanchy, *From Memory to Written Record, England 1066–1307*, 2nd edn Oxford 1993; for women's devotional literacy in particular, see the survey by Julia Boffey, 'Women's authors and women's literacy in fourteenth and fifteenth-century England', in Carol M. Meale (ed.), *Women and Literature in Britain 1150–1500*, Cambridge 1996, pp. 159–82.
9. In quoting from *Ancrene Wisse* I have used the translation in Anne Savage and Nicholas Watson, *Anchoritic Spirituality*, Mahwah New Jersey 1991. There is a good modern treatment of the medieval English anchoritic movement in Ann K. Warren, *Anchorites and their Patrons in Medieval England*, Berkeley and London 1985.

On the mediating role of anchoresses in the emergence of a devotional literature for lay people, see Bella Millett, 'Women in No Man's land: English recluses and the development of vernacular literature in the twelfth and thirteenth centuries', in Meale, *Women and Literature in Britain*, pp. 86–103.

10. Savage and Watson, *Anchoritic Spirituality*, p. 64.
11. In the Latin Bible, the Penitential Psalms are numbers 6, 31, 37, 50, 101, 129 and 142, and the fifteen Gradual Psalms are Psalms 119–33. They were known as the 'Gradual' Psalms because in the Latin text they are each headed 'Canticum graduum', a song of 'degrees' or 'ascents'. In early Christian and medieval legend, these psalms were recited by the infant Virgin Mary as she ascended the steps of the Temple, hence the special appropriateness of their place in Books containing the Hours of the Virgin. In citing the psalms the Vulgate number is given first, then the Hebrew numbering followed in most modern bibles is given in brackets.
12. Donovan, *The De Brailes Hours*.
13. Ibid., p. 24. The name has been conjectured from the presence of a sequence of illuminated initials in the Gradual Psalms, depicting the (rarely illustrated) story of Susannah and the Elders from the Book of Daniel. A kneeling woman, evidently the intended owner of the book, is shown in some historiated initials of the Penitented and Gradual Psalms, Litany and at the end of Compline of the Hours of the Virgin.
14. Ibid., pp. 120–4.
15. Ibid., pls. 2, 15, 16, fig. 6.
16. Reproduced in ibid., fig. 86, p. 126.
17. The much lower figures in Donovan, *The De Brailes Hours* exclude Hours combined with Psalters. Professor Morgan's database, followed in the text, lists 30 Hours (including Psalter-Hours) to the end of the thirteenth century, and 104 for the following century.
18. Contents listed in Donovan, pp. 183–4.
19. Christ's College Cambridge Ms 8: contents itemised in Donovan pp. 196–200, and more fully in M. R. James, *A Descriptive Catalogue of the Western Manuscripts in the Library of Christ's College Cambridge*, Cambridge 1905, pp. 9–27.
20. Lucy F. Sandler, *Gothic Manuscripts 1285–1385*, Oxford 1986, pp. 53–5, discussion of the Norwich Hours of *c.* 1310–20, Norwich Castle Museum Ms 158.926. 4f.
21. Discussions of thirteenth-century books of hours for women in Donovan, *The De Brailes Hours*, pp. 183–200; Smith, *Art, Identity and Devotion*, *passim*. This association with women would be a constant in the history of the Book of Hours, and would survive even the advent of print. Something like a quarter of the surviving Books of Hours printed for England before 1500 have been written in by women – Mary C. Erler, *Women Reading and Piety in Late Medieval England*, Cambridge 2003, p. 119.
22. The Psalter-Hours persisted in England, though in declining numbers. Professor Nigel Morgan's database yields the following figures for surviving manuscript Psalters and Hours (including Psalter-Hours) for England.

13th c.	Psalters: 137
	Hours (including Psalter-Hours): 30
14th c.	Psalters: 118
	Hours (including Psalter-Hours): 104
15th c.	Psalters: 150
	Hours (including Psalter-Hours): 610
1500–35	Psalters: 11
	Hours (including Psalter-Hours): 28

It should be borne in mind that the Psalter remained a canonically required book, which till well into the fifteenth century parishes might be expected to own, and this has a bearing on the continued production of Psalters. The collapse in manuscript production after 1500 is striking.

23. Smith, *Art, Identity and Devotion*, pp. 152–248.
24. Discussion of the devotional function of some of these early sequences in Smith, *Art, Identity and Devotion*, *passim*.
25. For the birth and infancy set, see Wieck, *The Book of Hours*, pls. 1–8 and pp. 60–6, and for the Passion sequence, ibid, pp. 66–71; for a good fifteenth-century example with both Infancy and Passion sequences before the Hours, Fitzwilliam Museum 53 fos 26v–27 ff.
26. Examples in Wieck, *Painted Prayers*, pp. 99 ff.; pls. 7, 15, 17, 27, 28, 29, 31–3, 40, 48 below.
27. *Horae Eboracenses* (1920) pp. 81–2, and Eamon Duffy, *The Stripping of the Altars*, New Haven and London 1992, pp. 238–48.

28. York Minster, Add Ms 2, Bolton Hours, *passim*; Ker and Piper, vol. IV, pp. 786–91; Kathleen Scott, *Later Gothic Manuscripts*, vol. II, pp. 119–23; Richard Marks and Paul Williamson (eds), *Gothic: Art for England 1400–1547*, London 2003, pp. 59, 278; Patricia Cullum and Jeremy Goldberg, 'How Margaret Blackburn taught her daughters: reading devotional instruction in a Book of Hours', in Jocelyn Wogan-Browne (ed.), *Medieval Women: Texts and Contexts in Late Medieval Britain*, Turnhout 2000, pp. 217–36, where the authors' identification of Margaret Blackburn as the commissioning patroness of the volume is perhaps overconfident; S. Rees-Jones and F. Riddy, 'The Bolton Hours of York: female domestic piety and the public sphere', in A. Mulder-Bakke and J. Wogan-Browne (eds), *Household, Women and Christianities*, Turnhout 2006, forthcoming. Henry IV planned but did not complete a House of Bridgettines on the site of the Hospital of St Nicholas at York.
29. S. Ringbom, *Icon to Narrative. The Rise of the Dramatic Close-up in 15th Century Devotional Painting*, Abo 1965; idem, 'Devotional images and imaginative devotions. Notes on the place of art in late medieval private piety', *Gazette des Beaux-Arts*, series VI, 73, 1963, pp. 159–70; Robert Scribner, 'Popular piety and modes of visual perception in late medieval and reformation Germany', *Journal of Religious History* XV, 1989, pp. 448–69.
30. Reproduced in facsimile in *The Hours of Mary of Burgundy*, ed. Eric Inglis, London 1995, fo. 14v, 43v; the first illustration, of Mary of Burgundy at prayer, was one of the points of departure for the important essay on prayer and the book of hours by John Bossy, 'Prayers', *Transactions of the Royal Historical Society*, 6th Series, 1, 1991, pp. 137–48, discussed below pp. 97–98.
31. Savage and Watson, *Anchoritic Spirituality*, pp. 64–5.
32. Cited in Smith, *Art, Identity and Devotion*, pp. 1–2.
33. Ibid, pp. 20–8: For the Pabenham-Clifford (Grey Fitzpayne) Hours (Fitzwilliam Museum Ms 242), see M. R. James, *A Descriptive Catalogue of the Manuscripts in the Fitzwilliam Museum*, Cambridge 1895, pp. 389–99; F. Wormald and P. M. Giles, *A Descriptive Catalogue of the Additional Manuscripts in the Fitzwilliam Museum*, Cambridge 1982, pp. 157–60; L. F. Sandler, *Gothic Manuscripts 1285–1385*, London 1986, pp. 36–7; Paul Binski and Stella Panayatova, *The Cambridge Illuminations*, London 2005, pp. 191–3. The reattribution to Pabenham-Clifford was made by John A. Goodall, 'Heraldry in the decoration of English medieval manuscripts', *Antiquaries Journal*, 77, 1997 pp. 180–1.
34. John B. Friedman, *Northern English Books, Owners and Makers in the Middle Ages*, Syracuse 1995, pp. 17–19.
35. For example the Hastings Hours (BL Add Ms 54782 (*c.* 1480) or BL 17012 (late 1490s) – for the latter see pls. 109, 110.
36. Nicholas Rogers, 'Patrons and purchasers: evidence for the original owners of books produced in the Low Countries for the English Market', in B. Cardon, I. Van der Stock and D. Vanwijnsberghe (eds), *'Als Ich Can': Liber Amicorum in Memory of Professor Dr Maurits Smeyers*, Corpus of Illuminated Manuscripts vol. 11–12, Low Countries Series 8, Leuven 2002, vol. 11, pp. 1165–81, summarising part of his invaluable unpublished 1984 University of Cambridge M. Litt. thesis, 'Books of Hours produced in the Low Countries for the English Market'; Jonathan J. G. Alexander, *Medieval Illuminators and their Methods of Work*, New Haven and London 1992, pp. 125–6.
37. I paraphrase Deschamps' lines, quoted more literally in Eric Inglis (ed.), *The Hours of Mary of Burgundy*, pp. 60–1.
38. Both books described and illustrated in Marks and Williamson, *Gothic*, pp. 274, 278. The Browne Hours are in Philadelphia Free Library, Widener Ms 3; cf. Rogers, 'Patrons and Purchasers' p. 1167 (book commissioned in the 1420s for a London grocer); N. R. Ker, *Medieval Manuscripts in British Libraries*, vol. I, pp. 205–7 (*Horae* commissioned in 1479 for a Bristol merchant); N. R. Ker and A. Piper, *Medieval Manuscripts in British Libraries*, vol. IV, pp. 727–30 (Book of Hours made for a parishioner of All Saints, York), pp. 786–91 (Bolton Hours).

39. These examples from Rees-Jones and Riddy, 'The Bolton Hours of York', with my thanks to Felicity Riddy.
40. Reproduced in Marks and Williamson, *Gothic*, cat. no. 213; Lorne Campbell (ed.), *National Gallery Catalogues: The Fifteenth-Century Netherlandish Schools*, London 1997, p. 377. Similar (later) examples from the reign of Henry VIII reproduced as *Gothic* cat. no. 276 and pl. 49 (Knyvett altarpiece) – though here, to judge by the double columns, the lay patrons appear to be reading breviaries rather than Books of Hours; cat. no. 135 (Withypole altarpiece). For the Hastings Hours, see D. H. Turner (ed.) *The Hastings Hours, a 15th century Flemish Book of Hours made for William Lord Hastings*, London 1983. For a suggestion that this manuscript was in fact made for Edward V and given by him to Sir William Hastings, see Pamela Tudor Craig, 'The Hours of Edward V and William, Lord Hastings: British Library Manuscript Additional 54782', in D. Williams (ed.), *England in the Fifteenth Century*, Woodbridge 1987, pp. 351–69, queried in J. J. G. Alexander, 'Katherine Bray's Flemish Book of Hours', *The Ricardian*, 8, 107, 1989, pp. 308–17. For the Hours of Sir John Donne, now in the library of the Catholic University at Louvain, see Marks and Williamson, *Gothic*, cat. no. 215, pp. 338–9.

Chapter 2

1. F. J. Furnivall (ed.), *The Fifty Earliest English Wills in the Court of Probate*, Early English Text Society 1882, pp. 5, 102; for Agnes Hull's bequest, see P. J. Goldberg, 'Lay book ownership in late medieval York', *The Library*, 6th Series 16, 1994, pp. 181–9, at p. 185. And compare Margaret Hungerford's bequest to her grand-daughter in 1478 of her 'matins boke . . . covered with blewe velwette and clasped with silver and gilte with my worde 'Myne assured trouthe', Meale, *Women and Literature in Britain*, p. 147; Anne M. Dutton, 'Passing the Book: testamentary transmission of religious literature for and by women in England, 1350–1500', in L. Smith and J. H. M. Taylor (eds), *Women, the Book and the Godly*, Cambridge 1995, vol. 1, pp. 41–51.
2. Pierpont Morgan Library, PML 1034 (STC 15959) final flyleaf, recto.
3. Bodleian Ms Don.d.206, *passim*; information from Professor John Barron, who is preparing a study of the book for the *Bodleian Library Record*.
4. Sidney Sussex Ms 37, fos. 154v–6.
5. Ushaw College Ms 43, fo. 136.
6. Rogers, 'Books of Hours', p. 48.
7. Duffy, *The Stripping of the Altars*, pp. 209–32, and below, ch. 8.
8. An example illustrated in Christopher de Hamel, *A History of Illuminated Manuscripts*, London 1994, p. 169.
9. Inglis (ed.), *The Hours of Mary of Burgundy*, fo. 14v.
10. This is true of many of the books discussed in Rogers, 'Books of Hours', *passim*.
11. Examples of cheap mass-produced manuscript illustrations from fifteenth-century books for the English market in Alain Arnould and Jean Michel Massing (eds), *Splendours of Flanders*, Cambridge 1993, cat. nos. 32, 33, 39. Two such late-fourteenth century books from the same workshop are CUL Ii 2 6, and BL Sloane Ms 2683. See pls. 14, 15, 53–60 infra. And for the illustrations for the Netherlandish books for England in general, see the exhibition catalogue *Vlaamse miniatures voor van Eyck c. 1380–1420*, Leuven 1993. (Thanks to Nigel Morgan for this reference).
12. The publishers were Philip Pigouchet and Simon Vostre; representative pages by the Master of Anne of Brittany in Marks and Williamson, *Gothic*, p. 345, and Wieck, *Painted Prayers*, pp. 33, 57; I. Netteboven, *Der Meister der Apokalypsenrose der Sainte Chapelle und die Pariser Buchkunst um 1500*, Turnhout 2004. (Thanks to Nigel Morgan for this reference).
13. Pierpont Morgan Library, New York, Ms M. 700, De Bois Hours, fos 30, 146v, 147, 147v: Smith, *Art, Identity and Devotion*, pp. 254–5.
14. Lambeth Palace Library Ms 474 ff., 181–3v: for a transcription and translation of the prayer, Anne F. Sutton and Livia Visser-Fuchs, *The Hours of Richard III*, Stroud 1990, pp. 76–8.
15. Scott, *Later Gothic Manuscripts*, vol. II, p. 164;

several women's signatures occur through the book, and obits suggest it went on being used into the 1540s.

16. CUL Ee.1.14 fos 119v–120r: Binski and Panayotova, *Cambridge Illuminations*, no. 82, pp. 193–4. For the same prayer customised for an owner named John, see New York, Pierpont Morgan Library Ms M. 487, fos 219–22v.
17. G. C. Moore Smith, *The Family of Withypoll*, Walthamstow Antiquarian Society, Official Publication no. 3, 1936, pp. 13–23.
18. M. R. James, 'Description of the ancient manuscripts in the Ipswich Public Library', *Proceedings of the Suffolk Institute of Archaeology and Natural History*, vol. xxii, 1938, p. 87; Ker, *Medieval Manuscripts*, II, pp. 991–2; for the printed book, see Alan Coates et al., *A Catalogue of Books printed in the Fifteenth Century now in the Bodleian Library*, III, Oxford 2005, pp. 1391–3.
19. If one accepts that the depictions of the biblical Susannah are allusions to the 'Susanna' who owned the book.
20. Binski and Panayatova, *Cambridge Illuminations*, pp. 192–3.
21. De Hamel, *Illuminated Manuscripts*, p. 170.
22. Duffy *Stripping of the Altars*, ch. 6; for printed Books of Hours for the English market, the standard reference work is Edgar Hoskins, *Horae Beatae Mariae Virginis or Sarum and York Primers with kindred Books . . . an Introduction*, London 1901; see also, Helen C. White, *The Tudor Books of Private Devotion*, Madison Wisconsin 1951, and C. Butterworth, *The English Primers 1529–1549*, Philadelphia 1953.
23. Harthan, *Books of Hours*, p. 37; for Annunciations with Bible or Breviary, see Otto Pächt, *Early Netherlandish Painting*, London 1997, Pl. 1 and fig. 3; for Annunciations with Hours or Psalter, see Isolde Lubbecke, *The Thyssen-Bornemisza Collection: Early German Painting 1350–1550*, figs. 84–5, and Pächt, *Early Netherlandish Painting*, figs. 65, 88; De Hamel, *Illuminated Manuscripts*, pl. 166.
24. Walters Art Gallery, Baltimore, Ms 267, fos 13v and 14: Wieck, *The Book of Hours*, figs 12a and 12b, and Plate 14, pp. 43, 74.
25. Lambeth Palace Library Ms 545, Lewkenor Hours, fos. 78v–79.
26. Ibid fo. 184v–185. Illustrated in Marks and Williamson, *Gothic*, p. 435; 'or sped', suggested by Erler, 'Devotional Literature', p. 513 seems a better reading of the inscription than the 'so goode' proposed by M. R. James and Claude Jenkins, *A Descriptive Catalogue of the Manuscripts in the Library of Lambeth Palace*, Cambridge 1930–2, pp. 747–50. For another such paste-in of a less elaborate card of the Cross of Bromholm, see Stonyhurst College Ms LVII, fo. 174.
27. Lambeth Palace Library Ms 545 fo. 193v.
28. Fitzwilliam Ms 55 fo. 57v.
29. *Hours of Mary of Burgundy* fos 1*v–2*. For a more sustained example of a 'virtual pilgrimage' in a Book of Hours, see Kathryn M. Rudy, 'A pilgrim's Book of Hours', *Studies in Iconography*, 21, 2000, pp. 237–79. I am grateful to Kathryn Beebe for alerting me to this article.
30. STC 15899, BL C 41 e 8: unpaginated back flyleaf. For illuminating discussions of late medieval and Tudor devotional card insertions and 'paste-ins', see Mary C. Erler, 'Pasted-in embellishments in English manuscripts and printed books *c.* 1480–1533', *The Library*, VI Series, vol. 14, 1992, pp. 185–206, and eadem, 'Devotional Literature', pp. 511–14.
31. Bodleian Douce Ms 24, unpaginated calendar *passim*: the charming note on her marriage occurs on the April page (Feast of the Translation of St Wilfred, 24 April); the notes testify to the Withypole family's court connections, for they seem to be replicated from similar additions to BL Ms Royal 2.A.XVIII, the Beaufort Hours, which Margaret Beaufort inherited from her mother Margaret Beauchamp, and the calendar of the Beaufort Hours contains an obit dated 1537 for Paul Withypole's daughter, Elizabeth Lucas: Scott, *Later Gothic Manuscripts* no. 37 at p. 131, and Coates et al., *Catalogue*, pp. 1391–3.
32. Fitzwilliam Ms 54, fos 2v, 3v.
33. Fitzwilliam Ms MacClean 89, back flyleaf.
34. CUL Ms Ee 1 14, Calendar for November.
35. C. Wordsworth and H. Littlehales, *The Old Service Books of the English Church*, London 1904, pp. 58–9; Colin Richmond, 'Margins and

marginality: English devotion in the later Middle Ages', in Nicholas Rogers (ed.), *England in the Fifteenth Century*, Stamford 1994, pp. 242–52, at p. 245.
36. Furnivall, *Earliest English Wills*, p. 58.
37. N. H. Nicolas (ed.), *Testamenta Vetusta*, London 1826, p. 148.
38. Bodleian Library, Douce 24, sigs A5r and D1r, Q10v, Coates et al., *Catalogue* pp. 1391–3.
39. Ushaw College, Durham, Ms 10: description in Ker and Piper, *Medieval Manuscripts*, vol. IV, pp. 516–19, and in E. Bonney 'Some prayers and prayer-books of our forefathers', *Ushaw Magazine* 12, 1902, pp. 273–87. See the satisfying and characteristically astute detective work by Rogers, 'Patrons and purchasers', p. 1169.
40. CUL Ii 6 4: see the similar inscription in York Minster Add Ms 67 f 125v.
41. Fitzwilliam Ms 56, fos. 1v, 159.
42. CUL Inc 4.J.1.2 [3750]; J. C. T. Oates, *A Catalogue of the Fifteenth-Century Printed Books in the University Library Cambridge*, Cambridge 1954, vol. 2, p. 685; Mary C. Erler, *Women, Reading and Piety in Late Medieval England*, Cambridge 2002, p. 119.
43. RSTC 15880, BL IA 41332.
44. RSTC 15881.3, Bodleian Arch n f 42.
45. RSTC 15889. For this and the two previous examples, Erler, *Women, Reading and Piety*, pp. 119–20.
46. Devonshire Collection, Chatsworth, Hours of Margaret Tudor, Queen of Scots, fos. 14, 32v: Marks and Williamson, *Gothic*, cat. no. 45, pp. 184–5; cf. British Library King's Ms 9 (Lovell Hours), fo. 231 (inscription by Henry VIII: and see Henry VIII's inscription to the owner of the Prayer-roll (now Ushaw College Ms 39), 'Willyam Harris I pray yow pray for me your loving master Prynce Henry', Ker and Piper, *Medieval Manuscripts*, vol. IV, p. 540.
47. R. Lockyer (ed.), *Thomas Wolsey, late Cardinal, his life and death written by George Cavendish his gentleman-usher*, London 1962, p. 141.
48. BL Add 17012 fos. 20v–21r.
49. Lady Joan Guildford married Sir Anthony Poyntz of Iron Acton.
50. BL Add 17012, fo. 192v.

Chapter 3

1. National Gallery, London, no. 2593.
2. Matthew 6:6.
3. Carol J. Purtle, *The Marian Paintings of Jan Van Eyck*, Princeton 1982, pp. 144–56.
4. Colin Richmond, 'Religion and the Fifteenth-Century Gentleman', in R. B. Dobson (ed.), *The Church, Politics and Patronage in the Fifteenth Century*, Gloucester 1984, p. 199.
5. On whom, see Clarissa Atkinson, *Mystic and Pilgrim, the Book and World of Margery Kempe*, Ithaca and London, 1983; Anthony Goodman, *Margery Kempe and her World*, London 2002, ch. 5.
6. M. J. Charlesworth (ed.), *St Anselm's Proslogion*, Oxford 1965, p. 110.
7. Above, p. 55.
8. See, for example, the title-page of STC 15973, published by François Regnault in 1531 (reproduced in Duffy, *Stripping of the Altars* pl. 93).
9. Reproduced in Oskar Batschmann and Pascal Griener, *Hans Holbein*, London 1997, p. 160.
10. S. B. Meech and H. E. Allen, *The Book of Margery Kempe*, Early English Text Society 1940, pp. 212, 221.
11. C. A. Sneyd (ed.), *A Relation of the Island of England*, Camden Society old series 37, 1847, p. 23.
12. Donovan, *De Brailes Hours*, p. 130 is mistaken in claiming that the Dominicans followed the Une of Rome. I am specially grateful to Nigel Morgan for clarification of this point.
13. Ann Hudson, *The Premature Reformation*, Oxford 1988; Nicholas Watson, 'Censorship and cultural change in late-medieval England: Vernacular theology. The Oxford Translation Debate, and Arundel's Constitutions of 1409', *Speculum* 70, 1995, pp. 822–64.
14. On the importance of language as the language of the Bible, Christopher de Hamel, *The Book: a History of the Bible in England*, London 2001, pp. 166ff.
15. See the examples collected in Sutton and Visser-Fuchs, *The Hours of Richard III*, figs. 12–19, plate 2.
16. Examples include the Gounter monument at Racton, the Ernley monument at West

Wittering, and the Sackville monument at Westhampnett, all in Sussex: the Sackville monument is illustrated in Duffy, *Stripping of the Altars*, pl. 9.
17. Lambeth Palace Library Ms 459 fo. 1r.
18. Latin text in *Horae Eboracenses*, pp. 83–4.
19. N. Davis (ed.), *Paston Letters and Papers of the Fifteenth Century*, Oxford 1971–6, vol. 1, p. 39.
20. Duffy, *Stripping of the Altars*, ch. 8.

Chapter 4

1. Above pp. 33–55.
2. Analysis of the standard contents in Wieck, *Painted Prayers*, pp. 26–119; see also Duffy, *Stripping of the Altars*, ch. 7.
3. See, for example, Ker and Piper, *Medieval Manuscripts*, vol. IV, pp. 788 (item 8a) and 810 (item 7).
4. Above pp. 17–19.
5. For another Book of Hours with Talbot family associations in a similar narrow format see Ker, *Medieval Mss in British Libraries*, vol. II, pp. 111–18 (Blairs College Ms 1).
6. The two books are calendared and analysed in M. R. James, *A Descriptive Catalogue of the Second Series of Fifty Manuscripts in the Collection of Henry Yates Thompson*, Cambridge 1902, pp. 218–38; F. Wormald and P. M. Giles, *A Descriptive Catalogue of the Additional Manuscripts in the Fitzwilliam Museum*, Cambridge 1982, pp. 441–54; Marks and Williamson, *Gothic*, cat. no. 94, pp. 230–1, where the dedication miniatures of both books are illustrated.
7. Biographical details on John and Margaret Talbot from the ODNB article by A. J. Pollard.
8. *I Henry VI*, III. vi. 70.
9. *I Henry VI*, IV. ii. 11–12.
10. James, *Descriptive Catalogue*, p. 232.
11. Cf. the similar portrayal of John, Duke of Bedford, with Saint George in the sumptuous Bedford Hours, reproduced in Janet Backhouse, *The Bedford Hours*, London 1990, p. 54, and commentary, pp. 37, 55.
12. E.g. the opening rubric of the Fifteen Oes 'And also oure lord seithe he that seithe the ose orois-sones hor hertrth hem he schal se myne body and receive hit xv deyes before hys dethe', Fitzwilliam 40–1950 fo. 55v. The oes are so named because they all start with the words 'O Jesu'.
13. Fitzwilliam 40–1950, fo. 50.
14. Ibid, fos 81–2.
15. James, *Descriptive Catalogue*, pp. 223–4, 228–30. Fitzwilliam 40–1950 fo. 82.
16. Duffy, *Stripping of the Altars*, ch. 8.
17. On the Charlemagne prayer, see ibid. p. 273.
18. Fitzwilliam 40–1950, fo. 35, my translation.
19. Fitzwilliam 40–1950, fos. 108–14v.
20. Fitzwilliam 40–1950, fo. 115.
21. Fitzwilliam 40–1950, fo. 133. See below on CUL Ii 6. 2, and see also CUL Ff.6.8 fo. 1, for another version of this prayer. See also below pp. 81, 86–7, 129–31.
22. Fitzwilliam 40–1950, fos 107v, 132–5v.
23. Fitzwilliam 40–1950 fo. 135–135v: Marks and Williamson, *Gothic*, p 231.
24. Fitzwilliam 40–1950 fo. f 73. It precedes a hymn to the Virgin, *Salve Mater Misericordiae*.
25. Most of the contents of Talbot's book are replicated in his wife's book, and in another book from Blairs College now in the Scottish National Library, which seems to emanate from the Talbot affinity. For the overlap between these books see James, *Descriptive Catalogue*, *passim*, who asterisks the common material in the two Talbot books in the Fitzwilliam, and Ker, *Medieval Manuscripts*, vol. II, pp. 113–18.
26. RSTC 20195; cf. Susan Powell, 'Lady Margaret Beaufort and her Books', *The Library*, 6th Series, vol. 20, 1998, pp. 197–240, at p. 212.
27. RSTC 15875; this was taken as the basic copy-text in Edgar Hoskins's analysis of the English *Horae*. For its inclusion in this and other printed versions, see Hoskins, *Horae*, pp. 116, 187, 211.
28. Above, pp. 534.
29. RSTC 15912, fos cxxxvi (verso) ff. This edition is illustrated below, plate 84.
30. Fitzwilliam 40–1950 fo. 107v.

Chapter 5

1. A comparable analysis might be made from the additions to many other fifteenth-century Ms

Horae, for example St John's College Cambridge Ms E.26; CUL Ff 6 8; Sidney Sussex Ms 80; Fitzwilliam Museum 51; Ushaw Ms 10; Bodleian Ms Rawl liturgy, f2, Rawl liturgy e7 or e8; or Pierpont Morgan Library Ms M. 487. All of these, though less copious, have many features in common with CUL Ii 6 2. Fitzwilliam Museum Ms 56, a high-quality fifteenth-century Flemish book which by the reign of Henry VIII was in the hands of Robert Ratcliffe, Earl of Sussex, contains many prayers in Latin and English added before and after the main body of the book in several fine scribal hands, representing different devotional campaigns: the added material includes a devotion in English verse on the Psalms of the Passion beginning 'O Lord Omnipotent, Father of our creation' (fo. 123v ff.), and versions of the standard set of English prayers for a good death found in many printed Horae and perhaps copied here (fos 160 ff.) from a printed book.

2. Rogers, 'Books of Hours', p. 71.
3. Above, p. 67.
4. T. F. T. Baker (ed.), *Victoria County History of Middlesex*, vol. VII, Oxford 1982, pp. 216–17, 238: F. A. Wood, 'The Parish of Willesden' in *Transactions of the London and Middlesex Archaeological Society*, vol. IV, 1875, pp. 189–201.
5. The handwriting is clear and there seems little doubt that the words are written as transcribed here, but I can make no sense of them. Theobal appears to be a proper name: the copyist of the prayer was perhaps rendering an imperfectly understood formula of invocation.
6. Remedium = Latin for healing or remedy. Tetragrammaton = the Hebrew Name of God, YHWH, often invoked in magical prayers of this kind. Hosion = Greek for holiness, All three words are being invoked as *names* of power.
7. The Latin at this point (as in others) is obscure and perhaps in part nonsensical. It runs: 'Christi veritas, pax Christi, molitus Christi eleyson'. Molitus is a participle of the verb *molior*, to strive or labour, and is just possibly being used as if it were a fourth declension noun, and I have translated it accordingly. This ingenious conjectural solution to a puzzle which admittedly may simply be due to the undoubtedly shaky Latinity of whoever copied the prayer, was suggested to me by my colleague Dr Richard Rex.
8. For an extended discussion of these sorts of prayers, and the issues they raise, see Duffy, *The Stripping of the Altars*, pp. 266–98.
9. Ibid., pp. 278ff.
10. E.g. Ushaw College Durham ms 10, fo. 11 and BL Harley Ms 494 fo. 89v.
11. Duffy, *Stripping of the Altars*, p. 277.
12. Nicholas Rogers points out to me that the same verse was also inscribed on the noble (coin worth 6s 8d) first minted in Edward III's reign, where it served perhaps as a protection against theft.
13. Marcel Thomas (ed.), *The Rohan Master, a Book of Hours*, New York 1973, pl. 63 (the commentary on this plate overconfidently identifies the Divine Judge in this plate as God the Father, despite the fact that his halo contains the 'titulus' from the Cross, 'Jesus of Nazareth King of the Jews'). The titulus was also employed as a protective charm, like that embroidered on the cuffs of God's robe, and its inclusion in the halo may therefore not be an entirely secure indication that the being portrayed is Christ as described in the Book of Revelation, with white hair and beard, rather than God the Father: but combined with the fact that God here speaks a version of Christ's words to the dying thief, there is a strong presumption that this is what is intended.)
14. Duffy, *Stripping of the Altars*, p. 175.
15. Ushaw College Ms. 10 fo. 11.

Chapter 6

1. Jonathan Hughes, *The Religious Life of Richard III*, Gloucester 1997, p. 123.
2. John Bossy, 'Prayers', *Transactions of the Royal Historical Society*, 6th series, 1, 1991, pp. 137–48.
3. Colin Richmond, 'Margins and Marginality: English Devotion in the Later Middle Ages', in Nicholas Rogers (ed.), *England in the Fifteenth Century*, Stamford 1994, pp. 242–52. The quoted prayer is from Bodleian Library Gough Liturgical Ms 7, fo. 81v, a prayer-book compiled for George, Earl of Shrewsbury, *c.* 1500.

4. I translate from the version printed in *Horae Eboracenses*, Surtees Society, vol. cxxxii, 1919, p. 83.
5. Sutton and Visser-Fuchs, *The Hours of Richard III*, pp. 67–75; the prayer is printed and translated pp. 76–8.
6. CUL Ii.6.2 fo. 11.
7. *The Primer, or office of the blessed virgin Marie, in Latin and English: according to the reformed Latin: and with lyke graces privileged*, Antwerp 1599 (RSTC 16094) fos 227–229.
8. Hughes, *Religious Life of Richard III*, pp. 104–53.
9. Ibid., pp. 124–5, 137.
10. Ibid., pp. 132.
11. Ibid., pp. 123.
12. *Horae Eboracenses*, p. 48 note 1.
13. The Eggesford book described and the rubric attached to the prayer printed in Orme, 'Two early prayer-books from North Devon', pp. 346–9; the prayer is printed in full in *Horae Eboracenses*, p. 125.
14. Cf CUL Ii.6.2 fo. 11, CUL Ee 1 14. fo. 119, and many others.
15. C. Horstman (ed.), *Yorkshire Writers*, London 1895, pp. 376–7: Hughes notes the presence of the prayer and the preamble in the Thornton Mss (*Religious Life of Richard III*, p. 133), but insists that Thornton in using the prayer would have had in mind 'his enemies, neighbours who resented his spiritual and social progress', a speculation for which there appears to be no evidence, and which seems at odds with the startling specificity of the many ills named in the rubric.

Chapter 7

1. Beinecke Library, Yale, Ms Vault More: Louis L. Martz and Richard R. Sylvester (eds), *Thomas More's Prayer Book, a Facsimile Reproduction of the Annotated Pages*, New Haven and London 1969. More's Book of Hours was published by François Regnault in 1530, and is RSTC 15963, Hoskins, *Horae*, no. 89.
2. *Thomas More's Prayer Book*, p. 200.
3. *Thomas More's Prayer Book*, p. 194.
4. *Thomas More's Prayer Book*, p. 200.
5. Garry E. Haupt (ed.), *The Complete Works of St Thomas More*, vol. 13, New Haven and London 1976, pp. 228–31.
6. *Thomas More's Prayer Book*, pp. 194, 189.
7. Note by L. Martz and R. Sylvester, *Yale University Library Gazette*, vol. 43, 1968, p. 68.
8. This is evident from the grubby state of the relevant pages in Beinecke Library, Yale, Ms Vault More (More's Prayer-Book) fos xcix ff.
9. *Thomas More's Prayer Book*, pp. 185–7 and pls 3–21.
10. Bede Camm, *Lives of the Martyrs*, London 1904–5, pp. 459–9.
11. CUL Dd 6 1, fo. 142v.

Chapter 8

1. Above, pp. 41–3.
2. Much of the attention paid to these books has been devoted to their English material, with a consequent neglect of their Latin religious content. Apart from the foundational study by Helen C. White, *The Tudor Books of Private Devotion*, Madison Wisconsin 1951, see Edwyn Birchenough, 'The Prymer in English', *The Library*, Series IV, vol. 18, 1938, pp. 177–94; C. Butterworth, *The English Primers*. The best short treatment is Mary C. Erler's admirable discussion in 'Devotional Literature', pp. 499–510; see also Mary C. Erler, 'The *maner to live well* and the coming of English in François Regnault's Primers of the 1520s and 1530s', *The Library*, 1984, pp. 229–43; some relevant discussion of illustrations in printed Books of Hours for the English market in Martha W. Driver, 'Pictures in print: late fifteenth and early sixteenth-century English religious books for lay readers', in M. G. Sargent (ed.), *De Cella in Seculum: Religion and Secular Life and Devotion in Late Medieval England*, Woodbridge 1989, pp. 229–44.
3. Above, pp. 79–81.
4. Cf. RSTC 15973, a small octavo Latin Book of Hours printed by Regnault in 1531, with RSTC 15970, half the size, containing identical text, and the same sequence of illustrations, but simpler and cruder in execution.

5. The illustrative programme of some of these books is discussed in Duffy, *Stripping of the Altars*, pp. 227–31.
6. RSTC 15926. See the copy of this edition in The Pierpont Morgan Library, which has a clasped binding with the monogram of the owner, Katherine Brown, and sensational blue and gold illumination on the title-page. PML 15433.
7. Ibid, fo. cxxiii. The blockprint of St Brigid from *The Dietary of Ghostly helth* is reproduced in Duffy, *The Stripping of the Altars*, pl. 61.
8. Erler speculates that Wynkyn de Worde may have struck a deal with Regnault *c.* 1528, withdrawing from the production of Primers to leave the field free for the Frenchman – 'Devotional Literature' p. 503.
9. Above pp. 110ff.
10. Beinecke Library, Yale, Ms Vault More, fos xxix (v), xxxiii (v) cxxiiii.
11. The same sequence is followed in RSTC 15968 (illustrated infra nos 71, 90, 93, 102, 110) and RSTC 15981 (illustrated infra nos 75, 77).
12. Ibid., fos cxix ff, cciiii ff.
13. This vernacular biblical material is the special subject of Butterworth's *English Primers*.
14. Examples printed in Hoskins, *Horae*, pp. 120–1.
15. Ibid., pp. 124–5.
16. On this sort of 'underground' devotional material in France, and official attitudes to it, see Virginia Reinburg's important unpublished 1985 Princeton Doctoral Dissertation, *Popular Prayers in Late Medieval and Reformation France*, chapter 4.
17. Hoskins, *Horae*, p. 134 (no. 81).
18. The rubric is printed in full from RSTC 15912, a Book of Hours of 1511, in Hoskins, *Horae*, p. 126.
19. Above, p. 79–80.
20. RSTC 15675.
21. On the Oes, see Duffy, *Stripping of the Altars*, pp. 249–56.
22. Ibid., pp. 320–1. These English prayers are printed in *Horae Eboracenses*, pp. 85–8.
23. Ker and Piper, *Medieval Manuscripts*, vol. IV, p. 790; Rees-Jones and Riddy, 'The Bolton Hours of York'; *Horae Eboracenses*, pp. 150–4.
24. M. R. James, 'Description of the ancient manuscripts in the Ipswich Public Library', *Proceedings of the Suffolk Institute of Archaeology and Natural History*, vol. xxii, 1935, pp. 95–9.
25. Hoskins, *Horae*, pp. 133, 190.
26. Rogers, 'Books of Hours', p. 362.
27. Erler, 'Maner to live Well', p. 232.
28. Leeds University Library, Brotherton Collection 15, fos. 1–6v; Ker, *Medieval Manuscripts*, III, p. 52.

Chapter 9

1. *Three Primers put forth in the Reign of Henry VIII*, Oxford 1848, p. 2.
2. RSTC 15986, *A Prymer in Englysche, with certeyn prayers and godly meditations, very necessary for all people that understonde not the Latyne tongue* [1534].
3. RSTC 160009, *The manual of prayers, or the prymer in Englysch & Laten . . . set forfth by Jhon by Goddes grace, at the Kynges calling, bysshoppe of Rochester at the commandemente of Thomas Crumwell* [1539]. Both Marshall's and Hilsey's Primers were usefully reprinted in *Three Primers put forth in the Reign of Henry VIII*, Oxford 1848.
4. RSTC 16034, *The primer, set foorth by the kynges maiestie and his clergie, to be taught lerned and read: and none other to be used throughout all his dominions*, 1545.
5. Butterworth, *The English Primers*, *passim*. Edwyn Birchenough, 'The Prymer in English', *The Library*, series IV, vol. 18, 1938, pp. 177–94.
6. P. L. Hughes and J. F. Larkin (eds), *Tudor Royal Proclamations*, New Haven and London 1967–9 no. 158, vol. I, p. 231.
7. Erler, 'Maner to live well' *op. cit.*, p. 239.
8. Hoskins, *Horae*, pp. 171–2.
9. See the preface to RSTC 15993, issued in 1536, printed in Hoskins, *Horae*, pp. 159–61.
10. Erler, *op. cit.*, pp. 241–3.
11. *Tudor Royal Proclamations*, no. 186, vol. 1, pp. 270–6.
12. Duffy, *Stripping of the Altars*, p. 418.
13. Bodleian Ms Laud Lat 15.
14. Sidney Sussex College, Ms 37, fos 2, 6v, 22v–33, 156.
15. Bodleian Library, Gough Missals 49 (RSTC

15970), fos li, cxx (verso), cxxii (verso), clxxxii (verso), clxxxviii, cxcvii, xcv (verso), clxxxiiij.

16. Bodleian Ms Aubrey 31, f4.
17. Pierpont Morgan Library, 1034 (RSTC 15959).
18. Richard Rex, 'Blessed Adrian Fortescue', *Analecta Bollandiana* Tome 115 (1997) pp. 307–53.
19. Hoskins, *Horae*, pp. 130, 355. This book is BL Add 17012. See pp. 55 above, and pls 38–9.
20. Duffy, *Stripping of the Altars*, p. 393.
21. BL C35 a 14 (STC 15978), fos. ccvl (v), calendar *passim*. The Jesu psalter is unpaginated but occurs at the end of the book.
22. BL C35 d 9 *passim* (STC 15954).
23. Fitzwilliam Ms 53, fos 181v–182.
24. H. B. Walters, *London Churches at the Reformation*, p. 193; J. Venn, *Alumni Cantabrigiensis*, I, p. 216.
25. *Catalogue of the Harleian Manuscripts*, vol. 1, p. 478.
26. British Library Ms Harley 935, fo. 108v. I am grateful to Nicholas Rogers for help in deciphering these difficult entries.
27. BL Harley 935, fo. 22.
28. BL Harley 935, fo. 23v–4.
29. Butterworth, *The English Primers*, table of variant readings, p. 303.
30. BL Harley 935, fo. 71v.
31. Ibid., fo. 66v.
32. Ibid., fo. 28v.
33. Ibid., fo. 30.
34. Ibid., fo. 98v.
35. e.g. CUL Ii.6.2 fol. 33v–4.
36. Above, pp. 87–95.
37. *Hoskins, Horae*, p. 237.
38. A suggestion I owe to Dr Tom Freeman.
39. Duffy, *Stripping of the Altars*, pp. 537–43.
40. As late as 1602 a protestant collection of prayers for all occasions *A Right Godly Rule, how all faithfull Christians ought to occupie and exercise themselves in their dayly prayers*, would take the official Catholic Book of Hours issued in Queen Mary's reign as its source text, though blatantly Catholic features like the real presence were silently edited out: RSTC 21446.7.

Chapter 10

1. RSTC 6428, *Christian Prayers and Meditations* London 1569. I have used the first edition of 1578, RSTC 6429. This collection, edited by Richard Day, reused the format and decorated borders which had been first used in an earlier and different collection of protestant prayers, Christian prayers and Meditations, London 1569, RSTC 6428. Both books are often referred to as "The Queen's Book" because of the frontispiece portrait of Elizabeth which appeared in both.
2. RSTC 6429 fols 31, 62: Helen White, *Tudor Books of Private Devotion*, *passim*; E. Duffy, 'Continuity and divergence in Tudor religion' in R. Swanson (ed.), *Unity and Diversity in the Church*, (*Studies in Church History*, vol. 32, Oxford 1996), pp. 171–205.
3. Thomas Ingelend, *a Pretie and Mery new interlude called The Disobedient Child* London 1570 (?) RSTC 14085 sigs c ii – c ii (v).
4. See for example the protestant prayer in BL Sloane 2683, fos 11–11v.
5. BL C 123 d 32 (STC 15908.5), fos xxxviiii (v), lxxx(v), clvi.
6. RSTC 16094: on these Counter-Reformation books, see J. M. Blom, *The Post-Tridentine English Primer*, Catholic Record Society, 1982.
7. Downside Ms 26529, fo. 101.
8. Downside Ms 18203, fos 1–16; Hoskins, *Horae*, no. 213: RSTC 16064.
9. Peter Holmes, *Elizabethan Casuistry*, Catholic Record Society, 1981, p. 24.
10. W. H. Frere (ed.), *Visitation Articles and Injunctions of the period of the Reformation*, vol. III, London, 1910, p. 289.
11. John Bossy, *The English Catholic Community 1570–1850*, London, 1975, p. 122; Alexandra Walsham, 'Domme Preachers', *Past and Present*, no. 168, August 2000, pp. 112–13; Adam Foxe, *Oral and Literate Culture in England 1500–1700*, Oxford 2000, p. 37. My thanks to Alex Walsham for this cluster of references.

BIBLIOGRAPHY

BOOKS OF HOURS CITED

In preparing the lectures on which this book is based I examined most of the manuscript and printed Books of Hours made for use in England currently held in the collections of the British Library, the Cambridge University Library, the Bodleian Library, and a selection of the College Libraries of Oxford and Cambridge, Lambeth Palace Library, the Fitzwilliam Museum, the Pierpont Morgan Library, and the libraries of Ushaw College, Stonyhurst College, and Downside Abbey. To keep the bibliography within usable bounds, I have included here only books directly cited in the text or notes. Printed Books of Hours are cited under the entry for the library in which they are held, giving first the RSTC number, then the printer or publisher, place of publication, and date, and finally the call number or shelf-mark.

Baltimore, Walters Art Gallery

Ms 267

Cambridge University Library

MANUSCRIPTS

Dd 6 1
Ee 1 14
Ff 6 8
Gg vi 25
Ii 6 2
Ii 6 4
Ii 6 7
Kk 6 10

PRINTED HORAE

RSTC 15675 (Wynken de Worde, London, 1494) Inc 4.J.1.2 [3750] (Parr Hours)
RSTC 15887 (Pigouchet, Paris, 1498) Rit d 350.1
RSTC 15912 (Kerver/Byrckman, Paris 1511), Sss 15 20
RSTC 15933 (Pynson, London, 1522) Sss 29 10
RSTC 15941 (Wynken de Worde London 1525) Rit e 352 1
RSTC 15968 (Regnault, Paris, 1530) Sss 60 19
RSTC 15973 (Regnault, Paris, 1531) Syn 8 53 95
RSTC 15981 (Regnault, Paris, 1533) Syn 8 53 97
RSTC 15993 (Le Roux, Rouen, 1536) Syn 7 53 19
RSTC 16068 (Valentin, Rouen, 1555) Syn 8 55 171
RSTC 16070 (Valentin, Rouen 15555) Syn 8 55 164
RSTC 16065 (Wayland, London 1555) Young 263

—— Fitzwilliam Museum

MANUSCRIPTS

Fitzwilliam Ms 40–1950 (The Talbot Hours)
Fitzwilliam Ms 41–1950 (Hours of Margaret Talbot)
Fitzwilliam Ms MacClean 89
Fitzwilliam Ms 53
Fitzwilliam Ms 54
Fitzwilliam Ms 56

—— Magdalene College

RSTC 15968 (Regnault, Paris, 1530) Pepys Library 1848
RSTC 15978 (Yolande Kerver, Paris, 1532) Pepys Library 23

Kings Primer 1545 (not in RSTC) Old Library
RSTC 16054 (R Grafton 1551)

—— St John's College

Ms E.14
Ms E.26

—— Sidney Sussex College

Ms 37
Ms 80

Durham, Ushaw College

Ms 10
Ms 43

Leeds University Library, Brotherton Collection

Ms 15

London, British Library
MANUSCRIPTS

Add Ms 17012
Add Ms 27924
Add Ms 54782 (Hastings Hours)

Harley Ms 494
Harley Ms 935
Harley Ms 2845
Harley Ms 2887
Harley Ms 2982
Harley Ms 2985
Harley Ms 3835

King's Ms 9

Royal Ms 2 A XVIII (Beaufort Hours, Microfilm)

Sloane Ms 2565
Sloane Ms 2683

PRINTED HORAE

RSTC 15978 (Kerver, Paris, 153) C.35.a.14
RSTC 15879 (Pigouchet, Paris, 1494) 1A.40311
RSTC 15880 (Pigouchet, Paris, 1494) 1A.41332
RSTC 15881 (Jehannot, Paris 1495) 1A.40910
RSTC 15899 (Wynken de Worde, London, 1503) C.41.e.8
RSTC 15908.5 (Wynken de Worde, London, 1510) C.123.d.32
RSTC 15926 (Vostre, Paris, 1520) C.41.e.9
RSTC 15954 (Regnault, Paris, 1527) C.41.e.31
RSTC 15978 (Kerver, Paris 1533) C.35.a.12

—— Lambeth Palace Library

Ms 459
Ms 474 (Hours of Richard III)
Ms 545 (Lewkenor Hours)

New York, Pierpont Morgan Library
MANUSCRIPTS

Ms G.50 (De Lisle Hours)
Ms M.700 (DuBois Hours)
Ms M.487

PRINTED HORAE

RSTC 15959 (Hardouyn, Paris, 1528) PML 1034
RSTC 15926 (Vostre-Higman, Paris, 1520) PML 15433

Oxford, Bodleian Library
MANUSCRIPTS

Bodleian Ms Aubrey 31
Ms Don d 206
Ms Gough Liturg. 7
Ms Laud Lat 15
Ms Rawl liturgy d1
Ms Rawl liturgy e7
Ms Rawl liturgy e8
Ms Rawl liturgy f2

PRINTED HORAE

RSTC 15880 (Pigouchet, Paris, 1495) Douce 24 (Withypole Hours)
RSTC 15881.3 (Jehannot, Paris, 1495?) Bodleian Arch n f 42

RSTC 15970 (Regnault, Paris, 1531) Gough Missals 49
RSTC 15881.3 (Jehannot, Paris, 1495) Arch B f 42

Stonyhurst College, Lancashire

Ms LVII
T7/26, S3/9 RSTC 15970, Regnault, Paris, 1531

OTHER PRINTED WORKS CITED

Jonathan J.G. Alexander, *Medieval Illuminators and their Methods of Work*, New Haven and London 1992
—— 'Katherine Bray's Flemish Book of Hours', *The Ricardian* 8 (107) 1989, pp. 308–17
Alain Arnould and Jean Michel Massing (eds.), *Splendours of Flanders*, Cambridge 1993
Clarissa Atkinson, *Mystic and Pilgrim, the Book and World of Margery Kempe*, Ithaca and London 1983
Janet Backhouse, *The Madresfield Hours*, Oxford 1976
—— *The Bedford Hours*, London 1990
T. F. T. Baker (ed.), *Victoria County History of Middlesex*, vol. VII, Oxford 1982
Oskar Batschmann and Pascal Griener, *Hans Holbein*, London 1997
Edwyn Birchenough, 'The Prymer in English', *The Library*, Series IV, vol. 18 (1938), pp. 177–94
Edmund Bishop, 'On the Origin of the prymer', *Liturgica Historica*, Oxford 1918, pp. 211–37
Paul Binski and Stella Panayatova, *The Cambridge Illuminations*, London 2005
J. M. Blom, *The Post Tridentine English Primer*, Catholic Record Society 1982
Julia Boffey, 'Women's authors and women's literacy in fourteenth and fifteenth-century England', in Carol M. Meale (ed.), *Women and Literature in Britain 1150–1500*, Cambridge 1996, pp. 159–82
E. Bonney, 'Some Prayers and Prayer-Books of Our Forefathers', *Ushaw Magazine* 12, 1902, pp. 273–87
John Bossy, *The English Catholic Community 1570–1850*, London 1975
—— 'Prayers', *Transactions of the Royal Historical Society* 6th Series, 1, 1991, pp. 137–48
Susan Brigden, *London and the Reformation*, Oxford 1991
C. Butterworth, *The English Primers 1529–1549*, Philadelphia 1953
Lorne Campbell (ed.), *National Gallery Catalogues: The Fifteenth Century Netherlandish Schools,* London 1997
Bede Camm, *Lives of the Martyrs*, London 1904–5
M. J. Charlesworth (ed.), *St Anselm's Proslogion*, Oxford 1965

M. T. Clanchy, *From Memory to Written Record, England 1066–1307*, 2nd edn, Oxford 1993
Alan Coates *et al.*, *A Catalogue of Books printed in the Fifteenth Century now in the Bodleian Library*, III, Oxford 2005
Patricia Cullum and Jeremy Goldberg, 'How Margaret Blackburn Taught her Daughters: Reading Devotional Instruction in a Book of Hours' in Jocelyn Wogan-Browne (ed.), *Medieval Women: Texts and Contexts in Late Medieval Britain*, 2000, pp. 217–36
N. Davis (ed.), *Paston Letters and Papers of the Fifteenthy Century*, Oxford 1971–6
Richard Day, (editor) and John (publisher), *a booke of Christian Prayers* 1578, RSTC 6429
Christopher de Hamel, *A History of Illuminated Manuscripts*, London 1994
—— *The Book: a history of the Bible in England*, London 2001
Claire Donovan, *The de Brailes Hours: Shaping the Book of Hours in Thirteenth-Century Oxford*, London 1991
Martha W. Driver, 'Pictures in print: Late Fifteenth and Early Sixteenth-Century English Religious Books for Lay Readers', in M. G. Sargent (ed.), *De Cella in Seculum: Religion and Secular Life and Devotion in Late Medieval England*, Woodbridge 1989, pp. 229-44
Eamon Duffy, *The Stripping of the Altars*, New Haven and London 1992
—— 'Continuity and Divergence in Tudor Religion', in R. Swanson (ed.), *Unity and Diversity in the Church, Studies in Church History* vol. 32, Oxford 1996, pp. 171–205
Mary C. Erler, *Women Reading and Piety in Late Medieval England*, Cambridge 2003
—— 'The maner to live well and the coming of English in François Regnault's Primers of the 1520s and 1530s', *The Library*, 1984, pp. 229-43
—— 'Pasted-in Embellishments in English Manuscripts and Printed Books *c.* 1480–1533', *The Library*, VI Series, vol. 14, 1992, pp. 185–206
—— 'Devotional Literature' in Lotte Hellinga and Joseph B. Trapp (eds), *The Cambridge History of the Book in Britain,* vol. III 1440–1557, Cambridge 1999, pp. 495-525
Adam Foxe, *Oral and Literate Culture in England 1500–1700*, Oxford 2000
W. H. Frere (ed.), *Visitation Articles and Injunctions of the period of the Reformation*, vol. II, London 1910
John B. Friedman, *Northern English Books, Owners and Makers in the Middle Ages*, Syracuse 1995
F. J. Furnivall (ed.), *The Fifty Earliest English Wills in the Court of Probate*, Early English Text Society 1882
P. J. Goldberg, 'Lay book ownership in late medieval York', *The Library*, 6th series, 16, 1994, pp. 181–9
John A Goodall, 'Heraldry in the Decoration of English medieval Manuscripts', *Antiquaries Journal* 77, 1997, pp. 180-1
Anthony Goodman, *Margery Kempe and her World*, London 2002
A Catalogue of the Harleian Manuscripts in the British Museum, London, 4 vols, 1808–12
J. Harthan, *Books of Hours and their Owners*, London 1977
John Hilsey, *The manual of prayers, or the prymer in Englysch & Laten . . . set forfth by Jhon by Goddes grace, at the Kynges calling, bysshoppe of Rochester at the commandemente of Thomas Crumwell* [1539], RSTC 16009
Peter Holmes, *Elizabethan Casuistry*, Catholic Record Society 1981
Horae Eboracenses, Surtees Society vol. cxxxii, 1919
C. Horstman (ed.), *Yorkshire Writers*, London 1895
Edgar Hoskins, *Horae Beatae Mariae Virginis or Sarum and York Primers with kindred Books . . . an Introduction*, London 1901
Ann Hudson, *The Premature Reformation*, Oxford 1988
Jonathan Hughes, *The Religious Life of Richard III*, Gloucester 1997
P. L. Hughes and J. F. Larkin (eds), *Tudor Royal Proclamations*, New Haven and London 1964–9
Thomas Ingelend, *A Pretie and Mery new enterlude: called The Disobedient Child*, London 1570(?) RSTC 14085
Eric Inglis (ed.), *The Hours of Mary of Burgundy*, London 1995
M. R. James, *A Descriptive Catalogue of the Manuscripts in the Fitzwilliam Museum*, Cambridge 1895
—— *A Descriptive Catalogue of the Second Series of Fifty Manuscripts in the Collection of Henry Yates*

Thompson, Cambridge 1902
—— *A Descriptive Catalogue of the Western Manuscripts in the Library of Christ's College Cambridge*, Cambridge 1905
—— 'Description of the ancient manuscripts in the Ipswich Public Library', *Proceedings of the Suffolk Institute of Archaeology and Natural History*, vol. xxii, 1935, pp. 95–9
N. R. Ker, *Medieval Manuscripts in British Libraries*, 5 vols (vols IV and V with A. Piper), Oxford 1969–92
V. Leroquais, *Les livres d'heures manuscripts de la Bibliothèque nationale*, Paris 1927, (*Supplément*, 1947)
R. Lockyer (ed.), *Thomas Wolsey, late Cardinal, his life and death written by George Cavendish his gentleman-usher*, London 1962
Isolde Lubbecke, *The Thyssen Bornemisza Collection: Early German Painting 1350–1550*, London 1991
Richard Marks and Paul Williamson, *Gothic: Art for England 1400–1547*, London 2003
Louis L. Martz and Richard R. Sylvester (eds), *Thomas More's Prayer Book, a facsimile Reproduction of the Annotated Pages*, New Haven and London 1969
S. B. Meech and H. E. Allen, *The Book of Margery Kempe*, Early English Text Society 1940
Bella Millett, 'Women in No Man's land: English recluses and the development of vernacular literature in the twelfth and thirteenth centuries', in Carol M. Meale (ed.), *Women and Literature in Britain 1150-1500*, Cambridge 1996, pp. 86–103
G. C. Moore Smith, *The Family of Withypoll*, Walthamstow Antiquarian Society, Official Publication no. 34, 1936
Garry E. Haupt (ed.), *The Complete Works of St Thomas More*, vol. 13, New Haven and London 1976
Nigel Morgan, *Early Gothic Manuscripts II, 1250–1285*, London 1988
I. Nettekoven, *Der Meister der Apokalypsenrose der Seinte Chapelle und die Pariser Buchkunst um 1500*, Turnhout 2004
N. H. Nicolas (ed.), *Testamenta Vetusta*, London 1826
J. C. T. Oates, *A Catalogue of the Fifteenth Century Printed Books in the University Library Cambridge*, Cambridge 1954
Nicholas Orme, 'Two early prayerbooks from North Devon', *Devon and Cornwall Notes and Queries*, vol. 36, 1991, pp. 345–50
Otto Pächt, *Early Netherlandish Painting*, London 1997
Susan Powell, 'Lady Margaret Beaufort and her Books', *The Library*, 6th Series, vol. 20, 1998, pp. 197–240
A Prymer in Englysche, with certeyn prayers and godly meditations, very necessary for all people that understonde not the Latyne tongue, 1534, RSTC 15986
The primer, set foorth by the kynges maiestie and his clergie, to be taught lerned and read: and none other to be used throughout all his dominions, 1545, RSTC 16034
The Primer, or office of the blessed virgin Marie, in Latin and English: according to the reformed Latin: and with lyke graces privileged, Antwerp 1599, RSTC 16094
Carol J. Purtle, *The Marian Paintings of Jan van Eyck*, Princeton 1982
Virginia Chieffo Raguin (ed.), *Catholic Collecting, Catholic Reflection 1538–1850*, Worcester MA 2006
S. Rees-Jones and F. Riddy, 'The Bolton Hours of York: female domestic piety and the public sphere', in A. Mulder-Bakke and J. Wogan-Browne (eds), *Household, Women and Christianities*, Turnhout 2006
Virginia Reinburg, 'Popular Prayers in Late Medieval and Reformation France', unpublished 1985 Princeton Doctoral Dissertation
Richard Rex, 'Blessed Adrian Fortescue', *Analecta Bollandiana*, Tome 115, 1997, pp. 307–53
Colin Richmond, 'Religion and the Fifteenth-century Gentleman', in R. B. Dobson (ed.), *The Church, Politics and Patronage in the Fifteenth Century*, Gloucester 1984, pp. 193–208
—— 'Margins and Marginality: English Devotion in the Later Middle Ages', in Nicholas Rogers (ed.), *England in the Fifteenth Century*, Stamford 1994, pp. 242–52
S. Ringbom, *Icon to Narrative. The rise of the dramatic close-up in 15th century devotional painting*, Abo 1965
—— 'Devotional Images and Imaginative

Devotions. Notes on the place of art in late medieval private piety', *Gazette des Beaux-Arts*, Series VI, 73, 1963, pp. 159–70
Nicholas Rogers, 'Patrons and purchasers: evidence for the original owners of books produced in the Low Countries for the English Market' in B. Cardon, I. Van der Stock and D. Vanwijnsberghe (eds), 'Als Ich Can': *Liber Amicorum in Memory of Professor Dr Maurits Smeyers, Corpus of Illuminated Manuscripts* vol. 11–12, Low Countries Series 8, Louvain 2002, vol. II, pp. 1165–81
—— 'Books of Hours produced in the Low Countries for the English Market', unpublished Cambridge M. Litt. Dissertation, 1984
S. E. Roper, *Medieval English Benedictine Liturgy. Studies in the Formation, Structure and Content of the Monastic Votive Office c. 950–1540*, New York and London 1993
Kathryn M. Rudy, 'A Pilgrim's Book of Hours', *Studies in Iconography 21*, 2000, pp. 237–79
Lucy F. Sandler, *Gothic Manuscripts 1285–1385*, Oxford 1986
M. G. Sargent (ed.), *De Cella in Seculum: Religion and Secular Life and Devotion in Late Medieval England*, Woodbridge 1989
Anne Savage and Nicholas Watson, *Anchoritic Spirituality*, Mahwah New Jersey 1991
Kathleen Scott, *Gothic Manuscripts 1390–1490*, London 1996
Kathryn A. Smyth, *Art, Identity and Devotion in Fourteenth-Century England: three women and their Books of Hours*, London and Toronto 2003
C. A. Sneyd (ed.), *A Relation of the Island of England*, Camden Society old series 37, 1847
Robert Swanson, *Religion and Devotion in Europe 1215–1515*, Cambridge 1993
Anne F. Sutton and Livia Visser-Fuchs, *The Hours of Richard III*, Stroud 1990
Marcel Thomas (ed.), *The Rohan Master, a Book of Hours*, New York 1973
Three Primers put forth in the Reign of Henry VIII, Oxford 1848
Pamela Tudor Craig, 'The Hours of Edward V and William, Lord Hastings: British Library Manuscript Additional 54782' in D. Williams (ed.), *England in the Fifteenth Century*, Woodbridge 1987, pp. 351–69
D. H. Turner (ed.), *The Hastings Hours, a 15th century Flemish Book of Hours made for William Lord Hastings*, London 1983
Vlaamse Miniaturen vor van Eyck c. 1380–1420, Louvain 1993
Alexandra Walsham, 'Domme Preachers', *Past and Present* no. 168, August 2000
H. B. Walters, *London Churches at the Reformation*, London 1939
Ann K. Warren, *Anchorites and their Patrons in Medieval England*, Berkeley and London 1985
Nicholas Watson, 'Censorship and Cultural Change in Late-Medieval England: Vernacular Theology. The Oxford Translation Debate, and Arundel's Constitutions of 1409', *Speculum* 70, 1995, pp. 822–64
Helen C. White, *The Tudor Books of Private Devotion*, Madison Wisconsin 1951
Roger S. Wieck, *The Book of Hours in Medieval Art and Life*, London 1988
—— *Painted Prayers: the Book of Hours in medieval and Renaissance Art*, New York 1997
F. A. Wood, 'The Parish of Willesden', in *Transactions of the London and Middlesex Archaeological Society*, vol. IV, 1875, pp. 189–201
C. Wordsworth and H. Littlehales, *The Old Service Books of the English Church*, London 1904
F. Wormald and P. M. Giles, *A Descriptive Catalogue of the Additional Manuscripts in the Fitzwilliam Museum*, Cambridge 1982

INDEX

Plate numbers are given in bold italic.

PHOTOGRAPHIC CREDITS

Thanks are due to the institutions and individuals listed below for permission to reproduce the following plates:

Author: 41, 45
Beinecke Rare Book Library, Yale: 63, 64, 65, 66, 89
Bodliean Library, Oxford: 23, 34, 74, 75, 78, 85
Bristol Museum and Art Gallery: 22
British Library: 2, 3, 4, 15, 19, 20, 31, 32, 38, 39, 54, 68, 69, 70, 99, 100, 103, 104, 105, 106
Cambridge University Library, reproduced by kind permission of the Syndics: 6, 14, 21, 24, 35, 36, 37, 53, 55, 56, 57, 58, 59, 60, 67, 71, 72, 73, 76, 77, 80, 83, 84, 87, 88, 91, 92, 94, 95, 98, 101, 102, 108, 109, 110
Christ's College, Cambridge, reproduced by kind permission of the Master and Fellows: 1
Fitzwilliam Museum, Cambridge, reproduced by kind permission of the Syndics: 5, 7, 10, 11, 30, 33, 44, 47, 48, 49, 50, 51, 52
Free Library of Philadelphia, rare book department: 16, 17
Kunstmuseum, Basle: 43
Lambeth Palace, London: 28, 29, 61
Magdalene College, Cambridge, reproduced by kind permission of the Master and Fellows: 96, 97, 107 (Old Library); 81, 90, 93 (Pepys Library)
National Gallery, London: 13, 40
National Portrait Gallery, London: 62
Österreichische Nationalbibliothek: 9, 18
Dr Ruth Chavasse: 46
Scala: 25
Stonyhurst College, Lancashire, frontispiece
The Saint Louis Art Museum, Saint Louis: 42
The Walters Art Museum, Baltimore: 26
York Minster Library: 8, 12